THE SIGNS OF THE TIMES
AND THE RELIGIOUS LIFE

The Signs
of the Times
and the Religious Life

✝

by PAUL HINNEBUSCH, O.P.

SHEED AND WARD : NEW YORK

© *Sheed and Ward, Inc., 1967*

Library of Congress Catalog Card Number: 67–21912

Imprimi potest:
  Gilbert J. Graham, O.P.
  Provincial
  March 20, 1967

Nihil obstat:
  Thomas J. Beary
  Censor Librorum

Imprimatur:
  † Robert F. Joyce
  Bishop of Burlington
  April 21, 1967

The Nihil Obstat and Imprimatur are official declarations that a book or pamphlet is considered to be free of doctrinal or moral error. No implication is contained therein that those who have granted the Nihil Obstat and Imprimatur agree with the contents, opinions or statements expressed.

Manufactured in the United States of America

Contents

Introduction

On Christmas Day, 1961, Pope John the Optimist said, "Distrustful souls see only darkness burdening the face of the earth. We, on the other hand, like to reaffirm all our confidence in the Savior, who has not abandoned the world which he redeemed. Indeed, we make our own the recommendation of Jesus that one should know how to distinguish the 'signs of the times' (Matt. 16:4), and we see now, in the midst of so much darkness, a number of indications which seem to announce better times for the Church and for the human race."[1]

In Pope John's thinking, then, "the signs of the times" are signs of better things ahead, for they are signs that the redeeming power of Christ is still at work in this miserable world.

Vatican II declares that "the Church has always had the duty

[1] *Humanae Salutis,* convoking the Council (Ab, p. 704). Excerpts from the Message to Humanity and Pope John's Convocation of the Council are taken from *The Documents of Vatican II,* published by Guild Press, Association Press, The America Press, and Herder and Herder; copyrighted 1966 by The America Press. Used by permission.

of scrutinizing the signs of the times and of interpreting them in the light of the Gospel" (*GS* 4). God speaks to us, as it were, in the events and needs of the times, and by his Holy Spirit stirs up in his People a response to these needs. "The People of God believes that it is led by the Spirit of the Lord, who fills the earth. Motivated by this faith, it labors to decipher the authentic signs of God's presence and purpose in the happenings, needs and desires in which this People has a part along with other men of our age. For faith throws a new light on everything, manifests God's design for man's total vocation, and thus directs the mind to solutions which are fully human" (*GS* 11).

God speaks to us, then, not only in the word of revelation, but also in the signs of the times. In a sense, the word of revelation is completed in these signs, for in them we can discern the concrete way in which God is carrying out in our days the general plan revealed in the word of the Gospel.

The "signs of the times," then, are manifestations of the workings of the Holy Spirit in his People and in the world, in response to the needs of the times. The needs of our fellowmen in the contemporary situation, social and economic conditions, scientific discoveries and their technological applications, intellectual and cultural problems, current trends in every area of human life— all these indicate in some way the divine will for God's People. They are clues to the task which the Spirit of God wills to accomplish in the world today with the cooperation of his People.

For the Church must see to it that God's word becomes incarnate, as it were, in the world today. God's People themselves, in fact, are that incarnation. They are the People called into being and formed by the word of God. But not in the sense that the word alone determines what they must be. The word of divine revelation is not a die used to stamp out sons of God who are as identical as the thousands of copper cents stamped out each year in the United States mint. The specific cultures and varying conditions of differing peoples in changing centuries help determine the manifold manner in which God's word becomes manifest in them.

For "the life of Jesus" must "be made manifest in our mortal flesh" (2 Cor. 4:11). "The glory of God shining in the face of Christ" (2 Cor. 4:6) must in turn shine forth on the face of the Church to the whole world. This is the main theme of Vatican II. As the Fathers of the Council explained in their "Message to Humanity" (October 20, 1962), the Church must be renewed "so that there may radiate before all men the lovable features of Jesus Christ, who shines in our hearts that God's splendor may be revealed (2 Cor. 4:6)" (Ab, pp. 3–4).

The light of Christ must shine forth in every element of human life and culture. The one light of the natural sun is reflected in diverse hues and many degrees of brilliance by the various objects it strikes on the face of the earth, so that this light itself is revealed in endless variety. So, too, the word of divine revelation must be manifested in multiple ways in the lives of men. The divine word alone does not determine what men's lives should be. The very material into which this word is received determines to some extent how the word will be manifest.

The Eternal Word, the Son of God, assumed his human nature from the womb of a woman of Palestine, from the midst of the specific culture of the people of which she was a member, at a definite point of time in human history. These factors of time and parentage and culture made their distinctive contribution in determining what sort of existence Christ would have. By means of the human nature he assumed, the Word was the visible expression of the invisible God (Col. 1:15). But the Eternal Word thus spoken in time was modulated, as it were, by the Jewish features inherited from the Maiden of Nazareth, by the accents of the Aramaic language and culture into which he was born and educated, by the geographical and historical situation in which he existed, and from which he borrowed the imagery in which he expressed the word of his Gospel.

The pre-existing Eternal Word, then, in becoming man, was manifested as a man of his times—and yet as a man for all times, because he is an Eternal Person who conditioned everything he touched in time more than he himself was conditioned by these things. The Eternal Word ever shines through in the concrete situations of his human life on earth for the man of faith to see. "We saw his glory, glory as of the only-begotten of the Father" (Jn. 1:14). If, then, his human nature and all the elements of his concrete existence in place and time modulated the Eternal Word and brought it within the grasp of human understanding, at the same time the Word himself was fully master of the elements he assumed to himself, and fashioned them in perfect holiness, consecrating them, ordering them perfectly to the Father and his glory.

So, too, it is true that when the "word of our Lord which endures forever" (Isa. 40:8, d) takes root in the hearts of men by faith, it takes these men as it finds them: "Let every man remain in the calling in which he was called" (1 Cor. 7:20). The word is modulated or conditioned by the varying peoples and cultures and times into which it is received; and the finished product, the Light of Christ shining in the lives of men, is determined in no small way by these conditions.

Nevertheless, the word of the Gospel conditions men far more than it is conditioned by them. The Gospel word takes men as it finds them in the sense that it accepts and christianizes all that is good in them. It gives them Christ-life, it makes them Christ-like. But that Christ-life infused into men and into the milieu in which they exist so transforms them that they become, as it were, "a new creation" of a totally different order (Gal. 6:15). As God's creative word called all things out of nothingness, and called light out of darkness, so the word of divine revelation, the Gospel, the word which is Christ, shines into men's hearts and creates of them, as it were, a new world.

The word of God—when it is truly the word of God—is not

adulterated by thus dwelling in the hearts of men, by thus becoming incarnate in the lives which men live in their own times and cultures. Rather, it purifies these men, drawing them to Christ, drawing them away from all that is in opposition to his heavenly Father. They who bring the word of God to the world today must not adulterate it in adapting it to the signs of the times. "We, at least," says St. Paul, "are not, as many others, adulterating the word of God" (2 Cor. 2:17). The word of the Lord, which endures forever, must certainly be expressed in ways intelligible to the men of the times, in terms of their condition and culture. But if it is adulterated, it is no longer the divine word, and is deprived of its sanctifying and purifying power.

The Church, therefore, in scrutinizing the signs of the times, must judge them in the light of the Gospel, rather than judge the Gospel in the "light" of the times. In our eagerness to be in touch with the times, "up-to-date," we must beware of twisting the Gospel to fit the times, rather than purifying and sanctifying the times by the power of the Gospel. It is essential, therefore, that we thoroughly know the Gospel even while we study the times and try to meet them.

For these reasons, when Vatican II instructs religious to be alert to the times, well acquainted with social and economic and cultural conditions and ever ready to adapt to them, it insists at the same time that the first and highest rule of the religious life is Christ as proposed in the Gospel. And in renewing their religious life they must return to the authentic sources of Christian spirituality, and be faithful to the ideals and aims of their founders. For they must never adulterate the word of God in their efforts to live it in modern conditions. Otherwise they will not really bring Christ, the Light of the Nations, into our times.

Under our title, we should write a book endeavoring to interpret all the signs of the times specifically for religious, trying to show them how to adapt their lives accordingly. It is our purpose, however, to look at the signs of the times in a different way. The problems which are agitating many religious today are themselves signs of the times. The times are so confusing that people are end- lessly confused. Among these confused people are many religious. Because of the variety of complexities arising in swiftly changing modern life, says Vatican II, "many of our contemporaries are kept from identifying permanent values and adjusting them properly to fresh discoveries" (*GS* 4).

Many contemporary religious are unable to identify the per- manent values of the religious life, and so are making serious mistakes in their attempts to adjust to modern life. Sometimes they have allowed its thinking to adulterate the word of God as it should be expressed in their lives specifically as religious. In- stead of bringing the full light of the Gospel to purify their times, they have allowed the times to adulterate their living of the Gospel. And so, Vatican II calls them first of all to renew their lives according to Christ as presented in the Gospel, for without this spiritual renewal all adaptation to the times will fail in its purpose.

Many religious, we said, seem unable to identify the permanent values of religious life. And this is true of religious in both the conservative and radical groups. Some of the conservatives hold on to accidentals as though they were permanent values, while some of the radicals seem to deny that there are permanent values.

This book was written chiefly as an aid toward identifying the permanent values of the religious life by commenting on the statements of Vatican II which deal with these values. It is im- possible for religious to adapt their lives properly to modern times if they are not thoroughly convinced of these permanent values. Otherwise they will achieve not adaptation but destruc- tion.

The book is not a line-by-line commentary on the Council's documents on the religious life. Nor are the passages on which we comment treated in the order in which they occur in the documents. The topics treated and the order in which they are treated were determined in large measure by the specific questions agitating the religious with whom the author has been in close contact during the past year or two. He has found the same problems wherever he has given retreats for religious, from Texas to Pennsylvania and New York, from Louisiana to Illinois and Michigan. He has found them also in instructing novices and postulants, who echo the problems of their communities. He has found them as chaplain and spiritual director of sisters, in correspondence with religious in many places, in workshops for religious renewal, and as lecturer in Sisters' Formation conferences.

In this sense, the book is a response to the signs of the times, for as we have said, the problems agitating religious are themselves signs of the times. It is an effort to untangle the confusion resulting from blundering efforts to be fully abreast of the times without being able to identify permanent values.

In the past year or two, one question after another has been agitated among religious, depending upon which latest book or magazine article or newspaper column was being widely read. The resulting confusion is itself a strong argument for the necessity of that return to the authentic sources of Christian spirituality prescribed for religious by Vatican II. Religious who use only the latest paperbacks on Christian Atheism, situational ethics, and the like, for their reading and meditation, and neglect the Gospels and the Fathers of Christian spirituality, will, of course, be in perpetual confusion.

Many of the chapters of the book came into being in response to the agitation which was the fad of the moment. In July it was being said, "Religious life cannot possibly be a special consecration, since all Christians are consecrated in Baptism." In the fall, one heard the widespread cry, "Religious life is contrary to the Gospels," and "My conscience forbids me to live according to outmoded constitutions." At another time, the claim was being made that a vow of obedience is foreign to the Gospel. In December, there was the idea that teaching and nursing are no jobs for the modern religious. During the late winter, celibacy and the value of virginity were being questioned. In the springtime, Christian Atheism was casting its shadow upon the meaning of the religious life.

At other times, there was the fear that obedience destroys maturity and personality. Or again, there was a great deal of sentimentality in speaking of Christian love, as though some sort of sickly love of neighbor should replace the worship of God.

In response to these various questions, the author ever sought to bring to bear the light offered by Vatican II in its treatment of the religious life.

And that is how this book came to be. It is neither an exhaustive commentary on the Council's statements on the religious life nor a complete treatise on the religious life and the problems of adaptation and renewal. It is offered primarily as an aid toward identifying and living the permanent values of the religious life, which must be recovered and renewed if adaptation to the times is not to be in vain.

The author is greatly indebted to Father Elio Gambari, S.M.M., of the Sacred Congregation of Religious, for many of the insights developed in this book. Father Gambari and the author were co-lecturers at the Ninth Instructional Program in Spirituality, Sisters' Formation Conference, held in San Antonio, August 23–30, 1966. The book was recast in the light of Father Gambari's detailed commentaries on the part of the motu proprio _Ecclesiae Sanctae,_ which implements the Decree of Vatican II on the Appropriate Renewal of the Religious Life (August 6, 1966). In the original writing, the book had more of a polemic spirit, in reaction to that contemporary confusion of thought of which we have just spoken. In the rewriting, after Father Gambari's remarks, the book lost most of the polemic approach and became a more positive presentation of the Council's doctrine on the disputed points. Now that the Council has spoken with authority, the polemic spirit is less necessary.

The author also wishes to express his sincere gratitude to Sister Mary Henry Soniat, O.P., of St. Albert's Catholic Student Center, Southeastern Louisiana College, Hammond, Louisiana, for typing the manuscript and for other invaluable aid and encouragement.

We wish to give special thanks to Sister Mary Patrick Ryan, O.P., and to Sister Mary Carmelite, O.P., of Rosaryville, for typing the last third of the manuscript after Sister Mary Henry broke her arm (not in typing the manuscript!).

We are grateful also to the editors of the following periodicals for permission to use as chapters articles which originally appeared in their pages: *Sisters Today* for "Charisms and Religious Obedience" (Vol. 38, No. 5, January 1967); *Review for Religious* for "Epikeia and the Signs of the Times" (copyright 1967 by *Review for Religious*); *Dominican Calendar* for "The Living Book of Charity"; also to The Conference-a-Month Club for permission to use "Religious Chastity and Personal Fulfillment," which was the Club's recording in July 1966.

Besides the regular index to the book, we have provided also a special index of all the quotations we have made from the documents of Vatican II, indicating the special point in the quotation on which we have commented.

In quoting the documents of Vatican II, we have usually made our own translation from the official Latin texts, especially in those quotations dealing directly with the religious life. Many of the current English translations are unsatisfactory on several key points.

For the sake of brevity, most of the time we refer to the Council documents under their Latin titles, the two opening words of the document. For example, instead of saying, "The Pastoral Constitution on the Church in the Modern World," we say,

"Gaudium et Spes"; or instead of "The Decree on the Adaptation and Renewal of the Religious Life," we write, *"Perfectae Caritatis."*

All quotations from the documents of the Council are followed immediately by the initials of these titles, along with the number of the paragraph quoted; e.g., *LG* 8, paragraph eight of *Lumen Gentium,* The Constitution on the Church. When we quote the motu proprio *Ecclesiae Sanctae,* we write *ESr.* The small "r" refers to that part of the motu proprio which implements *Perfectae Caritatis,* the Council's decree on the religious life.

"Ab" after a quotation is a reference to *The Documents of Vatican II,* Walter Abbott, S.J., General Editor (New York: Guild, 1966).

The following is a list of the symbols used:

Ab - Abbott, *The Documents of Vatican II.*

AA - Apostolicam Actuositatem, Decree on the Apostolate of the Laity.

AG - Ad Gentes, Decree on the Church's Missionary Activity.

DH - Dignitatis Humanae, Declaration on Religious Freedom.

DV-Dei Verbum, Dogmatic Constitution on Divine Revelation.

ESr - Ecclesiae Sanctae, Motu Proprio of Paul VI, Implementing Four Documents of Vatican II.

GS - Gaudium et Spes, Pastoral Constitution on the Church in the Modern World.

LG - Lumen Gentium, Dogmatic Constitution on the Church.

OT - Optatum Totius, Decree on Priestly Formation.

SC - Sacrosanctum Concilium, Constitution on the Sacred Liturgy.

The Scripture quotations in this book are chiefly from the Confraternity translation; either *The Holy Bible,* copyright 1962 by The Confraternity of Christian Doctrine, or the revised version of the New English Missal. Other versions are noted as follows: d, the Douay; j, *The Jerusalem Bible,* copyright 1966 by Darton, Longman and Todd, Ltd., and Doubleday and Company, Inc.; k, *The New Testament,* translated by James Aloysius Kleist, S.J., and Joseph L. Lilly, C.M., copyright 1954 by Bruce Publishing Company; s, *The New Testament,* translated by Francis Aloysius Spencer, O.P., copyright 1937 by The Macmillan Company.

Rosaryville, Louisiana
October 31, 1966

THE SIGNS OF THE TIMES
AND THE RELIGIOUS LIFE

1. Epikeia and the Signs of the Times

"The Church has always had the duty of scrutinizing the signs of the times and of interpreting them in the light of the Gospel" (*GS* 4). The Church must ever be up-to-date, keenly aware of the contemporary situation, understanding the world of the here and now—its needs, its hopes, its expectations—so that in language intelligible to the contemporary mentality "she can respond to the perennial questions which men are asking about this present life and the life to come" (*GS* 4).

The world of today, however, is changing so profoundly and with such bewildering rapidity and is becoming so exceedingly complex, that much of mankind is hopelessly confused. "Influenced by such a variety of complexities," says Vatican II, "many of our contemporaries are kept from accurately identifying permanent values and adjusting them properly to fresh discoveries. As a result, buffeted between hope and anxiety, and pressing one another with questions about the present course of events, they are weighed down with uneasiness" (*GS* 4).

What is the remedy for this anxiety and uneasiness, this inability accurately to identify permanent values? In our day, perhaps as never before, even the most sacred of values are being questioned. Even in the religious life, affected by the spirit of the times, we detect much insecurity and inability to distinguish the permanent from the ephemeral, the absolute from the relative. And yet religious, as servants of the Church's mission of salvation, should be among the leaders in the Church's work of interpreting the signs of the times in the light of the Gospel, and of "accurately identifying permanent values and adjusting them to fresh discoveries."

To direct religious in their share in this task, the Council laid down guidelines in *Perfectae Caritatis*. This document reasserts all the permanent values of the religious life which have been called into question, and gives principles for adapting them to the world today.

But knowledge of basic values and of principles is not enough; much more is needed. There is a special virtue—we might call it a crisis virtue—which forms in us right attitudes and correct procedures for dealing unerringly with swiftly changing times and situations. This crisis virtue is epikeia.

Epikeia is a firm will to act according to the intentions of the lawgiver, for the common good, in those cases where following the letter of the law would harm the common good, or in those cases where the law does not adequately cover a situation.

In a world which is changing with such bewildering rapidity, religious are certain to run into frequent situations which are not covered by existing laws. They will discover that they are no longer equipped with a set of laws capable of directing their actions in practically any situation in which they find themselves; for a profoundly changing world has produced situations which no one could have dreamed of when their existing legislation was drawn up.

Nor should confused young religious too severely condemn their elders for not adapting their life sooner to modern times.

Even if their superiors had been the most alert people on earth, they still could hardly have kept abreast of the times, because the changes have taken place in the world with such explosive rapidity.

The great problem, therefore, is: What does one do when old laws and procedures and customs are no help, but seem to be even a hindrance in a new situation? What is to be our guide while we are waiting for our laws to be revised and adapted to the times, in accordance with the will of the Council? What will guarantee that we will make the right adaptations and not bungle the work of revision? And even when the revision has been completed, how can renewal "be encouraged in a continuing way" (ESr 19)? What will prevent legislation and customs from again becoming ossified? The answer to all these problems is the virtue of epikeia.

This virtue, we said, more badly needed than ever, will give us certain basic attitudes and manners of proceeding in cases in which existing laws are no help. Epikeia received little attention in the oxcart days, when life was so leisurely that it changed less in the course of five centuries than it now changes in the course of five years. In those days of little change, existing laws were usually quite adequate to govern most of our actions, and so Lady Epikeia did not have too much work to do. But in our times, she will have to be one of the busiest of all virtues. Therefore, we need to be introduced to her, if she has not yet been formed in our lives.

Who is this Lady Epikeia? The Greeks gave this virtue her name. Aristotle knew her well and even described her for us. Thomas Aquinas drew her portrait clearly in two articles in the *Summa*.[1] Yet she is practically unknown to most of us, and the average English dictionary does not even carry her name. Since her task is so crucial in our present crisis, her name, "epikeia," ought to be granted full citizenship in our language and inscribed

[1] 2a–2ae, Q. 120.

in the rolls of citizenship—our dictionaries. But above all, the idea expressed in this word should take its rightful place in our moral thinking, so that we may carefully cultivate the virtue it signifies. She is already slightly known in English as "equity," but this word carries many legalistic connotations. That is why we suggest that we take over officially her Greek name, "epikeia."

What, then, is epikeia, and how do we acquire it and exercise it?

Epikeia's Family

In the kingdom of the virtues, ruled by Queen Charity, Lady Epikeia belongs to the noble family of justice. Her name, however, seems at first sight to deny these family ties, for it is made up of two Greek words which mean "above what is just." Does she belong, then, to a more noble family than justice? No, her name merely means that she is an elder sister of legal justice. "Epikeia does not set aside what is just in itself, but that which is just as by law established."[2] Legal justice acts according to law, epikeia acts when the law is inadequate in achieving justice in a particular situation.

When many human beings live and work together, their relationships need to be regulated by law, which directs all their actions in an orderly way to the common good. Anyone who truly loves his fellowmen loves the common good; and consequently, in charity he willingly follows the direction of the law in achieving that common good. Legal justice, the virtue which prompts one to live willingly according to law in order to achieve the common good, is therefore an expression of charity.

But laws regulate human actions, and since human actions

[2] Thomas Aquinas, *Summa Theologica,* First Complete American Edition, literally translated by Fathers of the English Dominican Province (New York: Benziger, 1947), 2a–2ae, Q. 120, a. 1, ad 1. All the quotations from the *Summa* are from this edition.

are contingent upon circumstances and no two situations are ever quite alike, human actions are innumerable in their diversity. Therefore, it is not possible to lay down rules of law which apply in every single case. Legislators in framing laws attend to what commonly happens. For though it is true that each situation is unique in some details, it is true on the other hand that varying situations do have a great deal in common, and so workable laws can be made to direct human actions to the good of the whole community. Ordinarily, therefore, human action according to law brings order and justice into human relationships.

When Epikeia Works

But now and then there are unusual situations in which action according to the letter of the law would defeat the intention or spirit of the law and harm the common good which the law intends to establish. "For example, the law requires deposits to be restored, because in the majority of cases this is just. Yet it happens to be injurious sometimes; for instance, if a madman were to put his sword in deposit, and demand its delivery while in a state of madness, or if a man were to seek the return of his deposit in order to fight against his country. In these and like cases, it is bad to follow the law, and it is good to set aside the letter of the law and to follow the dictates of justice and the common good. This is the task of epikeia, which we call equity."[3]

It is clear, then, that in all ordinary cases, the virtue of legal justice, inspiring human action according to the law, guarantees the justice required for the common good. But epikeia, the sister of legal justice, takes over in extraordinary cases, where the law defeats its own purpose, or is an inadequate guide because it did not foresee certain situations.

In our unsettled, rapidly changing times, the extraordinary cases—those in which the law is inadequate—have become much

[3] *Ibid.*, a. 1.

more frequent, and therefore epikeia will have to work overtime until laws have been revised to take care of all the new kinds of situations which now arise. It is very important, then, that we become better acquainted and more intimate with this virtue. She works, we said, only in situations where the letter of the law is inadequate.

Epikeia's First Characteristic

Exactly how does epikeia work? When a particular law does not cover a situation, epikeia acts according to a higher principle, namely, the intention of the lawgiver. She considers carefully what goals the lawmaker had in mind in making the laws; then she wisely plans her action in this situation in such a way that she will effectively achieve these same goals, fulfilling the purpose of the law without the help of the law.

For example, when Lady Epikeia is a Dominican, and finds herself in a new situation where her Dominican Constitutions or customs have no law covering the case, then she must ask herself, or the superiors—whom she should consult if possible—should ask themselves, How would our Father and Lawgiver St. Dominic act in this case? Epikeia, whether of the superior or of the subject, can answer this question only if she is very intimately and lovingly acquainted with St. Dominic and his spirit and ideals, and the specific goals which, under the inspiration of the Holy Spirit, he has set for the Order. Such loving knowledge is an indispensable part of Dominican epikeia.

This is why Vatican II in its decree on religious life lays down as a basic principle of adaptation the necessity of maintaining the specific spirit and goals of each religious congregation. Revision of laws will be prudent and correct only to the extent that the revised laws effectively embody the spirit and achieve the goals of the founder in the contemporary situation.

Or again, this is why the Council devoted so large a part of the decree on religious life to reasserting the permanent values of religious life, listing, for example, in paragraph five what all religious institutes have in common. In giving the evangelical counsels, Christ the Lawgiver set these changeless goals for religious, and the Church made them more explicit in legislating practical ways of living them, intending that they be achieved in the specific way outlined by each religious founder. Epikeia, in making adaptations to changing times, must ardently love these goals and intentions of Christ and the original lawgivers, and find effective ways of achieving them in modern situations. Christian epikeia, then, requires that one have what St. Paul calls "the mind of Christ" (1 Cor. 2:16), and this is possible only if one has the Holy Spirit of Christ. We shall return to this idea.

The first characteristic of epikeia, then, is a sincere will to fulfill the intentions of the lawgiver, inspired by a great love of the well-being of the community and of the Church. The religious lawgiver always intends the common good of the community and of the Church.

Epikeia Respects Legal Justice

In admiring the beauty of epikeia, we must beware of slighting her sister, legal justice. Epikeia, we said, is often a crisis virtue. But when, with her help, laws have been revised to fit the new times, then legal justice will take over again, achieving the common good intended by the lawgiver by inspiring action according to the new laws. Let us examine more closely the sisterly relationship of these two virtues, lest we ever succumb to the temptation to pretend we are exercising epikeia, when in reality we are trying to get out of fulfilling the letter of the law which ought to be fulfilled in legal justice.

"Epikeia," we said, means "above the just," the just as prescribed by law. It would seem, then, at first sight that epikeia gives greater freedom than her sister legal justice, who always lives according to the law. But this is not so; legal justice is every bit as free as epikeia. Legal justice is not the slave known as legalism. Legalism is a vice masquerading as the virtue legal justice. True legal justice is free, for she is ever inspired by love, love of the common good of the community, into which she brings peace and order with the help of law.

In her ardent love for the common good, legal justice is just like her sister epikeia. They are true sisters indeed, very much of one mind and one heart. They are social virtues, very community-minded, working for the common good, though in differing ways. That is why they are such ideal handmaids of Queen Charity. Charity, in her love of all mankind, knows that she must foster the good of all, and this good can be achieved only with the help of justice, in the harmony of a well-ordered community. Legal justice, inspired by charity in living according to the law, ordinarily does a beautiful job in maintaining the just order in which alone community love can thrive. Epikeia, we said, works for exactly the same goal, though in different circumstances. When the letter of the law defeats its own purpose, we said, epikeia acts according to the true spirit of the law by fulfilling the intentions of the lawgiver.

But legal justice also acts according to the spirit of the law in carrying out the letter. For she is not legalism, who sometimes carries out the letter contrary to the spirit. "Without doubt he transgresses the law who by adhering to the letter of the law strives to defeat the intention of the lawgiver."[4] An example of this would be the religious who insists on his rights prescribed by law, even though the apostolate suffers.

Action according to the letter of the law is virtuous only when such action fulfills the intention and the spirit of the lawgiver. But most of the time the letter of the law adequately manifests this intention of the lawgiver, and therefore the letter can be fulfilled in the spirit. When a law adequately covers a situation and

4 *Ibid.*

effectively leads to the common good intended by the lawmaker, then the intention and the spirit of the law is best achieved precisely in carrying out the letter. This is the role of legal justice and is no place for epikeia. Epikeia must never be presented as an excuse to escape the letter of the law when the letter ought to be observed, and especially when lawful authority insists upon the letter.

Since, then, legal justice is truly a virtue and not a masquerader, she ever acts in the true spirit, and precisely by carrying out the letter. For love—love of the common good—transforms observance of the letter of the law from mere legalism into a beautiful virtue, legal justice, handmaid and expression of charity. Only in those cases where the letter of the law clearly defeats the intention of the lawgiver does legal justice step aside so that her sister epikeia may find a course of action in full accord with the intention of the lawgiver.

Epikeia Is Not Vitiated by Selfishness

Although a sincere love of the intention of the lawgiver is an essential characteristic of epikeia, this in itself is not enough for her perfection. One needs in addition a mature unselfishness, lest one claim to be using epikeia when in reality one is only seeking an excuse for ignoring a law which hinders one's selfish goals. Both Sts. Peter and Paul warn against using freedom from the law as a cloak for malice (1 Pet. 2:16; Gal. 5:13). A person can tell himself he is seeking the common good in justice inspired by charity. But the selfishness still in him may lead him to interpret his mere personal advantage as though it were for the common good of all.

We see, then, the danger of too easily claiming that a law does not apply in a case and pretending to be practising epikeia in acting apart from the law. One of the great blessings of law is the fact that it points out the paths which save us from mere self-seeking; a willing conformity to law mortifies one's selfish tendencies. It is obvious, then, that one needs a rather high degree of all the moral virtues before he can safely exercise epikeia entirely on his own. Ordinarily, because of the danger of selfishness creeping in, one should take counsel with wiser heads than his own, and the normal person with whom to take this counsel is the superior, the one who has the care of the common good. Epikeia is not a substitute for true obedience; epikeia cannot act contrary to the expressed will of a superior, unless one has solid evidence that the command of the superior is sinful. We hear only too frequently these days of religious masquerading their disobedience as though it were epikeia, claiming that their constitution does not apply here and now.

Obedience too belongs to the justice family, and has good sisterly relations with epikeia. Together they are concerned about the common good intended by the lawgiver, which is also the concern of all right exercise of authority. Since ordinarily the intention of the lawgiver finds its best expression in the law and in government according to the law, conscience must ordinarily form itself according to law and authority, and an appeal to conscience in countering these can proceed only from a genuine epikeia with an absolutely sincere love of the intention of the lawgiver, unvitiated by pride or sensuality of any kind. "You have been called to liberty, brethren," says St. Paul; "only do not use liberty as an occasion for sensuality, but by charity serve one another" (Gal. 5:13).

Epikeia and the Holy Spirit

Epikeia, finally but most importantly, is attentive not only to the intention of human lawgivers, but above all seeks ever the intentions of the divine Lawgiver. One's epikeia is not Christian unless one acts according to what St. Paul calls "the mind of Christ." Only a few lines before, the Apostle had called such a one a "spiritual man," contrasting him with what he calls "the sensual man," who does not "perceive the things that are of the Spirit of God, for it is foolishness to him" (1 Cor. 2:14). The spiritual man is he who is led by the Holy Spirit to a penetration of the divine purposes in our regard: "the things of God no one knows but the Spirit of God. Now we have received not the spirit of the world, but the spirit that is from God, that we may know the things that have been given us by God" (1 Cor. 2:11–12).

Only under the living guidance of the Holy Spirit can we accurately scrutinize the signs of the times and interpret them in the light of the Gospel. For although in the Bible God has revealed to us the Good News and the overall plan of salvation, the details of the continuing working out of salvation until the end of time are still in large measure hidden, and are being unfolded to us only gradually. One of the chief ways in which God manifests the directions in which he is leading his People is the "signs of the times" (Matt. 16:4). "The signs of the times," we have seen, are the current events of history in which God is giving signs of whither he is leading his People. Let us consider again the words of Vatican II:

> The People of God believes that it is led by the Lord's Spirit, who fills the earth. Motivated by this faith, it labors to decipher authentic signs of God's presence and purpose in the happenings, needs and desires in which this People has a part along with the other men of our age. For faith throws a new light on everything, manifests God's design for man's total vocation, and thus directs the mind to solutions which are fully human (*GS* 11).

Ours, then, is a living God, ever active in his universe, ever Lord of history, even in these bewildering times in which so many of our contemporaries can no longer distinguish permanent values. Just as the Spirit of Yahweh moved over primeval chaos and brought order into it, so the Holy Spirit who has been breathed upon us by Christ is renewing the face of the earth, accomplishing the purposes of divine love. Just as in the Babylonian exile God was fashioning the holy remnant into a spiritual Israel according to his own heart, so in the trials of our times he is purifying a people acceptable to him.

Christian epikeia must ever be attentive to discern these workings of God in the seeming chaos where old patterns of law and custom do not seem to work. But only those who have "the mind of Christ" can discern these things. One does not have Christian epikeia to the extent that he does not have "the mind of Christ," and he does not have the mind of Christ to the extent that the workings of the Holy Spirit are hampered in him by disorderly emotion, willful ignorance, pride, bad will. One who does not consistently practise Christian mortification in these areas can hardly be a master in epikeia, for he is not open to the mind of Christ, the divine Lawgiver.

Thus we have a supremely important characteristic of Christian epikeia: its attentiveness to the eternal Lawgiver and Ruler of the universe, Christ the Lord. He rules us by his Holy Spirit, whose grace is the New Law: "I will make a new covenant . . . I will place my law within them and write it upon their hearts . . . I will put my Spirit within you and make you live by my statutes" (Jer. 31:31f.; Ezech. 36:26f.). Christian epikeia is humble and wonderfully docile to the Holy Spirit; and we mean docility in the strong and vigorous sense manifest in the etymology of the word. The term docility derives from *docere,* "to teach." Docility is the virtue of one who is learning well; it is the active cooperation of a student with the teacher; it is alert receptiveness to enlightenment.

Christian epikeia is ever awake to the inspirations of the Holy Spirit; it repeatedly consults the eternal Lawgiver and Ruler who "reacheth from end to end mightily and ordereth all things sweetly" (Wis. 8:1). It receives his Gift of Counsel whenever reason and even the light of faith are insufficient in charting a course where law is an inadequate guide.

The surest guarantee that we will ever be open to this divine light is sincere fidelity to conscience, seeking, like Christ, to do always the things that please the Father. We can please him, however, only by working within the framework he has established for us; and this he has revealed to us in the word of revelation. This word is made alive and relevant for us only "under the action of the Holy Spirit" (*DV* 10). The Word of God is found in its fullness in sacred tradition, Sacred Scripture and the living teaching authority of the Church, which "are so linked and joined together that one cannot stand without the others, and all together and each in its own way under the action of the one Holy Spirit contribute effectively to the salvation of souls" (*DV* 10). "Thus God who spoke of old uninterruptedly converses with the bride of his beloved Son. . . . Through the Holy Spirit . . . the living voice of the Gospel resounds in the Church" (*DV* 8).

It is clear, then, that the interpretation of the signs of the times in the light of the Gospel is impossible except under the action of the Holy Spirit, to whom all who claim to be exercising epikeia must be closely attentive. And since the full Gospel light, the fullness of the Word, is in tradition and in the teaching authority as one with the Sacred Scriptures, we see why Vatican II insists, in the decree on religious, that "the adaptation and renewal of religious life includes the constant return to the sources of all Christian life" (*PC* 2). "Drawing therefore upon the authentic sources of Christian spirituality, members of religious communities should resolutely cultivate both the spirit and practice of prayer" (*PC* 6).

In prayer we become alive to the Holy Spirit, who shows us in the authentic sources the light of the Gospel as it bears on present trends. Only in the light of the Gospel in the Church's ever continuing tradition can we rightly interpret the present and extrapolate into the future, prudently revising our laws to meet what is ahead. For God's plan is one, unified, and the signs of the present times can be fully understood only in the light of what God has done in times past, for it is all the unfolding of one consistent work of salvation. If religious are to make their contribution to the Church's work of helping the world solve its problems according to God's will for a better world, then under the action of the Holy Spirit they must search into the sacred tradition and the present teaching of the Church—"the treasury out of which the Church continually brings forth new things that are in harmony with the things that are old" (*DH* 1). But at the same time, they must study the signs of the times. The Decree on Adaptation and Renewal of Religious Life says:

> Institutes should promote among their members an ade-quate knowledge of the social conditions of the times they live in, and of the needs of the Church. In such a way, judging current events wisely in the light of faith, and burning with apostolic zeal, they may be able to assist men more effectively (*PC* 2, d).

And in the paragraph on the formation of young religious, the decree says:

> In order that the adaptation of religious life to the needs of our times may not be merely external and that those employed by rule in the active apostolate may be equal to their task, religious must be given suitable instruction, de-pending on their intellectual capacity and personal talent, in the currents and attitudes of sentiment and thought prev-alent in social life today. This education must blend its ele-ments together harmoniously so that an interested life on the part of the religious concerned results (*PC* 18).

We see, then, how precious a virtue is Christian epikeia, with her attentiveness to the purposes of the divine Lawgiver and ever present Ruler, and her consequent ability to interpret the signs of the times in his divine light. Epikeia will have a prominent role to play throughout the period of experimentation in legislation prescribed by *Ecclesiae Sanctae (ESr* 6), for all experimentation must ever be guided by the intention and spirit of the original lawgivers, Christ and the founder. Only a firm virtue of epikeia in those who revise laws will guarantee the proper revision. And only true epikeia will guarantee that, in the meantime, before the revision is completed, superiors will make right decisions. Moreover, even when the adaptation has been accomplished and legislation has been revised, there will still be a role for epikeia in a rapidly changing world; for, says *Ecclesiae Sanctae,* "suitable renewal cannot be made once and for all, but should be encouraged in a continuing way, with the help of the zeal of the members and the solicitude of the chapters and superiors" *(ESr* 19). A continuing spirit of epikeia will prevent legislation and customs from again becoming ossified.

True epikeia will always enable subjects to act rightly in those situations where they are without either adequate law or direction of superiors. A person strong in epikeia never sits by helplessly, doing nothing, saying, "There is no law to cover the situation; I don't know what to do; the superior is not here." Epikeia meets the challenge, assumes responsibility, finds and executes the right course of action. She is truly free and responsible. Our era, which prides itself on its concern for freedom and responsibility, should therefore acclaim Lady Epikeia's full citizenship in the kingdom of the virtues under Charity, Mother and Queen of all virtues.

2. Your Life— A Search for Christ

"To reap the fruits to be derived from the Council"—these are the opening words of *Ecclesiae Sanctae, II,* that momentous document which will profoundly change the life of every religious institute in the Church, if the religious carry out its directions.[1]

The Council has planted the seed; religious must water it and cultivate it, and reap an abundant harvest. "To reap the fruits to be derived from the Council, religious institutes must first of all promote a spiritual renewal, and then prudently and diligently proceed to the appropriate renewal of their life and discipline" *(ESr,* Introd.). That is, their life—their whole way of living—must be updated, adjusted to the needs of the Church today. This requires that their discipline—their rules and constitutions, their customs and religious observances—must be adapted to these needs.

This renewal and adaptation, says the document, has to be in

[1] *Ecclesiae Sanctae, II,* is entitled, "Norms for the Implementation of the Decree of the Second Vatican Council *Perfectae Caritatis.*" This motu proprio of Pope Paul VI is dated August 6, 1966.

18

accord with "the teachings and prescriptions of the Council" (*ibid*). Indeed, there is no other way to true renewal and adaptation. The Holy Spirit was at work in the Council. Each of the sixteen documents of Vatican II ends with a paragraph assuring us that all that the document contains has been "established in the Holy Spirit." The Council documents give divine direction to the renewal which the Holy Spirit himself wills to accomplish in the whole Church. Therefore, religious too must make effective in their lives what the Holy Spirit has begun. The religious life needs to be brought into conformity with what the Council has prescribed for the entire Church. All legislation and all customs of religious communities "are to be suitably revised and brought into harmony with the documents of this sacred Synod" (*PC 3*). The renewal of the religious life is truly a vital part of the renewal of the whole People of God.

Therefore, in the motu proprio all religious institutes are instructed to "study assiduously and reduce to practice the teachings and prescriptions of the Council, especially of the constitution *Lumen Gentium*, Chapters Five and Six, and the decree *Perfectae Caritatis*" (*ESr*, Introd.). We cannot bring about in the religious life the type of renewal and adaptation willed by the Holy Spirit for our times without a thorough familiarity with all sixteen documents of the Council, but above all, those parts dealing explicitly with religious.

"The Lovable Features of Jesus Christ"

But what is the starting point of it all? What is the goal set by the Holy Spirit and the Council Fathers for this work of universal renewal? On October 20, 1962, nine days after the opening of Vatican II, the Council Fathers sent a message to all mankind explaining why they had gathered together:

In this assembly, under the guidance of the Holy Spirit, we wish to inquire how we ought to renew ourselves, so that

we may be found increasingly faithful to the Gospel of
Christ. . . .

Hence, obeying the will of Christ, who delivered himself
to death "that he might present to himself the Church, not
having spot or wrinkle . . . but that she might be holy and
without blemish," we as pastors devote all our energies and
thoughts to the renewal of ourselves and the flocks committed to us, so that there may radiate before all men the
lovable features of Jesus Christ, who shines in our hearts
"that God's splendor may be revealed" (2 Cor. 4:6) (Ab,
pp. 3–4).

There we have the purpose of the renewal of the Church:
"That there may radiate before all men the lovable features of
Jesus Christ. . . . that God's splendor may be revealed." The
Church has so to renew herself in the holiness of Christ that she
"will be able to show herself to the whole world and say, 'Who
sees me, sees Christ,' as he said of himself, 'He who sees me, sees
also the Father' (Jn. 14:9)"[2] The key document of the Council,
Lumen Gentium, declares in its opening words, "Since Christ is
the Light of the Nations, this sacred Council gathered together in
the Holy Spirit ardently desires to enlighten all men with His
brightness, shining on the face of the Church" (*LG* 1).

The Church is the sacrament of Christ, the sign and instrument of his presence in the world. The whole purpose of her
renewal and updating is that she may live more effectively
Christ's own holiness, that through her he may shine forth to the
whole world and be present in the world for its salvation and
sanctification. There are, then, two aspects of the goal of the
renewal and adaptation of the Church: a more perfect living of
the life of Christ by the Church—such is the goal of the spiritual

2 Pope Paul VI, "Opening the Second Session," *The Pope Speaks,* IX (1964),
p. 133. This excerpt and the quotations which follow are reprinted with permission from *The Pope Speaks* Magazine, Washington, D.C.

renewal—so that she may make him more effectively present in the world of today—such is the goal of the adaptation of the renewal to our times.

Let us consider some of the Council's statements telling religious that they are to live the life of Christ, and make him present in the world today.

The first and supreme rule of the religious life is the following of Christ as proposed in the Gospel (*PC* 2a). "The more ardently religious unite themselves to Christ through a self-surrender involving their entire lives, the more vigorous becomes the life of the Church and the more abundantly her apostolate bears fruit" (*PC* 1). In other words, the life of the whole Church benefits from the total gift of self to Christ made by the religious. And since the effectiveness of the Church's apostolate depends upon the holiness and fervor of the union of her members with Christ, the intimate union with Christ achieved in a faithful living of one's religious consecration is most fruitfully apostolic.

The entire decree on the religious life is framed between two statements asserting the Church's great esteem for the religious life as a way of following Christ more closely, and the consequent apostolic fruitfulness of this intimate union with Christ: "All who are called by God to practise the evangelical counsels and faithfully profess them, consecrate themselves in a special way to the Lord, following Christ, the virgin and poor man who by obedience unto the death of the cross redeemed men and made them holy. They are so impelled by the love which the Holy Spirit has poured into their hearts, that more and more they spend themselves for Christ and for his body the Church. . . . The life consecrated by the profession of the counsels is of surpassing value and has a necessary role to play in the circumstances of the present time" (*PC* 1).

These are words from the opening paragraph of the decree. The closing paragraph repeats the Church's esteem for the religious life: "This sacred Synod has high regard for the charac-

ter of their life—virginal, poor and obedient—of which Christ
the Lord is himself the model. The Council places steady hope in
the immense fruitfulness of their labors, both the unseen ones
and the obvious" (*PC* 25).

On May 16, 1966, Pope Paul VI, speaking to religious women,
gave a beautiful commentary on the Council's teaching concerning the religious life as the living of Christ's own life. "Your
life," he said, "means a search for Christ—Christ placed at the
summit of all thoughts, Christ lived and witnessed in the world,
Christ seen and served in your brethren. Your life is the imitation of Christ, bringing to full development the consecration received in holy baptism. As the Council said in the Dogmatic
Constitution on the Church: 'The religious state more faithfully
imitates and continually represents in the Church the manner of
life which Christ, as the Son of God, accepted in entering this
world to do the will of the Father, and which he proposed to his
disciples who followed him' (*LG* 44)."[3]

Recent attacks on the religious life have claimed that it is not
in keeping with the Gospel. It may be true that the Gospel does
not contain a detailed description of the religious vows, but it
does present to us the living Christ, the virginal, poor and obedient Christ. Christ himself is the living Gospel; *his* is the life
which religious have vowed to live.

The religious state, then, represents in the Church Christ's
own life in virginity, poverty and obedience. On a previous occasion, Pope Paul had pointed out that the purpose in updating
religious life is to make it possible for religious to live the life of
Christ more effectively in our times, and thereby make Christ
and his sacrificial life present in the world today.[4] Indeed, we
are told in the Decree on the Missionary Activity of the Church
that the presence of the Church in any given place, and there-

3 *The Pope Speaks*, XI (1966), p. 110.
4 *The Pope Speaks*, X (1965), pp. 331–332.

fore the presence of Christ, is incomplete without the presence of the religious life (*AG* 18, 40).

We see, then, what a key role the spiritual renewal of religious will play in achieving the goal of the whole Church's renewal, namely, the more perfect living of Christ's life by the Church, "so that there may radiate before all men the lovable features of Jesus Christ," drawing all men to him. "Let religious diligently see to it," says the Council, "that day by day through them the Church will be better able to manifest Christ to believers and non-believers alike" (*LG* 46).

We see from these various quotations how intent the Council and Pope Paul have been in restoring full confidence in the excellence of the religious life and its outstanding value in the Church today. They have labored so hard to restore esteem for this way of life, not so that religious might think they are better than other Christians, but so that they might realize and assume their tremendous responsibility in the Church, their obligation to live the holiness of Christ in an outstanding way and thus bear witness to Christ, making him shine forth in the Church and to the world.

In his endeavor to give religious a high esteem for their way of life, Pope Paul has said to them: "The Church loves you, for what you are and what you do for the Church, for what you say and what you give, for your prayer, your renunciation, the gift of yourselves.

"Do you perhaps hold doubts about the Church's love for you? No, indeed." How could you, after all the wonderful things recent popes and the Council have said about the religious life? They said these things "to show you how much the Church of our times cherishes you, and how much it expects of you."[5]

After giving and explaining many reasons why the Church loves and esteems religious, the Pope asks: "But do you love the Church? Do you love the Church of the Council?" Love for the

5 *The Pope Speaks*, XI (1966), p. 109.

Church, he explains, must be expressed by a generous response to the Council's appeal for spiritual renewal and adaptation, "in order to present to the world the Gospel message in its untainted beauty, in its missionary impulse, in its apostolic approach toward souls to be saved."[6]

If, then, the Church loves religious because theirs is so efficacious a way of living the life of Christ and making him present for the salvation of the world, religious must show their love for the Church by courageously reforming themselves in such a way that they will more effectively fulfill in our times this tremendous responsibility in the mission of the Church.

The Pope had said earlier in this talk: "The Church loves you above all for the religious state you have chosen, because you have desired the better part."[7] Christ, of course, is the better part. Religious have chosen this better part not in the sense that they alone have chosen Christ—for every fervent Christian has chosen him—but in the sense that they are totally intent upon him, vowed to follow him more closely in the way of the counsels, the way which the Son of God himself lived when he came into this world, the way of celibacy, poverty, and obedience.

"Your life," Pope Paul continues, "means a search for Christ . . . a continuous stretching forth toward him, in accordance with the Pauline thought: '. . . I press on hoping that I may lay hold of that for which Christ has laid hold of me.' "[8]

Christ has laid hold of religious so that each may live his own life, and that consequently his own lovable features may shine forth more brightly on the face of the Church.

[6] *Ibid.*, p. 111.
[7] *Ibid.*, p. 109.
[8] *Ibid.*, p. 110.

3. The Sign Value of the Religious Life

If there is any one characteristic of the religious life which receives strong new emphasis in Vatican II, it is what Pope Paul calls its "sign value"—the value of the religious life as witness to the truth. Repeatedly throughout *Lumen Gentium* we are told that religious should be "a sign to all the members of the Church" (*LG* 44), "an outstanding witness of the Church's holiness" (*LG* 39), a manifestation of Christ "to believers and non-believers alike" (*LG* 46), "a splendid and shining testimony" guiding the laity in their work of sanctifying secular life (*LG* 31). In short, the whole being of religious should speak a message. In a striking way, they should continue Christ's prophetic office: his office as teacher and witness to divine truth.

But this newly emphasized sign value is inseparable from the very oldest emphasis in religious life, namely, the following of Christ. Above all, religious should be signs of Christ, clear manifestations of his presence among men for their salvation. "Let religious diligently see to it," says the Council, "that day by day through them the Church will be better able to manifest

25

Christ to believers and non-believers alike" (*LG* 46). In other words, religious have the mission to strive to live the life of Christ ever more perfectly, so that in them especially the Church may show Christ to the world. For one can be a sincere and effective *sign* of Christ only if one *lives* Christ's *life* in full reality.

Therefore, in his address, "Religious Life and Aggiornamento,"[1] Pope Paul says, "First of all we have to reaffirm the true and genuine meaning of religious life as a following of Christ in accordance with his words and example, 'If anyone wishes to come after me, let him deny himself, and take up his cross, and follow me' (Matt. 16:24)." Then, in striking words from St. Augustine, the Pope describes the poverty, the humility, the self-denial, the obedience of the Savior's life, which, he says, "must be embraced by anyone who wants to follow Christ more faithfully and more closely in religious life." Moreover, the Pope emphasizes the need of a profound spiritual life, cultivated in silence, in detachment, in prayer and in study, and the necessity of "an effective practice of the evangelical counsels" accomplished in the "humble and punctual observance of the rule, which should be authoritatively brought back to its spirit and reaffirmed and modified as the times require."

The purpose of this renewal of spirit and adaptation to the times, says the Pope, is "to make it easier in our day for individual religious to conform in this way to their divine Model. It certainly is not a question of an aggiornamento that aims at catching up with the secular world. Rather, it is a sincere and loving pursuit of anything that will be of help and encouragement to a more faithful extension in the world of Christ's presence, his example, and his sacrificial life that was expended for the glory of the Father and the salvation of the brethren."

We should note these last words carefully. We hear much these days about the necessity of religious being present in the world.

---

[1] *The Pope Speaks,* X (1965). The quotations which follow in this chapter are from this address, in *ibid.,* pp. 330 ff.

By really living the religious life, the religious is a presence in the world of Christ and his sacrificial life. The world must see Christ in the religious.

"This," says Pope Paul, "is the main thing that the men of today want from religious." Religious have to be visible signs of Christ, and they can be such only if they live in reality his sacrificial life in the service of the Father and of his fellowmen. In some remarkable words, the Pope goes on to say that the widespread criticism of the religious life in the Church today and the many attacks on it are perhaps due to a deep disappointment with it. "It must be said," says the Pope, "that some people's hostility may well be the unconscious complaint of one who, along his earthly path, has met a soul consecrated to God, and could not see Christ in him, as he longed to do from the bottom of his heart."

Pope Paul is hinting that if religious life has lost much of its old-time prestige in the Church, it must be because religious are not following Christ closely enough in his unselfish, sacrificial life. Consciously or unconsciously, the world is disappointed in not seeing in religious the sign and reality of Christ. The heart of man, hungering for happiness, often does not know where to look for it. Hopefully groping in the dark for true values, man is sorely disappointed when in his search he comes across someone who claims to have the true values, but is not living them as if he were convinced of it. And so his groping hope, disappointed just when it seemed to be on the verge of discovery, turns in resentment upon the way of life which claimed to be the answer, but was not really lived as though those professing it were convinced of this. This, Pope Paul suggests, is the explanation of some of the hostility to religious life in the Church today. This is why some have lost confidence in it and have denied its value as a special consecration.

Even when the world is deliberately seeking values which are not the true ones, deeper down in the depths of their souls unconsciously they are groping for the true ones, and perhaps would recognize and embrace them if they saw them expressed strikingly enough in fervent Christians. Not finding this, without even knowing why, they can resent a person consecrated to God in whom they do not really see Christ.

And so Pope Paul goes on to say that religious have to be aware of the world's true needs and genuine hopes and expectations, of which the world itself may not be aware. If religious beautifully illustrate in their whole being the true answer to the unconscious hungerings of every man, then souls will be won to Christ. Perhaps the world is pursuing wrong values because there has not been enough striking witness to the true values. "It is clear," says the Pope, "that temporal prosperity must not be looked upon as the supreme good in life; and in this regard, the religious has the great responsibility of showing the world the ideal of evangelical poverty, the model of a perfect Christian, the eschatological anticipation of the Kingdom of God on earth. . . .

"This seems to Us to be the most urgent and up-to-date 'sign' value that religious life is called upon to offer the community of the faithful." Those who profess the evangelical counsels, the Pope continues, "ought to shine forth before their brethren for their total detachment from earthly realities."

This bearing witness to heavenly realities by total detachment from earthly realities is the so-called eschatological function of religious life. The word "eschatological" derives from a Greek word meaning "last." Religious, by their life of detachment even from the good things of this life, are to bear witness to the last things, the things to come, the heavenly perfection of the People of God.

"This," says Pope Paul, "is the shining teaching of the Sacred Council," and he quotes *Lumen Gentium*: "The People of God have no lasting city here; they look forward to one that is to come. Since this is so, the religious state, giving its members greater freedom from earthly cares, more clearly reveals to all believers the heavenly benefits already present in this world. It also bears witness more clearly to the new, eternal life won by Christ's redemption and more clearly foretells the future resurrection and the glory of the heavenly kingdom" (*LG* 44).

In the providence of God, this eschatological value of the religious life is being emphasized at a time when the Church's so-called incarnational mission in the temporal world is being taken more seriously than ever before. The Church has to be in the world as a kind of extension of Christ's incarnation, as a continuation of his presence in the world to save men (cf. *LG* 8). Precisely because of the new emphasis on the apostolate of the laity and the Church's mission to sanctify even the temporal order through their labors, the value of the special consecration of religious has been called into question. Some have even gone so far as to deny that religious profession is a special consecration. Religious have been called Pharisees, accused of setting themselves apart from other Christians, observing petty rules of their own in a "better than thou" attitude, as though holiness were for them alone. It has even been said that religious violate the Gospel by their claim to a special consecration, for the whole world has been consecrated by Christ's incarnation.

It was to counteract exaggerations like this that the Council twice reasserted that religious profession *is* a special consecration, and by its indissoluble permanence is a sign of Christ permanently united to his Bride, the Church (*LG* 44; PC 5). It is exceedingly important that we recover this notion of religious profession as something most sacred and permanent, to be held in profound reverence.

The inability to see the role and value of religious consecration in the world today is due to the inability to see that the eschatological and incarnational aspects of the Church are not contradictory but complementary. The Council therefore found it necessary to assert that while religious bear witness to the heavenly kingdom to come by their voluntary sacrifice of the goods and pleasures of this world, they also eminently fulfill the incarnational function of the Church. They truly do make Christ present in the world for the salvation of mankind. "The religious state," says the Council, "more faithfully imitates and continually represents in the Church the manner of life which Christ, as Son of God, accepted when he entered the world to do the Father's will" (*LG* 44). By living their modernized rule in its true spirit, says Pope Paul, they will achieve "a more faithful extension in the world of Christ's presence, his example, and his sacrificial life."

Precisely by making present in the world the reality of Christ's sacrificial life of self-denial, religious have their fullest sign value, bearing witness to the heavenly realities, and thus in an eminent way serve the salvation of their fellowmen by showing forth the true nature of Christ's kingdom. Moreover, their sacrificial life as an incarnational continuing of Christ's sacrificial life has true redemptive value in the world today.

And far from there being opposition between the mission of the laity in the world to sanctify the secular order, and the special consecration of religious which seems to set them apart from the world, the sign value of religious consecration, according to the Council, is actually a help to the laity in their mission to sanctify and offer to God the temporal order. For in the chapter on the laity, *Lumen Gentium* declares: "Religious by virtue of their state give splendid and striking testimony that the world cannot be transformed and offered to God without the spirit of the beatitudes" (*LG* 31). In other words, good religious by their witness to the heavenly realities help the laity to make a more accurate judgment of the true value of the earthly realities in the midst of which their apostolate lies.

The Council has some even stronger words in defending religious against the accusation that they are shirking their incarnational responsibility to the world by setting themselves apart in a special consecration. Pope Paul quotes these words, after saying that religious detachment, bearing witness to the heavenly realities, "does not mean that the religious forgets about the world or is indifferent to the world's anxieties and suffering and eagerness for greater justice and charity. 'For,' once again the Council points this up, 'even though they sometimes do not have direct contact with their contemporaries, they are present to them in a deeper way in the heart of Christ, and they cooperate with them spiritually, so that the building-up of the earthly city may always be grounded in the Lord and directed toward him, lest those who build it should labor in vain' (*LG* 46)."

What could be more incarnational than to be "in the heart of Christ"? To be in the heart of Christ is to be concerned about the salvation of the whole world. By their prayer and sacrificial life, religious help the Church to deeply root in Christ its mission in the world, and they direct this work of the laity to God both by their witness to the heavenly realities and by their prayer and sacrifice for its success.

Religious must strive earnestly, then, to achieve their full sign value in the Church, diligently laboring to live the sacrificial life of Christ, so that daily more efficaciously the Church may be able through them to present Christ to believers and non-believers alike. If religious have disappointed the world, it is chiefly because they have taken the cross out of their lives. Until they put the cross back in and once again make Christ's sacrificial life present in the world, they are going to be unhappy and frustrated, and more and more of them will drop out of their communities. For without fervent, closer following of Christ, religious consecration is an empty and meaningless word, and open to the accusation of Pharisaism. Those accusations about celibates being nothing but frustrated old maids would have no legs to stand on if religious were truly faithful in following Christ in his loving self-sacrifice for others.

When religious fully recover the spirit of self-denial which is essential to the following of Christ, then too they will recover the spirit of deep joy traditionally characteristic of true religious. Such is the paradox of Christianity—the one who has most perfectly died with Christ in true asceticism is the one who is fullest of the joy of the risen Christ. Lack of Christian joy denotes lack of the cross of Christ in one's life.

Which is better, the daily frustrations and unhappiness of rebellion against the various elements of the religious life, or the superabounding joy of a life of sacrifice willingly and generously embraced in the unquestioning simplicity of true love of Christ?

4. Is a Religious
Rule a Holy Rule?

All religious used to reverence their rule as "the *holy* rule." Of late, however, most religious have awakened to the fact that many of the prescriptions of their rule have become obsolete. Some prescriptions, indeed, seem ridiculous. It is therefore difficult to give them reverence, especially when they seem to hamper apostolic charity, or seem to interfere with living the Gospel in its full spirit.

In consequence, there is a growing irreverence not merely for the obsolete prescriptions and customs, but for the whole body of legislation. In some quarters, the very suggestion that the rule should still be referred to as the *holy* rule leads to scoffing.

Worse still, because some customs of some religious seem to be poorly adjusted to the living of the Gospel in the world of today, the religious life itself has been branded as contrary to the Gospel. The claim is made that there is no justification in the Gospel for the religious life, and that the making of a vow of obedience is contrary to the freedom of the Gospel.

Vatican II, fortunately, aware of these attacks upon the re-

33

ligious life, took pains to reassert firmly that the religious life is a gospel way of living: "The evangelical counsels of chastity consecrated to God, poverty and obedience are based on the words and example of the Lord" (*LG* 43). "The religious state imitates more closely and perpetually represents in the Church the form of life which the Son of God accepted in entering the world to do the will of the Father, and which he proposed to his disciples who followed him" (*LG* 44).

Moreover, in *Ecclesiae Sanctae,* all religious institutes are not only empowered but commanded by the Church to eliminate everything obsolete from their discipline, and to revise their legislation to bring it into full harmony with the needs of the Church and the world today (*ESr* 14).

Nevertheless, full reverence for the religious rule as a *holy* rule will not be easy to restore. We propose in this chapter, however, to take a step toward that restoration.

According to Vatican II, not only is the religious life an authentic way of living the Gospel, but the religious legislation is itself an expression of the Gospel. The various religious families in the Church, the Council says, are like so many branches of a tree which has grown "from this divinely given seed," the evangelical counsels, which are based on the words and example of the Lord (*LG* 43). "The authority of the Church, under the guidance of the Holy Spirit, has taken care to interpret these counsels and regulate their practice and from them institute stable forms of living" (*LG* 43).

This interpretation and regulation by legislation results in effective, concrete ways of living the Gospel in its fullness.

It was not the Church's legislation, however, which brought the religious life into existence; this life is not the invention of the Church. It is no mere juridical state resulting from law. Rather, the religious life grew spontaneously from Christian living. Under the inspiration of the Holy Spirit, it sprouted from the living Gospel, that is, from the life of the Church as handed down in a living continuity from the Apostles. The religious life, then, is truly a gospel way of life, and not a mere juridical institution.

Out of this living experience of the evangelical counsels, and theological reflection upon this experience, there gradually grew up a theology of the religious life. Church authority, judging the continuing living experience of the religious life in the light of these evangelical and theological principles, legislated accordingly, and approved the legislation of new founders. Consequently, life according to this legislation is truly gospel-living. The Church's approval of a religious institute and its legislation guarantees the institute as an authentic way of living the Gospel.

For the Church is the divinely appointed interpreter of the Gospel not merely by explaining its meaning in words, but also by regulating by law the practice of the gospel life, showing us concrete ways of expressing the gospel truth in everyday living. Her laws not only keep the living of the Gospel within true limits, but direct it into positive channels of fulfillment.

Our Lord said, for instance, in a general principle, "Unless you shall do penance, you shall all likewise perish" (Lk. 13:3,d). Mother Church presents to the charity of Christians precise ways of carrying out this particular principle of the Gospel by her legislation concerning penitential exercises. Lest her children procrastinate and keep putting off penance until it is too late, her love prescribes for them definite times, such as Lent, when her children's love for Christ Crucified should express itself in concrete works of penance. Such legislation, proposed to our love, and obeyed in the spirit of the Gospel, guarantees the living of this particular truth of the Gospel. The same is true in the case of the law of Sunday Mass. Here, says Mother Church, is your love's way of participating in the sacrifice of your Savior, your way of putting on his likeness—his humility, his obedience, his love of the Father and of mankind—your way of offering that worship to God which is due him from all creatures.

The same things are remarkably true of the legislation which the Church has enacted or approved for religious. Religious founders are men and women, in the midst of the life of the Church, who are inspired by the Holy Spirit to give vivid expression to the life of Christ, in some concrete situation in the continuing life of the Church. Christ is needed here or there, to take care of this or that need of the people for whom he has died. Inspired by love of Christ and by love of his needy ones, religious founders, under divine inspiration, find concrete ways of providing for that special need of the Mystical Body, ways of expressing Christ and making him present again. "The hierarchy, following with docility the prompting of the Holy Spirit, accepts the rules presented by outstanding men and women and authentically approves these rules after further adjustments" (*LG* 45).

Such approved legislation guarantees the continuation and permanence of this specific, authentic way of living the Gospel. In giving her approval, the Church exercises her divine authority as interpreter of the Gospel and regulator of its living. A religious rule is thus an expression of the Gospel. The rule guarantees that by following the rule in the right spirit—the Gospel spirit—the religious leads a life according to the Gospel.

We see, then, why a religious rule is called holy and is held in great reverence. The Church, in approving a rule, declares infallibly: "This is an authentic way of living the Gospel of Jesus Christ in all its fullness." For the Church officially interprets the Gospel not merely by explaining it in words, but even more by giving concrete ways of living the Gospel in everyday life, stabilizing that gospel-living by prudent laws.

Since the Church's legislation is an authoritative interpretation of the Gospel for daily living, it follows that our reverence for the Church's legislation is a participation in our reverence for the Gospel. Obedience to the Church's laws is truly a profession of faith in the Gospel itself. This is eminently true of the laws of religious life, which point out such a superb way of living the Gospel. When one vows to live in obedience according to this legislation, one is truly making a magnificent act of faith in response to the Word of God, a commitment of one's whole being to Christ in faith. Everything done in true religious obedience is a living profession of faith in the Gospel. Therefore, *Perfectae Caritatis* can say, "Religious, under the motion of the Holy Spirit, subject themselves in faith to their superiors who hold the place of God. . . . In the spirit of faith and love for the divine will, they should humbly obey their superiors according to their rule and constitutions" (*PC* 14).

Such obedience day after day is a vivid expression of Christ's own obedience to the Father, and of the Church's obedience to her divine Spouse; it is faith expressing itself in love's response. It is loving God by obedience, and obeying God by love.

Is an Outmoded Rule Still a Holy Rule?

If the legislation of a religious institute should become obsolete because of changing times, is the legislation still holy, is it still an authentic interpretation of the Gospel?

Ordinarily, a religious rule as a whole does not become outmoded, but only certain prescriptions in that legislation. There is a twofold standard for judging whether a particular prescription of the law is obsolete, or is still an authentic interpretation of the Gospel for the times. In religious legislation, we said, we are dealing with the application of the Gospel in concrete ways of everyday living. Therefore, an interpretation of the Gospel expressed in laws must take two things into consideration: the Gospel principles, and the life situations which we judge in the light of those principles to find ways of living them according to the Gospels. The life situations, we might say, are the material with which we are dealing, the Gospel is the form we wish to build into that material; we wish to give the gospel-form to human life. We must, therefore, study both the form and the material, both the Gospel and contemporary human life, if we are to have legislation expressing the gospel truth which our life should have. Laws, and the ways of living which they regulate, are therefore the gospel truth and fully deserve to be received in reverent faith, when they accurately express the Gospel in everyday life. Changed life-situations sometimes require changed legislation.

Some writers, insisting that each religious institute in the Church came into being only in response to a concrete need or situation of the Church at some specific time in her history, have implied that since times change, religious institutes also become completely obsolete, and that the only thing that remains changeless in the religious life, the only thing that is essential, is the gospel principles themselves. Therefore, we should be ready to tear down completely the structure of the religious life and find totally new forms of gospel-living.

This radical reformism is far from the thinking of Vatican II. The religious life will not be abolished because, as the Council has stated, "the counsels are a divine gift which the Church has received from its Lord, and which it always safeguards with the help of his grace" (*LG* 43). By her authority, the Church interprets the counsels, regulates their practice, gives them authentic expression in "stable forms of living" in the various religious institutes (*LG* 43).

In approving a specific institute and its legislation, the Church is saying, "This institute, its aims, its ideals, its special character, its laws measure true to the Gospel." Because the great religious founders were led by the Holy Spirit, "the Church preserves and fosters the special character of her various religious institutes" and "by its vigilant and safeguarding authority, it is ever present with these same institutes that they may grow and flourish according to the spirit of their founders" (*LG* 44, 45).

In other words, the distinct characters and spirits of the various institutes remain authentic forms of gospel-living and should be retained and reverenced. These are the reasons behind the first two principles laid down for adaptation and renewal in *Perfectae Caritatis*:

"(a) Since the ultimate norm of the religious life is the following of Christ set forth in the Gospels, let this be held by all institutes as the highest rule.

"(b) It redounds to the good of the Church that institutes have their own particular characteristics and work. Therefore, let their founders' spirit and the special aims they set before them, as well as their sound traditions—all of which make up the patrimony of each institute—be faithfully held in honor" *(PC 2)*.

Renovation of religious life, therefore, does not mean the destruction of the whole structure of religious life to begin all over again. It is not to be a death to all old forms and a reincarnation in totally new forms. It is, rather, to be an adjustment of existing forms.

Ordinarily, therefore, a religious institute and its legislation as a whole do not become outmoded, but only certain elements in that legislation. And therefore the rule as a whole ever remains a holy rule, and deep reverence for it must be maintained throughout the process of modernizing the few or the many individual prescriptions which need modernizing.

For the good of the Church, then, religious institutes are to retain their distinctive characteristics and works. Here we have a more precise reason for holding the religious rule in reverence. The rule is an expression of the distinctive vocation of the institute, and every vocation from God is to be held in reverence. We have said that reverence for the rule, as an authentic way of living the Gospel, is an expression of reverence for the Gospel itself. God's word must ever be held in reverence. Moreover, a religious vocation is a personal word from God to the individual who receives it. The details of this word of vocation are expressed in the basic legislation of the institute to which one is called. Just as St. Paul in his call was told, "Arise, and go into the city, and it will be told thee what thou must do" (Acts 9:6), so a religious in his call is told, "Go to this institute and it will be told you what you are to do."

One is told what to do in the constitutions of the institute, one has a vocation to obey according to these constitutions (*PC* 14). Consequently, the constitutions are reverenced as an expression of God's own word to the institute and to those who are called to the institute. These constitutions are holy inasmuch as they are a distinctive precision of the Gospel, an authentic concrete way of living it, a way of rendering a specific service to God in the Church, a way of enriching the whole Church.

For these reasons *Ecclesiae Sanctae* is explicit in requiring that the revised constitutions express in clear juridical norms the character, purpose and means of the institute (*ESr* 12a). These norms will bring out the true relevance of the life of this religious institute to the life of the Church. Thus they are to be reverenced as a precise expression of one's personal vocation and of the vocation of the institute in the Church, and therefore as God's own holy word of call. Thus, the rule is a *holy* rule.

The Council's insistence that the special spirit and character of each religious institute be faithfully maintained is tantamount to saying that the spirit and character are not obsolete. They remain authentic expressions of the Gospel. Each institute, therefore, in revising its legislation in accordance with the needs of the times, must judge which of its laws still adequately give flesh to that spirit. In the past, this true spirit and character were embodied in the institute's legislation as approved by the Church.

Therefore, in considering in turn each item in its legislation with a view to renewal and adaptation, an institute should strive to see precisely how this item originally embodied the gospel spirit and the spirit of the founder, and how it should be adjusted or reworded to express this spirit with unmistakable clarity. The question should be asked: Which virtue of Christ, or of the founder in his authentic expression of Christ, is this item intended to foster in us; or how does this item effectively contribute to our participation in Christ's and the founder's apostolate in our times? In the final revision of the constitutions, it should be shown how these things do express Christ and the founder. Then the religious will have no fear of obeying this legislation with all their hearts, knowing that this is truly a holy rule, an authentic interpretation of the Gospel for our times, and containing within itself the seeds of continuing renewal according to the authentic spirit.

But even before the final revision of the legislation has been completed, the religious can in all sincerity consider their present legislation as holy, since each approved institute in the Church is an authentic way of living the Gospel. Even if some or many details in the legislation are obsolete and ridiculous, the legislation as a whole still expresses their distinctive spirit and character, approved by the Church as authentically inspired by the Gospel. It is their responsibility to seek and reverence this spirit and character, so that in the coming revision they will embody this true spirit in whatever new forms are necessary. The old constitutions should be reverenced in the meantime for the spirit which originally inspired them. Whenever the exercise of the virtue of epikeia requires that the obsolete letter of the law be not observed, the spirit and the intention of the lawgiver which originally inspired that letter are still to be reverenced. Thus reverence for the rule as a whole, though parts of it are obsolete, can and always should be maintained.

Superiors Should Grant Dispensations

In those cases where the observance of obsolete forms would hinder the true spirit and be a real obstacle to the spiritual life

or to the apostolate, superiors should willingly use their powers
to grant dispensations from these outmoded prescriptions until
the legislation is revised. Then no one need be tempted to make
unlawful innovations on their own in their impatience for
needed reform.

Such dispensations, however, should be no mere suspension of
laws which no longer work. Using the virtue of epikeia, the superior is obligated to find other, more effective ways of fulfilling
the intention of the original lawgiver. The ways thus found, and
tried on an experimental basis, will provide invaluable experience from which those authorized to revise the constitutions and
customs will be able to draw.

When this author was explaining to a group of religious the
norms given in *Ecclesiae Sanctae* for the implementation of *Perfectae Caritatis,* and pointed out that general chapters will have
the power to initiate experimental legislation, some of the
younger religious present were dismayed at the thought that it
would be two years before their institute's general chapter would
convene. "Does that mean," they asked, "that we will be unable
to experiment till then?" "Do we have to continue to live that
long under our outmoded legislation?"

The answer was: Not at all! Experimentation can and ought
to begin immediately in those areas where it is obvious that
present legislation is inadequate, by dispensing from the outmoded laws and trying other methods to find one which will
work. It is not only lawful for superiors to do this, but they are
obliged to do so by the virtue of epikeia. As the result of such
experimentation, through the use of dispensation, the general
chapter will be able to profit from valuable experience. Unfortunately, it is exceedingly difficult to convince superiors of their
power and *duty* to dispense when necessary. Revised constitutions
should contain explicit directives convincing superiors that they
have such a power and duty.

Religious Have Not Been Totally Faithless!

Those religious who have abandoned all reverence for their constitutions on the pretense that they are hopelessly outmoded are implicitly accusing their institute of infidelity to the divine Bridegroom. Let them ponder the very wise, oft repeated, observation of Pope Paul VI: The Church has not been unfaithful to her divine Spouse![1] To want to tear everything down to the skeleton of the gospel principles and start all over again amounts to accusing the Church of centuries of infidelity to her Lord. This is not so, says Pope Paul. We must hold in reverence "dogmas and laws which the Church has inscribed on the tablets of her fidelity to Christ the Lord"![2] On the whole, the Church and her religious have been faithful to Christ. The adaptations and renewal aim at a still more perfect fidelity, a struggle for continuing fidelity.

[1] Cf. Opening of the Second Session of the Council, September 29, 1963.
[2] Address of Pope Paul VI, July 28, 1965.

5. Evangelical and Theological Principles in Revised Religious Constitutions

The religious life, Vatican II tells us, is rooted in the very life of Jesus himself. "The pursuit of perfect charity through the evangelical counsels has its origin in the teaching and example of the divine Master" (*PC* 1). "Christ proposed to his disciples this form of life which he, as Son of God, embraced in entering this world to do the will of the Father" (*LG* 44).

Of themselves, these two passages say no more than that the religious life is based on our Lord's teaching and patterned on his example. But in reality, within the living organism of the Church the religious life is a living continuity with the very life of Jesus, as is all Christian life. The Council, we have seen, describes the many religious families in the Church as many fruitful branches of a great tree which sprang forth "from this divinely given seed," the evangelical counsels (*LG* 43).

The seed, however, is really the Word himself. In the first chapter of *Lumen Gentium,* the whole Church is presented as a growth from the word of Christ, and indeed from Christ himself. "The Word of the Lord is compared to a seed which is sown in

44

a field. Those who hear the Word with faith and become part of the little flock of Christ have received the kingdom itself. Then, by its own power the seed sprouts and grows until harvest time" (*LG* 5). The life-giving power of the seed is the Holy Spirit poured out by Jesus upon his Church, which is "the initial budding forth of the kingdom" (*LG* 5).

This life of the Church is in living continuity with Jesus himself: "The true vine is Christ, who gives life and fruitfulness to the branches, that is, to us. Through the Church, we abide in Christ, without whom we can do nothing" (*LG* 6). "All men are called to this union with Christ . . . from whom we go forth, through whom we live, and toward whom our whole life strains" (*LG* 3).

Obviously, then, the growth of the religious life within the Church from the seed of the counsels is a growth from Christ himself. The religious life originates in Christ not only because it is based upon his words and examples, but also because it is rooted in Christ himself, who is the source of the Holy Spirit. The Spirit gives one, ever continuing life to the whole Church, which expresses and continues Christ, the living Gospel.

Vatican II aimed at finding effective ways of living the Gospel in the world of today, practical ways of expressing the Gospel in contemporary living and in meeting the needs of modern man. We might say that the Council sought a contemporary "incarnation" of the Word of God in the life of today's mankind.

However, the Gospel which is to find expression in modern life is more than what is contained in the written Gospels; it is the living Gospel, the Gospel which has found expression in an unbroken continuity of life in the Church ever since the origins of the Church in Christ's own life.

Thus, the Council was not seeking a totally new incarnation of the Gospel in modern man, for there is only one incarnation of the Word of the Lord, namely, the Church, the living body of Christ. Renewal and adaptation are not a radical reformism which tears down all development in the Church to start anew from the Four Gospels, or from the Gospel as lived in the primitive Church. The renewal and adaptation sought by the Council must be in fidelity to the ever living Gospel which is the Church, the tradition in life, the tradition which is a life, handed down in unbroken continuity from the beginning. All renewal has to result from a return to the ever living sources of Christian life, and all adaptation is but another concrete expression of one, ever continuing life of the Church.

The various religious families, we said, are various expressions of the one same life derived from the God-given seed, the evangelical counsels. The governing authority of the Church has always exercised its duty of regulating and approving these various expressions of the way of the counsels (*LG* 43, 45). In the motu proprio *Ecclesiae Sanctae,* the governing authority has now given the mandate to adapt all these expressions in keeping with contemporary needs. One of the chief means of making this adaptation will be the revision of the constitutions of each institute in accordance with the decrees and directives of Vatican II.

In the opening words of *Perfectae Caritatis,* after referring back to the living roots of the religious life in Christ as treated in the Constitution on the Church, the Council states that it will now treat of the life and discipline of religious institutes, and will provide for their needs in our time (*PC* 1).

The key words here are "life and discipline." These same words occur also in *Ecclesiae Sanctae* in the introduction to the norms for the implementation of *Perfectae Caritatis:* "To reap the fruits to be derived from the Council, religious institutes must . . . proceed to the appropriate renewal of their life and discipline."

Life and discipline are intimately related. By *discipline* is meant rules and constitutions, customs and observances, which mold the *life* of religious. Life is never lived in the abstract, but always in the concrete. The discipline, the constitutions, determine the specific way in which the life of an institute is to find its concrete expression. Constitutions are meant to point out a practical, effective way of living the evangelical counsels. In making profession of the counsels, religious always vow to live them according to the constitutions of their institute, in a well-defined expression of the Christian life. For each religious institute is a distinctive expression of the same life of the Church, the gospel-living derived from Christ himself in unbroken continuity.

Ecclesiae Sanctae requires that the constitutions of religious institutes should contain the "evangelical and theological principles of the religious life and of its union with the Church" (*ESr* 12). That is, constitutions must show clearly how the life of the institute is in living continuity with the "living Gospel," the life of Christ as continued without interruption in his Mystical Body.

Constitutions, furthermore, must "loyally acknowledge and preserve in suitable and clear words 'the spirit of the founders and their particular goals and wholesome traditions, all of which constitute the heritage of each institute' " (*ESr* 12). That is, constitutions must mold the life of the institute in keeping with the distinctive charismatic inspiration of the founder, for the enrichment and building up of the body of Christ. The concrete expression which the life of the Church is to have in this institute must be faithful to this special inspiration of the founder.

The evangelical and theological principles of the religious life are to be presented in the constitutions not as abstract principles, but as concretized in the life of the institute. That is, they are to be presented in such a way that the religious will be able to see clearly that theirs is truly an effective gospel way of living, a living continuation of Christ's life in his Church. The principles are to be presented in such a way that in the very living of them as presented, the religious will be brought into effective union with the living sources of the Christian and religious life: Christ and his Church—the living Gospel—and the special charism of their founder. Or, to put it in another way, the religious life is to be presented in terms of the living Christ and the living Church, in terms of Christ's life being continued in the Church in the lives of these religious in the specific manner in which their founder envisaged it, in response to some need in the Church's life.

A good example of this manner of presentation of the evangelical and theological principles of the religious life and of its union with the Church is found in the Council's treatment of the religious vows in *Perfectae Caritatis* (12–14). Here, for example, obedience is treated as a continuation in the Church of Christ's own obedient service of the Father's saving will:

> In professing obedience, religious offer to God the total consecration of their own wills as a sacrifice of themselves, and thereby unite themselves more permanently and securely to the saving will of God. In this way they follow the pattern of Jesus Christ who came to do the will of the Father. . . . Thus they are more closely bound to the service of the Church . . . (*PC* 14).

The precise way in which the members of a religious institute will serve God's saving will in the Church will be specified in "the necessary juridical norms defining clearly the character, purpose and means of the institute" (*ESr* 12b).

We shall consider more concerning the evangelical and theological principles of the religious life in the following chapters.

6. The Four Values of the Three Vows

At the close of the preceding chapter, we pointed to paragraphs twelve to fourteen of *Perfectae Caritatis,* dealing with the religious vows, as a good example of how to present the evangelical and theological principles of the religious life in revised constitutions. In these paragraphs, the Council has precious little to say about the vows of poverty, chastity and obedience, but that little is precious indeed.

The key for unlocking the treasures contained in these brief paragraphs is found in the *Relatio* introducing the revised decree to the Council Fathers for their final vote. "In concise but pregnant words befitting a Council," says the *Relatio* in reference to *Perfectae Caritatis* 12–14, "the theologal, christological, ecclesial and ascetic import of the profession of the counsels is expressed; presupposed, however, and united with those doctrinal points which are given in the Dogmatic Constitution on the Church, chapters five and six."[1]

[1] *Relatio super Schema Decreti de Accommodata Renovatione Vitae Religiosae* (Rome: Typis Polyglottis Vaticanis, 1965), p. 5.

In our translation of the words of the *Relatio,* for *theologicum* we have

These four values—"the theologal, christological, ecclesial and ascetic"—are a key for a deeper understanding of what the three vows should be in renewed and adapted religious life. For numbers 12–14, says the *Relatio,* "indicate the way in which the renewal in the practice of the evangelical counsels is to be brought about."[2]

Since the religious vows are the element distinguishing the religious life from the rest of Christian living, the theologal, christological, ecclesial and ascetic import of the vows certainly pertains to those evangelical and theological principles of the religious life which are to be expressed in the constitutions of all religious institutes.

What, then, is meant by the theologal, christological, ecclesial and ascetic import of religious profession?

The *theologal* import is the meaning or value of the three vows in fostering the direct, vital, personal relationship of the religious with God in the living activity of the theological virtues of faith, hope and charity. The *christological* import is their value in the following of Christ, the living of his life. The *ecclesial* import is their value in the life of the Church and in her pastoral and apostolic mission. The *ascetic* import is their value in exercising the religious in the virtues and in the detachment without which the first three values cannot be attained.

(Besides the four values of the religious life mentioned in the *Relatio,* there are many other values, but all of them can be

---

used "theologal" rather than "theological," since "theologal" connotes existential God-centeredness as distinct from the abstract-analytic nuance of "theological." (See E. Schillebeeckx, *Christ the Sacrament of the Encounter with God* [New York: Sheed and Ward, 1963], p. 16, note 14.) In translating *ecclesiologicum* we have used "ecclesial" rather than "ecclesiological," which is cumbersome; and rather than "ecclesiastical," which has too many hierarchical connotations. In current usage "ecclesial" has come to express the entire life of the whole Church, the whole People of God.

2 P. 7.

reduced to one or other of the four. The eschatological value, for example, is one aspect of the theologal value, for it is by faith, hope and charity that we already possess the heavenly or eschatological realities. The witness or "sign value" is really the same as the eschatological value, for we bear witness not to earthly realities which are obvious but to the hidden, heavenly realities possessed in faith.

The *Relatio* does not speak explicitly of an apostolic and pastoral value of the vows, since this is included in the ecclesial value. The inclusion of the pastoral and apostolic value within the ecclesial value emphasizes that there is no apostolate apart from the Church. Every apostolate is a mandate from the Church, a service rendered in and to the Church and regulated by the Church.

The charismatic value belongs to the ecclesial value, for a charism is a grace given for the building up of the Mystical Body of Christ.

The incarnational value belongs to the ecclesial and christological values, for it is a making Christ present in the world today.)

We shall treat of the theologal value of religious profession chiefly in the chapter entitled "Dynamic Consecration" and in the chapter entitled "Consecrated Chastity—'God Alone.'" We have already touched on the christological value in Chapter Three, "Your Life—A Search for Christ," and shall return to it repeatedly throughout this book.

We shall say much about the ecclesial value of the religious life in the chapter entitled "The Profession of Holiness," which shows how the profession of the vows situates the religious life at the very heart of the mystery of the Church and her pursuit of holiness.

Perfectae Caritatis intends to guarantee that full attention be paid to the ecclesial aspect of the religious life. The *Relatio* reminds us that in the Council's debate on the Schema on religious in 1964, "certain of the Fathers were especially solicitous for a true adapted renewal of religious life which would be effectively adjusted to the Church and the needs of souls in our times."[3] This, of course, is in full accord with the pastoral approach which Pope John and the Holy Spirit intended that the Council should take. The entire Decree is a tissue of references to this ecclesial, pastoral, apostolic value of the religious life; for example, "Let religious, living and thinking ever more in union with the Church, dedicate themselves wholly to its mission" (*PC* 6). We shall develop the apostolic element of the ecclesial import of the vows in the chapter entitled "The Apostolic Value of Religious Consecration."

The ecclesial apostolic value is intimately dependent upon the christological value: "The more fervently religious are joined to Christ by this total life-long gift of themselves, the richer the life of the Church becomes, and the more vigorous and successful its apostolate" (*PC* 1).

If the ecclesial value is the flowering of the christological value, the christological value is achieved only within the theologal value—or, as one of the Council Fathers called it, the pneumatic value—that is, only in the Holy Spirit who impels us to union with Christ in faith, hope and charity: "Driven by love with which the Holy Spirit floods their hearts, religious live more and more for Christ and for his body which is the Church" (*PC* 1).

The word "pneumatic," from the Greek for spirit, refers to the workings of the Holy Spirit. His presence in us, however, is expressed principally in the workings of faith, hope and charity, and that possibly explains why the Council preferred the word

3 P. 6.

"theologal" to "pneumatic" to express this aspect of religious life.

If it had been the Council's teaching that the religious life is primarily a charism for the benefit of others, perhaps it would have used the word "pneumatic" (although "pneumatic" includes both the theologal and the charismatic elements). The religious life, however, is more deeply theologal than charismatic, for religious profession "constitutes a special consecration which is deeply rooted in that of baptism and expresses it more fully" (*PC* 5). As we shall see in Chapter Fourteen, the dynamic response to baptismal grace in religious consecration involves the lively exercise of the theological virtues. The religious life, as a full response to baptism, is a striving to live the Christian life of sanctifying grace in all its fullness; and so it belongs primarily to the order of sanctifying grace and its living expression in faith, hope and charity.

The charismatic value of the religious life is secondary to this. The religious vocation is primarily a call to holiness, at the very heart of the Church's call to holiness; but holiness is essentially God's life in us, participated in sanctifying grace, and lived basically in faith, hope and charity. The graces of the religious vocation are therefore first of all for the sanctification of the religious himself; in the Church, of course, and in the exercise of one's mission in the Church. These graces are not merely charisms or graces directed primarily to the sanctification of others, just as the charisms of the laity are secondary to the graces of their personal sanctification, by which they participate in God's own life. We shall deal with the charismatic value of the religious life in a later chapter, "Charisms and Religious Obedience."

In stating the purpose of religious life, the decree refers only to the christological and theologal values: "The purpose of the religious life is to help the members follow Christ (christological)

and be united to God (theologal) through the profession of the
evangelical counsels" *(PC* 2e). However, the following of Christ
necessarily involves both the ascetic and the ecclesial values. For
it is impossible to follow Christ without asceticism or self-denial;
and to follow him is to get involved in his mission of salvation
continued in the Church.

Therefore, in another place the decree brings out all these
aspects explicitly. "By professing the evangelical counsels, religious respond to a divine call, so that by being not only dead
to sin (Rom. 6:11), but also renouncing the world"—the ascetic
value—"they may live for God alone"—the theologal value, union
with God. The decree then goes on to speak of the ecclesial
value: "Since the Church has accepted their surrender of self,
they should realize that they are also dedicated to its service"
(PC 5). The next sentence speaks of the ascetic value, the exercise of the virtues, involving self-denial. "This service of God
ought to inspire and foster in them the exercise of the virtues,
especially humility, obedience, fortitude, and chastity. In such
a way, they share in Christ's emptying of himself and his life
in the spirit." This reference to the christological value is then
developed in a sentence which, in four successive clauses, refers
to all four values: "Faithful to their profession, then, and leaving
all things for the sake of Christ (ascetic), religious are to follow
him as the one thing necessary (christological), listening to his
words (theologal), and solicitous for the things that are his
(ecclesial)."

In the next sentence, in one breath the Council speaks of the
union of the theological and ecclesial values: the contemplation
of God is to be united with apostolic love. The sentence after
that shows how the apostolic love flows forth from the theologal
"life hidden with Christ in God" *(PC* 6).

These examples show how inseparable are the four values of
the religious vows. If we seek out in the Constitution on the

Church and in the decree on religious life everything that is said concerning the three vows, and write in the margin the word theologal, or christological, or ecclesial, or ascetic each time that value is stressed in a sentence or phrase, we will see how intimately connected the four values really are. Sometimes all four are referred to in one same sentence or one same paragraph. One cannot rightly and fully cultivate any one of them without simultaneously cultivating the others. The more explicitly, then, we keep all four in mind, the better our chances of renewing our religious life in the manner intended by the Council and the Holy Spirit.

We said that the Council wills that religious relate their lives more intimately to the Church and her pastoral mission. But this cannot be rightly done if any of the other three values is neglected. To exaggerate the ecclesial or apostolic value at the expense of the theologal value, for example, would weaken the Church and the very apostolic value which should be strengthened. That is why the decree says that religious are to cultivate in all circumstances the theologal "life hidden with Christ in God, from which flows and is impelled the love of neighbor for the salvation of the world and the building up of the Church" (*PC* 6).

But if we emphasize the ecclesial-apostolic value, not at the expense of but solidly rooting it in the theologal value, we will strengthen both the theologal and the apostolic value. For we can give to others only in proportion to our receiving from God. And to serve the Church and her mission in the love flowing from the life hidden with Christ in God is to express and strengthen the love and faith and hope by which one's life is hidden with Christ in God.

"Hidden *with Christ* in God." This scriptural phrase used in the decree reminds us that all four values of the vows are united in the christological value. In Christ we go to God, in Christ we go to neighbor, in Christ we die to self to be freer to go to God and to neighbor. And therefore the Decree can lay down as the supreme rule of religious life "the following of Christ set forth in the Gospel" (*PC* 2a).

Rightly understood, the following of Christ in love is the highest motive we can have for doing anything. For love tends to express itself by striving to become like the beloved. Imitation is love's highest compliment to the beloved, for one must really esteem the goodness of the beloved when he thinks so much of him that he will die to his own ways to be like the beloved.

But to follow Christ is not merely to copy him; it is to participate in his own life, it is to live his life again, reproducing him, as it were, and making him effectively present to others. It is to follow him to the Father, it is to follow him to the service of neighbor. His death to self (ascetic) in service of neighbor (ecclesial) was first of all a going to the Father in love (theologal). For his obedience in laying down his life for love of men was an expression of his love for the Father. "I lay down my life for my sheep. . . . Such is the command I have received from my Father" (Jn. 10:15, 18), ". . . that the world may know that I love the Father, and that I do as the Father has commanded me" (Jn. 14:31).

By his self-giving to the Father in love, Jesus redeemed his Church. Thus the theologal value of our Lord's life is poured forth in its ecclesial-apostolic value; and inseparable from both values is the ascetic value, in which he died to self to live to God and thereby work the salvation of all. In our case too, the ascetic value is inseparable from the theologal and ecclesial values, for only by dying to self in Christ can our life be hidden with Christ in God and flow forth from God in effective charity for neighbor.

These reflections show how beautifully the Holy Spirit has reconciled the seemingly conflicting viewpoints expressed in the warm debate on the Schema on religious life which took place in the Council in November 1964. A strong emphasis on the ecclesial-pastoral-apostolic value of religious life, if rightly rooted in the christological, theologal and ascetic values, will serve only to strengthen these roots, which will flower and bear fruit abundantly, simultaneously in the personal holiness of the religious and in the salvation of others.

7. Love Is the Fulfillment of the Law

Revised constitutions, we have seen, are to express clearly the evangelical and theological principles of the religious life. The most fundamental evangelical principle, of course, is the law of charity, the basic principle of all Christian living. Not only should this basic principle be declared in religious constitutions, but their every single word and prescription should be penetrated through and through with its spirit. Every single part of the legislation needs to be evaluated in the light of the law of charity.

Since laws are directions for achieving a goal, we can judge the value of any piece of legislation only in the light of the goal which that legislation intends to achieve. Absolutely every law of Christianity and of the religious life has charity as its goal. The ultimate purpose of every Christian law, and therefore of all government according to that law and of all obedience to that law, is love of God with our whole heart and soul and mind and strength, and of our neighbor as ourself. "On these two com-

58

mandments depend the whole law and the prophets" (Matt. 22:39).

If some religious—in ruling or in obeying—sometimes seem to forget this, their founders who gave them these laws did not forget it. Because they did have this so clearly in mind, their legislation won the approval of the Church, which was a declaration that this is a gospel way of living, a way of fulfilling the new law of charity. St. Bernard says, for example, "Since all the observances prescribed by the legislation of the religious life are for the sake of charity, none of them should ever be allowed to militate against charity." Blessed Humbert de Romanis, in his commentaries explaining the spirit and purpose of Dominican legislation, quotes this principle of St. Bernard to show why dispensations are readily granted in the Dominican Order. "The laws of our Order," says Humbert, "must not be observed so rigidly that they impede the very purpose for which the Order was originally established," namely, the love of God and of neighbor.[1]

Our Lord himself laid down this principle of dispensation when he said that man is not made for the sabbath, but the sabbath for man, and pointed out how even under the Old Law such dispensations were granted, as for example when the sacred loaves of proposition, which ordinarily could be eaten only by consecrated priests were given to David and his famished fugitives (Matt. 12:1–8).

Commenting on the opening words of the Rule of St. Augustine, "Above all things, dearly beloved, let God be loved and then neighbor," Blessed Humbert, echoing the words of Jesus, says: "On these two commandments are founded all the others (Matt. 22:39), and without these two, all other laws are worthless."[2] And Humbert points out that religious legislation is of two kinds: those laws which directly lead to love of God, and

[1] *Opera de Vita Regulari* (Rome: Marietti, 1956), Vol. II, p. 38.
[2] *Ibid.*, Vol. I, p. 56.

those which directly lead to love of neighbor.[3] All religious legislation either prescribes works of virtue which bring about this love of God and neighbor, or prescribes remedies for the obstacles to this twofold love.

In studying their legislation with a view to adapting it to the world of today, therefore, religious should ask themselves concerning each law they wish to revise or enact or abolish: "What does this law teach us about loving God and neighbor? How does it help us to charity?" That should be the spirit behind each thing they do. And charity, too, is the only lawful reason for dispensation from any point of the rule.

"Love," says St. Paul, "is the fulfillment of the law" (Rom. 13:10). He does not mean that love abolishes or replaces law, but rather that love is the goal of all law. Love is the fulfillment of the law. A thing reaches its fulfillment in achieving its purpose. It is the purpose of all Christian law to teach us how to love. Christian laws are directions for loving. They point out ways of expressing love for God and for neighbor. Love therefore, has to be the motivation for observance of law if the law is to achieve its fullness and fulfillment.

To bring out this point, our Blessed Savior said, "On these two commandments—love of God and love of neighbor—*depend* the whole law and the prophets." What is meant by the word "depend"?

The fullness or fulfillment of all other commandments depends upon charity in the way that man's human actions depend upon their motivation. Our motives determine what we will do and the manner in which we will do it. Man acts humanly only when he acts for a motive. For he does nothing unless he is moved by love of a goal. He has a purpose to achieve, a fulfillment he desires to attain. Because he wills this goal, he acts accordingly. His will moves him to seek and carry out effective

3 *Ibid.*, Vol. I, p. 60.

means for attaining the goal. The way he acts, then, *depends* upon his goal.

Therefore, when one's goal is to love God above all things, the means he takes to achieve that goal are said to depend upon that love. In this sense, the proper fulfillment of all other laws depends upon charity. The other laws point out the means for attaining this goal, which is love of God and neighbor. And love is the motivation for carrying out these means.

Christian law does not merely point out evils to be avoided, but positive acts of virtue to be accomplished in order to love well. Charity, following the guidance of law, directs all the virtues to its own goal: namely, God loved above all things. Each human action thus becomes, not just a means to this love, but an expression of this love, an embodiment of this love.

The way love expresses itself is necessarily regulated or ruled by the condition of the beloved. If, for example, a beloved is in need, then love's fitting expression is to come to his aid, tactfully and reverently; tactfully and reverently, for genuine love esteems the beloved, holds him dear, values him highly, labors to increase his worth if he is deficient, and rejoices in his worth to the extent that he already has it.

Esteem for the beloved must therefore regulate the ways of expressing love for him. True esteem ever respects the reasonable wishes of the beloved. When the beloved is God, love's esteem ever reverences his will, and so love's expression can only be in accordance with his will, his directions for loving him. That is why love of God does not make law superfluous, but rather, love requires a law to guide it. Love asks, "Lord, what will you have me do to express my love?" And he replies to me, "If you love me keep my commandments, my directions for loving" (cf. Jn. 14:21).

There we have the purpose of Christian law: to point out the acceptable ways of expressing love's esteem, love's reverence for God and for neighbor. This law proposes to our love the exercise of a multitude of virtues, a multitude of positive good actions. If you would like to express your love, feed the hungry, be patient with your adversary, be kind to friend and enemy alike, be temperate, be prudent, be obedient, always give to others what is just, have fortitude's strength in facing danger for the faith, for country, for the benefit of your fellowmen in need.

In short, Christian law points out the virtues in which love is made operative, the virtues without which love cannot exist or act. Love is the fullness of the law. Law achieves its purpose, its fulfillment, when we carry out the virtues it prescribes as the expression or embodiment of our love for God and neighbor.

All these truths are brought out magnificently in that classic expression of the theologians, "Charity is the form of all the virtues." The end always gives form to the means; it gives shape to the plan for achieving the end, and therefore forms or shapes the action directed by that plan. In making something, for example, the end or purpose determines the form in which the thing is made. If we make a building and its purpose is to be a convent, we will make it in one way, but if its purpose is to be a gymnasium, we will make it in another way. The end determines the whole shape or form of the building and all that is done in achieving that form. The end puts its form into the building.

But the end forms the means and the product not only in making *things,* but also in living the life which we build by our human actions. The end gives form not only to what we do, but also to the manner in which we do it. This is what we mean when we say that charity is the form of all the virtues. Charity, as it were, communicates itself to the things we do when motivated by charity, charity puts itself into our acts of virtue, gives form to them, gives love's shape to them, gives love's life, love's perfection to them. We might almost say that charity turns everything we do into love.

To say that I express my love in acts of virtue is to say that I embody my love in them, my love penetrates their very being and

communicates itself through them. I love, then, by virtuous action: I love by obeying, I love by chaste living, I love by doing
justice to my fellowman. I love truly only when I express my love
in virtue, and my virtue is truly virtue only when it is love's
expression, only when love is its form, its life. Such is the meaning of that classic expression, "Love is the form of all the virtues." Love is their perfection, love is their fullness. Without love
they are not truly virtue. To carry out the *works* of virtue to a
"T" without charity is not Christian virtue at all, "it profits me
nothing" (1 Cor. 13:3). We see, then, that the letter of the law is
not enough, to carry out the prescribed *acts* of virtue is not
enough, to keep the religious rule is not enough. It is enough
only when charity's life, charity's form, is in everything we do.
Since only love is the fullness of the law, I truly obey only by
loving, I truly love only by obeying.

If works of *virtue* are dead without love, *love* is helpless without works of virtue. For love's true expression, we said, is virtue.
Love is fully operative only in acts of virtue. Only through acts
of virtue can we love God with our whole heart and soul and
mind and strength. Only virtue gives love its full integrity.
Young people worry a lot these days about their love being
integral or whole, and they ought to—for God commanded that
we love him with our whole heart and soul and mind and
strength; that is, we must put our whole being into love. And
the only way we can do this is by expressing love in all the
actions of all the powers of our being.

But not any action of these powers is the fitting expression of
love; only those actions which express true esteem for the beloved, only those which reverence his dignity, his will. Virtuous
acts alone fit this description, they alone can be the true vehicle
of love. Each faculty of our being must therefore be perfected
by its own special virtues so that love can use that faculty to the
full in expressing itself well. I can love God well only in the
temperance and fortitude of my emotions, only in the justice of

my actions toward neighbor, only in the humility and reverence of my submission to my Creator, only in the prudence of everything I do. "Charity is patient, is kind; charity envies not, boasts not of itself, is not arrogant, is not rude, is not self-seeking, is not provoked to anger, takes no account of evil treatment, rejoices not over wickedness, but rejoices with the truth. Charity bears everything, believes everything, hopes everything, endures everything!" (1 Cor. 13:4–7).

We see, then, why love ever needs a law, pointing out the ways of virtue, disciplining us in virtue. Love is ever under discipline, for esteem for the beloved ever regulates love's expression. To say that man can love without law is like saying that doctors can give health without medical books, without experience, without therapy, without instruments, without hospitals. To expect the fulfillment of the law without law is to expect the impossible. The more eagerly we seek perfect love, the more thoroughly we must submit to love's discipline. Religious, specially consecrated to the pursuit of perfect love, willingly, joyfully, take on the stricter discipline of a religious rule, ever seeing love as the goal of this law of discipline.

And therefore, in their discussions and meditations on their constitutions, with a view to the adaptation and renewal of the religious life, religious must look for the love in their legislation. They know it is there. Their founders have put it there. The Church has said it is there in saying that each approved religious institute is a gospel way of living, a way of expressing and living the love which is the New Law of Christ.

8. Epikeia versus Situation Ethics

The spirit of contextual or situation ethics has influenced the current thinking of many religious. Along with the good insights of this trend, some have accepted also its erroneous exaggerations. The situationist claims that there is only one law—the law of love. In the last chapter we spoke of the relationship of law and love, and shall have more to say on this in the two chapters following this one. In the present chapter we shall treat some preliminary notions which will give deeper contemporary meaning to what we shall say in the following ones.

Epikeia, treated in our first chapter, is part of the true answer to some of the difficulties which gave rise to situation ethics. There is a world of difference between the genuine freedom and responsibility characteristic of epikeia and the counterfeit freedom and responsibility of situation ethics. At an opposite extreme from that other sham, legalism—to which in part it is a reaction—situation ethics masquerades as the true morality.

Epikeia sets aside only human law; and she does this only when observance of the letter defeats the intention of the law.

But she does not put aside the divine law. Situation ethics, however, is lawless, in the sense that she boldly claims that in certain contexts or situations, she will act directly contrary to God's commandments; e.g., by abortion, she will kill an infant, and this murder she will call "agape"—Christian love! There is only one law, she says, the law of love. All the other commandments may at times have to give way to this only law.

Certainly every Christian agrees with Christ that love is the first and the greatest commandment, and that the second is like it, and that on these two depend all the others. But, in saying categorically that love is the only law, situation ethics is falsifying Christ's truth, taking his law of love out of the total context (for all her claims of being ever contextual or situational!). She rationalizes everything in the name of love.

She masquerades likewise in claiming that in making her decisions she is exercising moral responsibility to the full. She rejects laws because she claims that they hamper one's responsibility in making right decisions. Laws, she says, are prefabricated decisions imposed upon me, which may not fit my situation.

In truth, however, moral responsibility is not the power to make morality, but only to live it. Adam, in eating of the tree of knowledge of good and evil, was usurping the power to make morality, which God had reserved for himself. Adam's disobedience was a refusal to rule himself in freedom according to the directives of a God-given plan.

Jesus Christ did not arrogate to himself the right to determine or alter the eternal plan made for him in heaven. "As for sitting at my right hand and at my left, that is not mine to give you, but it belongs to those for whom it has been prepared by my Father" (Matt. 20:23). "Of that day or hour, no one knows, neither the angels in heaven, nor the Son, but the Father only" (Mk. 13:32). In other words, Jesus, Servant of Yahweh, did not come to make the plan of the kingdom, but to carry out that plan, in intelligent responsibility and love, in fidelity to the Father, and in alertness to the Holy Spirit, by whom he was ever led. Jesus ever made his human decisions in the light of his divine mission: "Did you not know that I must be about my Father's business?" (Lk. 2:49). Thus he fulfilled the commandment of love: "that the world may know that I love the Father, and that I do as the Father has commanded me" (Jn. 14:31).

The situation ethicists claim that there is only one law: the commandment to love. Jesus clearly makes a distinction between love and commandments, even while intimately and inseparably uniting them. In Semitic parallelism, his statement "I love the Father" is synonymous with "I do as the Father has commanded me." His love of the Father is embodied, expressed, perfected, in the fulfillment of the Father's will.

God's will lays down the conditions without which love cannot exist, conditions without which the two greatest commandments —love of God and love of neighbor—cannot come to fulfillment. Nor are these conditions, these other commandments, arbitrary. They spring from the very nature of the case. Love of God cannot exist in a heart divided from him by certain contrary loves. "If you love me, keep my word," i.e., fulfill my conditions for love. Keep my word; that is, my Gospel; my total message, not just love, its heart; my message of love, but love fulfilled in service, love fulfilled according to the conditions I have laid down for its existence and growth and perfection.

The Gospel—and we mean not just the Four Gospels, but the total biblical message—clearly prescribes many moral commandments inseparable from the love upon which they depend and which is their fulfillment.

The kingdom of God consists in love, for God reigns where his law of love is fulfilled. But God's inspired writer, the Apostle Paul, gives us God's word that "the unjust will not possess the kingdom of God. Do not err; neither fornicators, nor idolaters, nor adulterers, nor the effeminate, nor sodomites, nor thieves, nor the covetous, nor drunkards, nor the evil-tongued, nor the greedy will possess the kingdom of God!" (1 Cor. 6:9–10). If such cannot possess the kingdom of God, this must mean that these things destroy the love in which the kingdom consists. The divine laws, forbidding these sins which are destructive of charity, are commandments without whose fulfillment love is impossible.

Situation ethics, on the contrary, claims that in certain contexts, love justifies fornication, abortion, and the like. They cite examples such as the case of the German woman who procured her release from a Russian concentration camp by committing adultery; and this, they claim, was justified by her love for her husband and children, for only in this way could she return to them.[1]

Christian love, however—the love commanded by Christ—is a universal love; it is more than love of self, or husband, or family. It extends to all mankind, and therefore does nothing which will harm the community of men. Therefore, it observes the commandments or conditions laid down by God to guarantee the universality of this love. Adultery, divorce, abortion, lying, cheating, fornication, injustice of all kinds, are irreconcilable with charity, because they harm the whole community, love of which is necessary to genuine charity.

Because of these commandments of God, of course, individuals must frequently suffer for the sake of the common good. The situationist calls for compassion for these individuals, a compassion which would allow them to break the commandments of God to escape their difficult situation; as long as they are motivated by love, a love which, the situationist claims, excuses them from sin.

The Scriptures condemn this sort of false compassion, which harms the good of the community. In second Maccabees, in compassion springing from old friendship, certain officials endeavored to save Eleazar from martyrdom by offering him the

---

[1] Joseph Fletcher, *Situation Ethics* (Philadelphia: Westminster Press, 1966), p. 164.

opportunity to pretend to eat pork, and thus save his life (2 Macc. 6:21). But Eleazar rose above this narrow love, and in love for the entire People of God refused to compromise the law of God, bearing witness to the divine holiness for the edification of the young. His was the true love. In his martyrdom, he loved all God's People and strengthened them in the love of God.

In the same way, anyone who has to suffer innocently because of the law of God—e.g., the innocent party in a broken marriage, who cannot remarry—is called to exercise heroism akin to that of Eleazar, bearing witness to the truth of God's conditions for genuine love. Such a one must be a martyr or witness to the higher purpose of God whose laws are for the good of the whole people, which is to be loved with a greater charity than one's love for an individual. Compassion for an individual does not justify the violation of the greater love.

There are always those who are too weak to be martyrs for the truth of God's love, and who, by sinning, give in to their weakness. But Christian compassion for them does not justify invention of a new morality to excuse them of all guilt.

In asking the innocent—and the guilty!—to suffer sometimes for the sake of God's law, and thus to bear witness to the holiness of God and his higher purpose, the Gospel is not presenting an impossible ideal, as some contextual ethicists claim. "Nothing shall be impossible with God" (Lk. 1:38). "I can do all things in him who strengthens me" (Phil. 4:13). "God is faithful, and will not permit you to be tempted beyond your strength, but with the temptation will also give you a way out that you may be able to bear it" (1 Cor. 10:13).

Situation ethics' meritorious insistence upon the importance of the context or situation is entirely acceptable to the virtue of prudence. Christian prudence, however, judges the whole situation in the light of God's commandments, the conditions which must be fulfilled for the existence of genuine love.

Vatican II, insisting upon the necessity of scrutinizing the signs of the times, is thereby insisting upon the necessity of studying the situation. However, it insists further that the signs of the times are to be evaluated in the light of the Gospel—the whole Gospel, not just the gospel law of love divorced from its attendant conditions, the rest of the commandments.

Epikeia, in its ability to put aside the letter of the law when necessary, is in no way to be confused with situation ethics, in spite of some superficial resemblance. Morality cannot be determined merely by the situation. In a situation where a law does not seem to answer the needs, epikeia, we have seen, carefully considers the intention of the lawgiver, and especially that of the eternal Lawgiver, seeking to carry out his plan for the accomplishment of the purposes of his love. The endeavor to conform one's actions to the providence of God is not an abdication of the responsibility to make decisions. but is an endeavor to cooperate to the full with that providence, which accomplishes its purposes precisely through our responsible cooperation.

To judge each situation in the light of the laws of divine providence, then, and to make one's decisions accordingly, in love, is the fulfillment of one's rseponsibility to respond to the purposes of divine love.

9. Love's Inner Binding Force of Conscience

Christian and religious legislation, we have seen, achieves its purpose only when it is carried out in love. This legislation is not imposed upon Christians but is proposed to their love's willingness. To the extent that we are unwilling in doing the good that we do, to that extent we are not fully human or fully Christian. For we are most truly human, and therefore most truly ourselves, when we put our whole heart into whatever we do, doing it with love's spontaneity.

For what is it that makes us specifically human, different from every lower species of creature? It is precisely our freedom. A thing is done in freedom when it comes from within, from our heart, from the very roots of our nature as beings capable of loving and acting from love. What is forced upon us from without is not free. What comes from without can, of course, be freely accepted from within, in love's embrace, and then this too is free, since love's full acceptance comes from the heart. Our will, the power to love, the power to act freely, is, as it were, the very root of our human nature. It is this which makes us specifically human, setting us apart from lower creatures. To act humanly, then, is to act freely, in love.

But if we are most truly human when we act from within, from motives of love, it is also our truest nature not to put our heart into anything until we are sure it is really good and worthy of our love. And therefore, to be fully human and truly free, it is not enough for our actions to come willingly from the heart; these acts of love must also be guided by right conscience to what is truly good and therefore really worthy of love. Love must be guided by truth.

The fully human act, then, is an act of reasonable love; and the truly Christian act is an act of supernatural love guided by faith enlightening our reason.

But herein lies the problem: how do we find what is truly good and worthy of love? I want to love. I want to become my true self by loving well. I want to achieve my full personality in loving, but I don't know what to love or how to love it. That is the great problem which seems to be torturing much of modern youth. The same trends of contemporary thought which have done our young people a great service in telling them to find true fulfillment in loving have at the same time seemingly deprived them of the standards for judging what is truly worthy of love by arousing in them a great mistrust of changeless truths, and of law and authority, whose whole God-given purpose is to show the way to the truly lovable. Love and initiative and spontaneity and personal fulfillment are often highlighted in such an exclusive way that the impression is given and taken that law and authority are the natural, irreconcilable enemies of love and personality.

This mistaken impression is a swing of the pendulum to an opposite extreme in reaction to another mistake, the mistake of the immediate predecessors of our contemporaries in their somewhat warped notions of conscience and of law, deriving from Kant's philosophy of the categorical imperative.

To solve the problem, then, of knowing clearly what things deserve to be done with all our heart, we have to arrive at more accurate notions concerning the nature of conscience and of obligations in conscience. We have to see that right conscience is love's true guide.

Conscience is reason in the service of love, making a judgment concerning the goodness of actions to be performed. Reason studies a situation seeking a good course of action, and makes a judgment, indicating to the will that *this* course of action is good, and therefore ought to be loved and carried out. A mature, well-educated conscience is able to say: "Do this with all your heart, put your love into it without fear that you are making a mistake in so loving." For right conscience, we said, is love's guide. It is right reason pointing out what is truly good and therefore worthy of being done with love's spontaneity.

When conscience is truly enlightened and mature, it does not so much say: "Do this willy-nilly because it is *duty*." It says, rather, "Do this because it is *good*. This is the good course of action, worthy of being carried out willingly in achieving love's true goals. In this way of acting lies your true good, and that is why you ought to do it with love."

In other words, conscience derives its binding force, not so much from a law and duty imposed from without, as from within our own being, from the inner law or dynamics of our very nature. The nature of any creature develops toward its full perfection according to a pattern or inner law built into that nature. We know, for example, what to expect of an acorn in its growth or progress toward its natural fulfillment. So too, there is an inner law of human nature which must be followed if a human person is to reach his true fulfillment and become truly himself. The inner law of man's nature requires that he develop freely in love, lovingly choosing what conscience indicates as the good course of action leading to fulfillment in accordance with his true nature. As the acorn is obligated to a set course of action by the inner law of its being, man is obligated by the inner law of his being to love what is rightly judged by his reason as his true good, leading to the true development of his nature and his grace. That is what we mean when we say that obligation in conscience springs not so much from a law imposed from without as from reason's own judgment, which says: "This is truly your personal good; that is why you ought to love it and do it."

This inner obligation of man's nature, which is the root of the binding power of his conscience, is in no way the enemy of freedom. For what comes from within man's being, in accordance with his true nature, is not opposed to his freedom. Only that is opposed to freedom which is forced upon him from without, against his nature and his true good. When he is acting in a fully human way, according to right reason, his will embraces spontaneously, lovingly, of its own accord, whatever conscience indicates in saying, "This ought to be done, for in this course of action your true good lies." It is only when a man from his heart, with love, carries out the judgment of right conscience, that his action is fully human, truly free. His course of action is in no way forced upon him; he chooses it from within. It is what St. Paul calls "doing the truth in love" (Eph. 4:15). St. Paul is speaking specifically, of course, of the supernatural perfection of this process. Reason, enlightened by faith, sees the truth about the supernatural vocation of human nature, judges the right way of action accordingly, and the will carries it out joyfully in the supernatural love called charity. "The truth," rightly acknowledged by conscience, "shall set you free."

When we understand conscience in the way we have explained, law and command do not weigh upon us as an unpleasant burden but are reason's good guide in making the correct judgment concerning one's true perfection—a perfection found within the community of human society and therefore to be regulated by the laws governing that society, as well as by the inner dynamics of one's own nature and personality. Since man by his very nature is social, the laws of his natural development require that he grow to fulfillment according to the laws of his human community, and according to the divine law governing the universe of which also he is a part. Love of his own perfection and fulfillment necessarily includes love of the society and the universe in which he lives; and above all, and first of all, love of the God in whom alone he and his fellowmen find their true human fulfillment. Man to his own self is true only in being true to all of these.

Resistance to the judgment of conscience, and to the laws and authority which help form conscience, is not a sign of freedom or an assertion of one's true personality. Such resistance, on the contrary, is a sign of slavery and of a warped personality. For one rejects the judgment of conscience only because he is the slave of pride, of bad will, of prejudice. His distorted heart is set on something other than his true good. Therefore, instead of his will freely embracing the true good indicated by conscience, his reason is put to work to explain and justify the course of action his bad will prefers. This is called rationalizing. Since by the very force of his nature man has to be rational, when he is irrational in his desires he deceives himself by rationalizing into thinking he is rational. His will thus enslaves his reason, forcing it to work to invent false reasons. The will itself is enslaved in giving itself in love to a false good.

The rationalizer is the sort of person who finds law and authority a burden and cries out that they are the natural enemies of freedom and personality. Law and authority are, of course, the enemies of bad will, of enslaved will, but their guidance is accepted with love's joy and freedom by the man of good will, who knows that this guidance frees him from any blindness engendered by his own disorderly emotions, which tend to mislead his will into loving the wrong things. The greatest enemy of true freedom, of course, is pride, whose exaggerated notion of one's own excellence blinds it concerning the way to true fulfillment.

The humble man, on the contrary, is free, for he is wise enough to see how easily his love could go astray if he rejected all external guidance; he sees how easily the spontaneity of his heart could follow the lead of occasional disorderly emotion, or the errors of his finite, poorly instructed reason. And so, he finds freedom from these dangers of enslavement by freely committing himself, with all his heart, to a guide outside his unaided reason and will. In humility's freedom from pride's prejudice, he clearly judges that it is good to surrender oneself to a wiser guide than self, and to remain loyal and faithful to that guide.

This is what has prompted humble and prudent men in all centuries to seek counsel from wiser heads than their own. This is what has prompted men to make a vow of obedience to follow expert spiritual directors, and thus religious communities came into existence. In love's freedom and spontaneity, they willingly bound themselves to obedience, for their mature consciences said: "This is a good course of action—to subject my ignorance, my inexperience, my weakness to one wiser than myself, to one endowed with God's grace, to teach me the ways of prudence and wisdom."

The great religious orders in the Church have digested and summed up the wisdom and experience of the great God-given spiritual leaders of the past. Each religious founder has profited by the experience of the religious who went before him. Therefore, in vowing to live in such a community, approved by the Church as a gospel way of living, I need have no fear of loving wrongly, as long as I am faithful to the ideals and essential means of holiness adopted by my order. The very grace of God inspiring me to make a vow of obedience has enabled me to make this judgment of conscience: "God wills that I vow to live in this way, according to this rule. It is therefore my personal *good* to do so; therefore, I must put my whole heart into fidelity to this vow."

Without this fidelity, I will be untrue to myself and untrue to God—untrue to God who by my grace of vocation to this way of life has indicated to me where my true fulfillment and personality lies, and untrue to myself in rejecting this way to fulfillment, which he has set before me. Only by loving fidelity to the vocation of God, putting my whole heart into living up to my commitment of self to him in faith and obedience, can I be true to myself.

And even if I should happen to find myself subject at some time or other to a bad superior who misuses his authority, I am still free in my obedience, for with all my heart, in freedom of conscience, I committed myself by vow to something and to Someone greater than this or that individual superior. I am free in loving God and in expressing my love for him in obeying even a second-rate superior. By my obedience, humbly and lovingly, I express my faith in the great gospel truth that the wisdom of God works even in the foolishness of men. In simplicity of heart, I give myself to this truth in faith, and obey in love's freedom. Thus I am open to receive the fullness of the divine Gift of Counsel, which infallibly instructs me: Do this! And I do it with all my heart, a heart filled with the divine love in the Holy Spirit!

10. Religious and the Liberty of the New Law

One is fully *human*, we have seen, only when he does everything from the heart, in love's willingness, guided by right reason. And one is fully *Christian* only when whatever comes from the heart comes also from the Holy Spirit dwelling in that heart. Truly human action springs from within, from a profound love guided by reason, obligating us to do what is in accord with our true nature. Truly Christian action also springs from within, from a divine love poured forth into our hearts by the Holy Spirit who is given to us. This love springs from our will and from the Holy Spirit as from one source. Christian action, the expression of this love, is in perfect accord with the new life to which we are born as children of God, participating in the heavenly Father's own life. Therefore, whatever is done in the love inspired by the Holy Spirit dwelling in our hearts is done in the freedom of the sons of God.

This is the freedom of the New Law. Everything is done in love's liberty, love's willingness. For the New Law is the grace of the Holy Spirit, expressed in faith working by charity. Foretelling this New Law through his prophets, the Lord had said, "I will place my law within them and write it upon their hearts; I will be their God and they shall be my people" (Jer. 31:33). "I will put my Spirit within you, and make you live by my statutes, careful to observe my decrees" (Ezech. 36:27).

The New Law is called law in the sense that it guides toward a goal, for all true law, by its very nature, is direction toward a goal. But the New Law is more than guidance. It is effective movement from within us toward that goal of eternal life. It is a power of God in us for reaching that goal; it is inspiration from the Holy Spirit himself dwelling in us. For the goal in this case is life with God himself, and is so infinitely surpassing all human knowledge and power and hope, that the indwelling Holy Spirit has not merely to guide us toward it from within, by the light of faith, but has to move us effectively toward it by his grace, which is expressed in the love which is charity.

But what is done in love is done freely, spontaneously. The New Law, then, is the law of love and freedom, for whatever is done in accordance with it comes from within, from the inner light and love of the Holy Spirit.

Whatever is done under the movement of the Holy Spirit, we said, is done in accordance with our supernatural nature as sons of God, leading us to our true fulfillment in God. It springs spontaneously from a love which cries out to God, "Abba, Father!" We can be true to ourselves, then, and achieve our fullest Christian personality, only by being true to the Spirit who dwells within us, by ever acting in unison with his graces.

A mature Christian conscience, therefore, seeks ever to make all its judgments in the light of the indwelling Holy Spirit, to find what is truly good in keeping with our divine sonship, so that we may perform all our actions joyously, willingly, in the full spontaneity of charity inspired by that same Holy Spirit.

Paradoxically, the freer and more spontaneous our charity becomes, the more strictly it binds itself to ever greater obligations.

It is the nature of conscience, we said, to bind us from within our being to do those things which effectively lead us to our true fulfillment. Conscience is a judgment of reason pointing out what ought to be done, and for a Christian, it is a judgment of reason enlightened by faith. The more clearly a man's reason sees where his true good lies, the more firmly, the more surely, without fear of error, that reason can say: This is the right course of action, this ought to be done. And as one develops toward his perfection, growing in his powers and in his facility in using them, he sees that he *can* do ever more, and consequently his judgment of conscience says: You *ought* to do more: your responsibilities to yourself, to neighbor, to God, increase with each new development of your powers.

Thus, a rightly maturing conscience progressively obligates us to ever greater things. If one's love matures in proportion to this growth in reason's understanding, love willingly takes on ever greater obligations, in increasing willingness and spontaneity. Thus we have the paradox: as love grows in freedom and willingness, it ever more strictly obligates itself to do greater things in love; it imposes an ever stricter law upon itself.

In one sense, the more perfect love becomes, the less it needs a law. A lover does not need a law to force him to do something he does not want to do. According to St. Paul, law is for the unwilling (1 Tim. 1:9). A mature lover does everything in love, no one has to force him to do anything. But in another sense, the more perfect love becomes, the stricter a law it imposes upon itself. Since increasing love is capable of doing ever more, in conscience it feels obliged to do more, and wants to do more, and willingly binds self to do far more than the minimum commanded by God or man, joyfully obligating self to do things which are only counseled or suggested to it.

All this is true even on the natural level. Even the conscience of a rightly maturing pagan becomes aware of ever increasing responsibilities and willingly assumes them. But how immeasurably more true this is of a man who lives fully according to charity and therefore fully according to the Holy Spirit. Since charity is divine love in us, it is infinite in its scope and aspirations. And therefore charity's conscience, enlightened and impelled by the Holy Spirit, obligates itself to undertake ever greater works of love. The only law of such a Christian conscience is divine love. This love can never do enough, and so it imposes upon itself increasing obligations, sweetly binding itself to do ever more, committing itself to still greater expressions of love, in response to God's renewed invitations.

In this way, the indwelling Holy Spirit becomes the mature Christian's personal law of love. "What else are the divine laws written by God himself on our hearts," says St. Augustine, "but the very presence of his Holy Spirit?"[1] The fully Christian conscience is always attentive to the lights and inspirations of the Holy Spirit, and is sweetly obligated by love springing from within to follow this Holy Spirit's indications in the freedom of the sons of God. Such a one no longer lives according to the minimum prescribed by the ten commandments, but his law is the maximum freely undertaken in generous love, a love which binds itself to do ever more.

This explains why lovers of God make vows. One vows to do something better, something beyond the call of minimum duty, something which one is not otherwise obligated to do. And therefore, a vow is a kind of personal law. In vowing, I impose a law upon myself, no one imposes it upon me. My conscience, sweetly constrained from within by love's eagerness to do more, freely, willingly, assumes this new obligation.

That is why religious obedience and a religious rule are not at all contrary to the liberty of the sons of God. The religious, says Vatican II, enjoys a "liberty strengthened by obedience" (*LG* 43). No one imposes the laws of religious life upon the

[1] *De Spiritu et Littera*, ch. 21 (quoted by St. Thomas Aquinas in his *Summa Theologica*, 1a–2ae, Q. 106, a. 1).

religious—not God, not the Church, not the religious community, not the superiors. The religious life, with its laws and regulations and precepts of superiors, is not imposed, but proposed to one's love, and willingly accepted by a love which feels bound from within to do ever more for God. Christ imposed the religious life upon no one; the way of the counsels, and therefore the rule for living the counsels, is freely accepted.

That religious is a slave, then, who looks upon anything he does as imposed upon him and does it grudgingly. But that religious enjoys Christian freedom who always remembers that he obligated himself in love to do everything willingly, joyously. The religious is fully faithful to Christ who called him, only when he lives his life freely, in love. Whatever he does grudgingly, considering it as imposed upon him, he does as a slave, and to that extent he is unfaithful to love's conscience which promised to do all things in love. The religious, then, freely imposes the law of religious life upon himself in love's liberty when he vows to live according to it. He makes it his own law, because his love's conscience feels obliged to do ever greater things in love for God. It is precisely because his love is so free, so generous, that he willingly undertakes these greater obligations. His love finds added strength, for now it is more disciplined, more perfectly orientated toward the truly great, freer from the danger of dissipating itself on frivolous things.

What a perversity it is, therefore, when religious do degenerate into living for the frivolous! We must remember, of course, that a thing is not necessarily frivolous just because it is small. Every life is necessarily made up of great things and of small, even a life consecrated to God. We must take care that both the little things and the big things of our daily life are genuine expressions of one magnanimous love of God. If the New Law is the grace of the Holy Spirit expressed in faith working through charity, everything we do must be enlightened by faith and inspired by charity. Every law in religious life must somehow give expression to this faith and charity, every law must indicate works of virtue in which the generous love of the religious can manifest itself in a fruitful way. When everything in the life, every regulation, every custom, leads to this, enlightened conscience and generous love have no hesitation in accepting from the heart the stricter obligations of such a life, in the full liberty of the sons of God.

Even though my love's generosity freely binds itself to these greater things, this does not necessarily mean that each detail of the vowed life will always be fully pleasing to me. But I willingly vow to live the life anyway, because my conscience judges that it is truly good to do so, and it is good to do so precisely because God's grace invites me to do so. For the inner law of my love's conscience is the indwelling Holy Spirit who inspires me to undertake these greater things in love. In calling me to religious life, he invites me to undertake generously what is sometimes an unpleasant discipline, but has as its ultimate purpose to purify and free and strengthen my love.

My conscience, in judging whether I shall make profession, in judging whether religious life is good for me as an individual, must realize that far more important than being able to see clearly the wisdom of this or that element in the life is the ability to see that God's grace is inviting me to undertake this life. And so, it is quite possible that some things in a religious community or its legislation and customs do not especially please me, and I may be inclined to think they are foolish; perhaps because they are contrary to my emotions, or to my restricted ways of thinking, or to my former habits. But, although some of the details of the life may not please me, I conscientiously vow to live the life anyway when I see that my doing so pleases God and that he is inviting me to it by his grace.

For when I make religious vows for the proper motives, I do it more because it pleases God that I do so, than because the life pleases me in all its details. I may not in conscience make such vows unless I am morally sure that God himself is inviting me to do so by his grace. Therefore, in vowing to live the life, I accept its unpleasant features along with its pleasant ones, remembering our Lord's words that his call is a yoke, a discipline, but that it is sweet. It is sweet because it is his will that I bear it for the purification and strengthening of my love for him.

Whether all the details of the life fully please me or not, once I vow to live the life according to the rules and constitutions I am bound in conscience to do so. I am bound by love to form my conscience according to the rules and constitutions which form the law of the community or institute into which I have entered. This does not hamper my Christian liberty, for in love's freedom I accepted that law which was proposed to my love, even its unpleasant aspects. Of course, if I carry out these unpleasant details only grudgingly with little love, I am not fully free, not fully Christian. I find full freedom only when I carry them out in love's willingness, because it is pleasing to God that I do so, for it is *his* love which has invited *my* love to take this sweet yoke upon myself. Although some of the details of themselves do not please me, nevertheless I willingly embrace them as part of the way to which the Lord has called me. I can give my whole heart to the way, I can be fully Christian and human in living all of it willingly, for it is clearly his will that I do so. Inspired by the Holy Spirit dwelling in my heart, I do everything willingly in divine love, in the full freedom of the children of God. "For whoever are led by the Spirit of God, they are the sons of God" (Rom. 8:14).

11. The Profession
of Holiness

Precisely where does the religious life fit into the mystery and the life of the Church? The answer to this has to be clearly known by those entrusted with the task of revising religious rules and constitutions to bring them into harmony with the decrees and directives of Vatican II. The motu proprio *Ecclesiae Sanctae* requires that revised constitutions should express "the evangelical and theological principles of the religious life and of *its union with the Church*" *(ESr 12a)*. Constitutions should show clearly how religious are to share in the life and the mystery of the Church. *"Participation in the mystery and life of the Church* is to be fostered by the means which are most suitable" *(ESr 16)*.

In the Life of the Church

Perfectae Caritatis lists various areas of the life of the Church in which all religious communities should participate: "According to its individual character, each should make its own and foster in every possible way the enterprises and objectives of the

Church in such fields as these: the scriptural, liturgical, doctrinal, ecumenical, missionary and social" (*PC* 2c). This explains why *Ecclesiae Sanctae* requires that religious study assiduously *all* the documents of the Council, in which these various objectives and enterprises are set forth (*ESr*, Introd., 15).

In the Mystery of the Church

But if religious communities must participate in these various manifestations of the life of the Church, even more profoundly must they enter into the inner mystery which is the Church—the mystery of holiness, the mystery of God's life in his People.

Where do religious fit into this mystery of holiness? The very location of the chapter on religious—Chapter Six—in the Constitution on the Church dramatizes the role of religious in the mystery of the Church. In Chapter Five, the Council speaks of the universal call to holiness, after treating, in Chapters Three and Four, of the various classes of members in the Church, namely, the hierarchy in its several degrees—pope, bishops, priests, deacons—and the laity.

Religious are not included among these various groups, for they are not just another class in the structure of the Church. "From the point of view of the divine and hierarchical structure of the Church," says the Council, "the religious state of life is not an intermediate one between the clerical and lay states. Rather, the faithful of Christ are called by God from both these states of life so that they may enjoy this particular gift in the life of the Church" (*LG* 43).

Religious do not so much fit into the hierarchical, organizational structure of the Church as into the very heart of the inner spiritual mystery of the Church—into the mystery of holiness. It is only after it has dealt with the universal call to holiness in the fifth chapter that the Council takes up the religious life in the sixth chapter. For religious are called to an existence at the very root and source of the Church's holiness.

The chapter on holiness opens and closes by extolling the way of the evangelical counsels—chastity, poverty and obedience. At the end of the opening paragraph of Chapter Five, we are told that the holiness of the Church "shines forth in a very special way in the practice of the counsels, customarily called 'evangelical.' This practice of the counsels . . . gives and should give in the world an outstanding witness and example of this holiness" (*LG* 39). The closing paragraph of the fifth chapter returns to this idea, saying, "The holiness of the Church is fostered in a special way by the observance of the counsels proposed in the Gospel by our Lord to his disciples. Among these, an eminent position is held by virginity or the celibate state" (*LG* 42). Then, urging all to imitate the charity and humility of Christ, the Council says that the Church rejoices at finding many men and women in her bosom who bear witness to this humility and charity of Christ and make it present in the Church by following Christ more closely in voluntary poverty and religious obedience (*LG* 42).

The entire chapter on holiness is thus framed between two repetitions of our Lord's own challenge to follow him to holiness in the way of the counsels.

This is the setting in which the Council speaks of the religious life, for the chapter treating of the religious life follows immediately. If Chapter Five ends with the challenge to enter the way of the counsels, religious, spoken of in Chapter Six, are they who have accepted the challenge, by a special grace of God. Voluntarily, in love, they have *vowed* to practise the counsels. Their vowed commitment to live the counsels has been made in such a way that these counsels are freely assumed as an obligation, and thenceforth for them they are no longer mere counsels. "This state of life," says Pope Paul VI, "is distinctively characterized by the *profession* of the evangelical counsels";[1] i.e., this vowed commitment to practise the counsels is the precise thing which distinguishes religious from other Christians. Religious life is constituted not merely by the counsels and their spirit, but by the counsels assumed as an obligation binding under vow.

By their vows, religious actualize the evangelical counsels in their lives. In a practical, specific way, they embody in their lives the fullest spirit of the Gospel. "The profession of the evangelical counsels," says Pope Paul, "stands at the high point of the practice of the Christian life, which is planted in germ form in baptism and developed through the sacramental organism and through fidelity to the grace of God."[2] "Profession is, as it were, an act of personal consecration which completes the consecration proper to baptism."[3]

By this spontaneous, free, personal commitment, religious become "professionals" in the living of the counsels, which express the fullest spirit of the Gospel. "This state in life," says Paul VI, "seeks to insure continued growth in charity until perfection is reached. Other states in life have different aims, different values, and different duties, which are, however, legitimate in themselves."[4] But since religious make the wholehearted pursuit of perfect charity their professed aim, their primary duty, they are truly professional seekers of holiness. They are no mere amateurs, giving only part-time attention to this, or working at it in a haphazard way. They have obligated themselves to live the counsels in the specific, effective way prescribed by their religious founder and outlined in their constitutions.

Vatican II, then, by making the chapter on the religious life a further development of the chapter on the universal call to holi-

---

[1] *The Pope Speaks,* IX (1964), p. 398.
[2] *The Pope Speaks,* X (1965), p. 332.
[3] *The Pope Speaks,* IX (1964), p. 398.
[4] *Ibid.*

ness, situates the religious life at the very heart of the Church's pursuit of holiness. The counsels are a closer, more effective way of following Christ, of uniting self to him, the source of all holiness.

Religious Profession:
A Deeper Participation in the Church's Bond with Christ

Vatican II found still another way to show even more beautifully how the religious life is located at the very heart of the inner mystery of the Church. It shows how religious profession is a most intimate participation in the indissoluble bond uniting Christ with his Bride, the Church (*LG* 44). The firmer and more stable bonds of religious vows, by which the religious strengthens and deepens his baptismal consecration, are not merely a living symbol of the permanent union of the Church with her divine Bridegroom, but they actualize, concretize, that union in the indissoluble bond of religious profession. In and through the closer bond of religious profession, the Church herself is brought closer to Christ and Christ is brought closer to the Church and to the world: for the more effectively her members are united to Christ, so much the more closely is the Church united to him— for she *is* her members. And the more closely she is united to him, the more effectively he can be present to the world through her. That is why the Decree *Perfectae Caritatis* says of religious: "The more ardently they unite themselves to Christ through a self-surrender involving their entire lives, the more vigorous becomes the life of the Church, and the more abundantly her apostolate bears fruit" (*PC* 1).

The more effectively the members of the Church are united to Christ, the more efficiently the Church can accomplish her mission to sanctify the world. But her most immediate fruits of holiness are produced in those members themselves who are united most intimately to Christ, the fountain of all holiness.

For the Church is fruitful in holiness by bringing men to Christ and Christ to men.

Since religious enter so intimately into the Church's union with Christ by their religious profession, the Church can produce some of her richest fruits of holiness in the religious themselves. If the whole world is the Church's plantation in which, by the seed of the word and the waters of grace, she grows fruits of holiness, the religious life by its nature is one of the most fruitful of all the Church's gardens, precisely because it brings its members so effectively into union with Christ, the fountain of all holiness—to the extent, of course, that religious live their life as it ought to be lived. In the religious life the Church's sanctifying word and power find the best soil—all other things being equal—because religious profession is such a total response to the call and grace of baptism, such a complete giving of self to Christ who calls.

That is why Vatican II says, "The holiness of the Church is fostered in a special way by observance of the counsels proposed in the Gospel by our Lord to his disciples. An eminent position among these is held by virginity or the celibate state . . . a unique fountain of spiritual fertility in the world" (*LG* 42). The Church sanctifies mankind to the extent that men surrender themselves to Christ in her. In those who make the complete self-surrender of the religious life, she is thus able to fulfill her sanctifying mission with a high degree of efficacy, and through them, in turn, to bring the waters of holiness to others.

In the garden of the religious life, then—when the life is lived as it ought to be—the Church produces some of her choicest fruits of holiness. Vatican II says, for example, of cloisters: "They brighten God's People with the richest splendors of sanctity. . . . They make this People grow by imparting a hidden apostolic fruitfulness" (*PC* 7). If a religious institute is not producing notable fruits of holiness in its members, then it is not living its life as it ought, and sorely needs a spiritual renewal.

When these great truths about the religious life are asserted in our days, we often hear the protest that to extol the holiness of the religious state is to discourage the pursuit of holiness in the laity, since one gives the impression that holiness is for religious alone. Vatican II counters this objection, saying: "The profession of the evangelical counsels appears as a sign which can and ought to attract all the members of the Church to an effective and prompt fulfillment of the duties of their Christian vocation" (*LG* 44). The beauty of holiness in the religious life edifies and encourages others to seek holiness in their own way.

Or, the objection is raised: to extol the holiness of the religious state leads to pharisaic triumphalism among religious. It makes them act as though they have a monopoly on holiness and are better than all others.

Possibly some religious do fall into this danger. But these, of course, are the ones who are not truly holy, who have not used well the means to holiness provided by the religious life. Genuine holiness is always accompanied by genuine humility. Even if there is some danger of such pride for some religious, the truth about the greatness of the religious life must nevertheless be preached, so that the religious life will be restored to its rightful esteem in the Church. The greatness of the life must be preached, not to cause pride among religious, but to awaken them to their weighty responsibility to be holy. Theirs is not a position of privilege in the Church, but of tremendous responsibility to God and to the Church. Their holiness is a service to be rendered the Church; they must be alerted to their obligation to be outstandingly holy in fidelity to their vocation to be signs of holiness, standard-bearers in the Church's pursuit of holiness.

There is still another objection raised to the extolling of the religious life. It is claimed that Vatican II has taught that religious are no different from other Christians, since there is a universal call to holiness. This is a half-truth. It is true to this extent: all Christians, clergy and laity and religious, are called to one same holiness, the holiness of sharing in God's own life by grace and charity. Religious are no different from other Christians in the sense that all seek one same kind of holiness. But religious definitely are different from others in the "professional" manner in which they seek holiness. By religious profession, they are vowed to live the way of the evangelical counsels, in the fullness of the gospel spirit, living in the manner in which Christ himself chose to live—poor, virginal, obedient.

So important is the role of the religious life in the Church that the Council's decree on the missionary activity of the Church, in listing the requirements for the fullness of the Church's presence in a missionary territory (*AG* 15–18), specifies that "right from the planting stage of the Church, the religious life should be carefully fostered—not only for the sake of the precious and absolutely necessary assistance to missionary activity which it offers—but because by a more inward consecration made to God in the Church it luminously manifests and signifies the inner nature of the Christian calling" (*AG* 18).[5]

In striving to live the Gospel in its heroic fullness and in its deepest mystery of holiness, religious are not pharisees but people endowed by God with a weighty responsibility to be leaders in genuine holiness. In being different from others in using their own effective means to holiness, they are promoting, not hindering, the holiness of the laity. They are called to live at the very heart of the mystery of the Church, participating intimately in the Church's indissoluble, mystical bond with Christ, the source of all holiness.

---

5 Cf. also: "The contemplative life belongs to the fullness of the Church's presence, and therefore should be everywhere established" (*AG* 18).

12. The Religious Life
and the Mystery of Mary

If we would like to know just where religious fit into the mystery of the Church, we have to look to Mary, for in her the whole mystery of the Church was first actualized and perfected.

What do we mean by the mystery of the Church?

The reality of the Church is something more than the hierarchy, the liturgy, the sacraments, the laws which govern her. At the very heart of the Church, beneath her visible social organization, is the inner mystery of the Church, the mystical, spiritual bond in which she is united to Christ. In this union with Christ, she has communion with God—Father, Son, and Holy Spirit.

"The intimate, the primary source of the Church's sanctifying effectiveness," says Pope Paul, "is to be found in its mystic union with Christ."[1] Only from Christ does holiness flow to the Church and to the world through the Church. But we cannot conceive of the Church's union with Christ "as separate from her

[1] Address in promulgating *Lumen Gentium*, November 21, 1964; quoted in *Marian Studies*, XVI (1965), p. 22.

93

who is the Mother of the Word Incarnate and whom Jesus Christ himself wanted closely united to himself for our salvation. Thus the loving contemplation of the marvels worked by God in his holy Mother must find its proper perspective in the vision of the Church. And the knowledge of the true doctrine on Mary will always be the key to the exact understanding of the mystery of Christ and of the Church."[2]

In other words, we cannot rightly understand Mary except in the light of her role in the Church, nor can we rightly understand the Church except in the light of Mary, in whose own person the Church was first perfected. That is why the Council's document on Mary, originally a separate one, was incorporated into the Constitution on the Church as its crowning chapter.

The Council calls Mary the type of the Church—the figure in whom the Church first reaches its actuality and perfection, and who is therefore the model for the entire Church (*LG* 63, 65). Mary is type of the Church precisely in its deeper mystery, its inner reality, its indissoluble mystical union with Christ, its virginal bond with him in faith, its maternal fruitfulness in him in charity. "As St. Ambrose taught, the Mother of God is a type of the Church in the order of faith, charity, and perfect union with Christ. In the mystery of the Church, which itself is rightly called mother and virgin, the Blessed Virgin Mary leads the way, showing forth in an eminent and singular manner the example of virgin and mother" (*LG* 63).

Mary lived—and still lives—the mystery of the Church to the full; she lives the mystery at its very heart—there where Jesus is. That is why she is the exemplar for all others in living this mystery.

"Mary occupies a place in the Church which is the most exalted after Christ, and closest of all to us" (*LG* 54). Mary is truly closer to all of us, the members, than we are to one another in

2 *Ibid.*

that Church, for she has a direct, maternal, life-giving influence in the life of every living member of the Church. She is effectively present to all by the power of her spiritual maternity (*LG* 62).

But the Council intends to emphasize also another way in which Mary is very close to all of us. She too "is redeemed by reason of the merits of her Son . . . because she belongs to the offspring of Adam she is one with all those who are to be saved" (*LG* 53). And therefore, though as Mother of God she is Mother of the Church, as one of the redeemed she is daughter of the Church. "She too is a member of the Church," says Pope Paul. "She is redeemed by Christ, she is our sister."[3]

And precisely because she is one of the redeemed, she so beautifully shows forth how all of us become the Church of the redeemed by entering into the mystery of salvation in faith and obedience and charity like hers, and thus achieve that mystic union with Christ in which alone we can receive the fruits of the redemption. "In her," says the Constitution on the Liturgy, "the Church holds up and admires the most excellent fruit of the redemption, and joyfully contemplates as in a faultless image that which she herself wholly desires and hopes to be" (*SC* 103). "In the most blessed Virgin, the Church has already reached that perfection whereby she exists without spot or wrinkle" (*LG* 65).

Mary not only presents to us the picture of the final fruits of union with Christ, but shows all the People of God how to enter deeply into that union, in order to be saved by Christ and to become a savior with him. Mary, like the Church and before the Church, is both saved and saving, and she is both only by reason of her intimate union with Jesus.

Pope Paul has pointed out how the Council, in its pastoral approach to divine revelation, "speaks of the message of Christ

[3] Address of Pope Paul VI, November 18, 1964; quoted in *Marian Studies,* XVI (1965), p. 26.

in relation to man. It considers man as taking part in the history
of salvation" and prepares the way for "a theology which refers
to humanity as seen in history and in concrete actuality."[4] That
is, the Council shows us divine revelation at work in man; it
shows us man as listening to God's word and responding to it
in faith, responding to it in living it, and becoming involved in
the work of redemption.

Mary: the Perfect Response to God's Word

That is exactly how the Council presents Mary to us—as the
perfect "Yes" to God's word, as personally involved in the work
of salvation, as totally consecrated to that work, and by her
personal involvement attracting the whole Church to a similar
involvement. "Since Mary has entered intimately into the history
of salvation, in a certain manner she unites all the great truths
of the faith in herself and echoes them forth. When she is
preached and venerated, she draws believers to her Son and to his
sacrifice, and to love of the Father" (*LG* 65).

That is, in the person of Mary we see all the truths of the faith
united as a concrete, living reality. In Mary, Christ's truth, the
Church's truth, shines forth as eminently livable and lovable, attracting and inspiring others to live that same truth.

This has always been one of the Church's chief ways of handing on the Gospel. She has passed it on from generation to
generation in the lives of her holy members, who lived it in the
likeness of Mary and Jesus. Thus Christian tradition, besides
being the handing down of the word of God in preaching and
teaching, is the handing on of a gospel life which is always being
lived in the Church in an unbroken continuity, and is being ever
more deeply understood in the very living of it. The wealth of

4 Address of Pope Paul VI to the International Congress on the Theology
of Vatican II, September 1966.

this "living tradition," says the Council, "is poured into the practice and life of the believing and praying Church. . . . This tradition which comes from the Apostles develops in the Church with the help of the Holy Spirit. There is a growth in the understanding of the realities and the words which have been handed down. This happens through the contemplation and study made by believers, who treasure these things in their hearts through a penetrating understanding of the spiritual realities which they experience, and through the preaching of those who have received through episcopal succession the sure gift of truth. For as the centuries succeed one another the Church constantly moves forward toward the fullness of divine truth until the words of God reach their complete fulfillment in her" *(DV* 8).

Thus, the word of revelation reaches its full and final development in the very life of the perfected People of God.

The Religious Life: A Living Gospel

Since the Gospel and the deeper understanding of it is thus passed on in the continuity of a living tradition and a tradition of living, we can understand why religious are directed by the Council to return to the traditional sources of the religious life, not only to the living Gospel which is Christ himself, but to that Gospel as lived by generations of religious. For we must remain in the full stream of the living tradition even while we develop this continuity of life in new directions in adapting to modern needs.

All the faithful are to share in this handing on of the Gospel by living it, showing, like Mary, that it is both livable and lovable. But in a special way this is the function of religious: "The profession of the evangelical counsels appears as a sign which can and ought to attract all the members of the Church to an effective and prompt fulfillment of the duties of their Christian vocation" (*LG* 44). The only gospel some people will ever read is the gospel according to you—the gospel they read in your life.

All Christians are to be a kind of continuation of salvation history. As God originally revealed himself in the salvation deeds he accomplished in the lives of his chosen People of old, so he continues to manifest that same truth to the world today in the saving wonders he is accomplishing in us through our union with Christ.

Mary in Salvation History

The Council, we said, presents Mary as involved in salvation history.[5] It shows how in the course of Old Testament history "the figure of the woman, the Mother of the Redeemer," became ever clearer; it shows how Mary sums up in her own person, as it were, "the poor and the humble of the Lord who confidently hope for and receive salvation from him"; it shows how in her person she contains, as it were, the Daughter of Sion, the whole People of God, living in expectation of the promise (*LG* 55).

But when the promise is finally fulfilled, and she receives and gives to the world "him who is life itself," she does so "not merely in a passive way, but as freely cooperating in the work of human salvation through faith and obedience" (*LG* 56). Mary becomes involved in the history of salvation as a person acting with full intelligence and love, making a free commitment in a fully responsible way. In giving the perfect response to God's word—"Behold the handmaid of the Lord; be it done to me according to thy word"—she consecrates herself to the Savior and to his redemptive work, she enters intimately into salvation history in the likeness of the Servant of Yahweh described by Isaia. "Embracing God's salvific will with a full heart and im-

[5] The second section of Chapter Eight of *Lumen Gentium* is entitled "The Role of the Blessed Mother in the Economy of Salvation."

peded by no sin, she consecrated herself totally as a servant of the Lord to the person and the work of her Son; and in subordination to him and along with him, by the grace of the almighty God, she served the mystery of redemption" (*LG* 56).

At the very heart of Mary's commitment, her consecration to the work of salvation, are her faith and her obedience. "For, as St. Irenaeus says, she 'being obedient, became the cause of salvation for herself and for the whole human race.' . . . 'The knot of Eve's disobedience was untied by Mary's obedience; what the virgin Eve bound through her unbelief, the Virgin Mary loosened by her faith' " (*LG* 56).

Religious and Salvation History

It is interesting to notice how the Council describes the religious vow of obedience in the same terminology it used in speaking of Mary's commitment of self to the work of redemption. Of religious obedience it is said: "Religious by the profession of obedience offer the full consecration of their own will as a sacrifice of themselves to God, and thereby are united more permanently and more securely to the salvific will of God . . ." (*PC* 14). Of Mary it is said: "Embracing God's salvific will with a full heart . . . she consecrated herself totally as a servant of the Lord to the person and work of her Son . . . and served the mystery of redemption." By religious obedience, we too enter more intimately into the service of the mystery of redemption, we are "more closely bound to the service of the Church" (*PC* 14). Because of our closer union with the saving will of God in obedience, God is better able to work his designs of salvation in us, and through us in others.

There is another remarkable way in which the Council's words concerning Mary are echoed in its words concerning religious profession. Several times the Council speaks of the indissoluble bond uniting Mary with Christ; e.g., "Holy Church honors with special love the blessed Mary, Mother of God, who is joined by an indissoluble bond to the saving work of her Son" (*SC* 103; cf. *LG* 53). This union of Mary with Christ in the work of salvation is shown in detail in three paragraphs of *Lumen Gentium* (*LG* 57–59). The Church too has an indissoluble bond with Christ. This bond with the divine Bridegroom found its first expression and fullest perfection in Mary's bond with him. Indeed, the Church's bond with him is a participation in Mary's own bond with him. For at the Annunciation, by her faith and obedience to the word, Mary made that bond in the name of the whole Church, as the representative of all of God's People.

The Council says that religious profession is a firmer and more stable participation in the indissoluble bond uniting Christ and his bride, the Church, a more perfect expression of this bond than is the baptismal consecration (*LG* 44). To participate more deeply in the Church's virginal consecration to Christ by fidelity to one's religious profession is to enter more fully into Mary's own virginal consecration to him and to his work of salvation.

Is it any wonder, then, that in its closing words of the decree on religious life, the Council refers all religious to Mary, presenting her life as the rule of life for all: "With the powerful aid of that most loving Virgin Mary, God's Mother, 'whose life is a rule of life for all,' religious communities will experience a daily growth in numbers, and will yield a richer harvest of fruits that bring salvation" (*PC* 25). Mary, like Christ, is the "religious rule" in a concrete, existential expression (cf. *PC* 2a).

It is clear that the spiritual renewal which the Church is asking of religious will be achieved only to the extent that they live the mystery of the Church as Mary lived it. They will be able to do this only with her efficacious maternal help, by which she is closer to all of us than we are to one another. Mary is the pattern and the Mother of renewal. With her we must go to the very heart of the mystery of the Church—there where Jesus is, as source of all holiness and salvation. We must enter ever more fully into Mary's indissoluble bond with Christ, which is the Church's bond with him. To enter into the mystery of salvation is to enter into Christ and be saved in him and become saviors with him—in the likeness of Mary, who, as saved, is daughter of the Church and our sister, but as savior with Christ, is Mother of the Church and our Mother.

13. "The One Whom the Father Has Consecrated"

"The following of Christ as proposed by the Gospel is the supreme rule of the religious life," says Vatican II (*PC* 2). But is not this the supreme rule of every Christian? Is there something unique about the manner in which religious follow Christ?

The distinctive mark of the religious, Pope Paul has told us, is the *profession* of the evangelical counsels. Religious are professional seekers of holiness. By religious profession, the way of the counsels is assumed as an obligation binding under vow. This profession is a special consecration which gives full expression to the baptismal consecration in which it is vitally rooted.

By reason of this special consecration, religious follow Christ precisely as the consecrated One—"the one whom the Father has consecrated and sent into the world" (Jn. 10:36). Religious highlight this aspect of Christianity in their lives. The baptismal consecration of every Christian is a participation in Christ's own consecration; religious profession expresses this consecration more fully.

102

Different Christians express different aspects of Christ—Christ the teacher, Christ the workman, Christ the preacher, Christ the suffering one, Christ in his humility, in his patience, in his works of mercy. But all religious—even when they express one or another of these characteristics just mentioned—express above all Christ the consecrated one.

We can understand the special consecration of religious, then, only in the light of Christ's consecration. The supreme rule of the religious life is the following of Christ the Holy One. To consecrate means to make holy. Religious, we have seen, exist at the very heart of the mystery of the Church's holiness. By consecration, a thing is made holy at the very roots of its being, so that everything springing from these roots might be holy. One has to *be* holy before he can act holy. "A bad tree cannot bear good fruit," says Jesus (cf. Matt. 7:17).

Consecration is holiness in being, and only God can work it in us. Consecration is a holiness planted by God in the depths of our being so that it may bear fruit in all of our living and action. "He who has begun this good work in you," says St. Paul, "will continue to perfect it until the day of Christ Jesus . . . I pray that you may be filled with the fruit that springs from holiness through the aid of Jesus Christ" (Phil. 1:6–11, k).

If consecration or holiness in being is God's work in us, we must respond to what he has begun, we must cooperate in its growth and expression, we must live true to the holiness which he has planted in us, and bring forth "the fruit that springs from holiness." This response, this cooperation, is holiness in action, holiness in living.

"The Holy One"

All this is supremely true of Christ, the Holy One par excellence. Jesus calls himself "the One whom the Father has consecrated and sent into the world." "The Holy One" is his proper name (Jn. 6:69, k). That is the meaning of his title, "the Christ." The Christ means the anointed one. A ceremony of anointing, however, is a ceremony of consecration.

Christ is anointed with divinity. That is, the totality of his humanity is consecrated by its hypostatic union with the divine Person of the Word. The whole being of Jesus is holy with the totality of God's holiness.

Whatever is consecrated is God's own, exclusively his. Christ's total human nature is God's own in a unique way. His body and soul are totally surrendered to the Word who is God. What is more God's own than this human nature which exists in the Word's own person, inseparably united to him as one thing with him, existing with his own divine subsistence? Christ's human nature, then, exists solely for his divine Person; it is consecrated to his Person. As the Word's own, this body and soul does not have and never did have any existence apart from the divine Person to which it is hypostatically united. It exists exclusively for him, that in it, God might be present among men as Man for their sanctification. Christ is truly "the Holy One," the source of all other consecration and holiness. He is holiness itself.

He is the one whom the Father has consecrated and *sent into the world;* that is, he is consecrated for a mission. Christ is God's own to do God's work. Consecration implies total availability. The *Father* has consecrated Jesus; Jesus exists only *for the Father* in total availability, to be used only as the Father wishes in accomplishing his work. He is consecrated to the Father's will to save mankind.

Jesus frequently expressed his consecration to the Father and to his mission: "I have come down from heaven, not to do my own will, but the will of him who sent me" (Jn. 6:38). "My food is to do the will of him who sent me, to accomplish his work" (Jn. 4:34). "He who sent me is with me; he has not left me alone, because I do always the things that are pleasing to him" (Jn. 8:29).

In this way, Jesus expressed his personal response to the consecration imprinted upon his very being. This response was his holiness in action, springing from his holiness in being. It was the living out of the consecration which had been bestowed upon his human nature when his divine Person was united to it in the instant of the incarnation. Because it was anointed with divinity from that very instant, our Lord's humanity was fully equipped for his mission. It remained only for him to live this consecration in carrying out that mission.

"Therefore in coming into the world he says . . . 'Behold I come to do thy will, O, God' " (Heb. 10:5, 9). Thus, consecration is not merely a quality of his being; it springs into living action, it expresses itself in his life. The very heart of his living consecration is manifest in the words, "I come to do thy will, O God." Jesus wills to exist for no other purpose, he willingly makes himself totally available to the Father in eager devotion. Devotion is love's readiness of will to do the will of the beloved. Love's devotion is the heart of living consecration. It is the living response to consecration in being. Devotion is the living giving of one's whole being to the saving will of God.

To sum up—God consecrated Christ's humanity in bestowing divinity upon it in the instant of the incarnation, equipping it for God's work of salvation; Christ responded to this consecration of his being by eagerly accepting his mission, consecrating his will and all of his action to its accomplishment.

Our Christian Consecration

Our very being, likewise, is consecrated by God in baptism, so that henceforth we are God's own, existing exclusively for him. "You are not your own, for you have been bought at a great price" (1 Cor. 6:20). The baptismal consecration is a share in Christ's own consecration. Not only do we belong exclusively to God as Christ does and in Christ, but we share in Christ's own holiness, we share in his own grace equipping him for carrying out his mission. "For in him dwells all the fullness of the Godhead bodily, and in him . . . you have received of that fullness" (Col. 2:9). "You alone are holy!" we sing to him in the *Gloria* of the Mass. He alone is self-existing holiness. All our holiness is ever flowing from his and ever dependent upon it.

Just as Christ's humanity is totally and inviolably holy because of its hypostatic union with the Person of the Word, so our very being is permanently consecrated by its baptismal union with his sacred humanity. The baptismal character is the mark of inseparable union with Christ in his paschal mystery, it is the power of coming into ever more intimate union with him. The baptismal character is a participation in the Church's indissoluble bond with Christ her divine Bridegroom.

But just as Jesus responded to the consecration of his being in devoted acceptance of his mission, so we must respond to the baptismal consecration of our being by our consecration in action; we must live true to baptismal consecration in the ardent devotion of a consecrated will.

The Religious Consecration

Religious profession, we have seen, is a fullness of voluntary response to the baptismal consecration, in love's eager acceptance of that consecration with all its implications. As in the case of Jesus, the very essence of this response is the consecration of one's will in love's devotion and fidelity. Such living devotion is the core of every Christian's true response to his baptismal consecration. Religious profession, however, is Christian devotion and fidelity irrevocably stabilized by vow, thus guaranteed against fickleness and cooling of devotion.

Man's devotion tends to be fickle. When the Scriptures declare that "every man is a liar" (Rom. 3:4), they are referring not so much to lying in speech as to the lying which is infidelity, the

failure to measure true to God and to what God expects man to be, the failure to measure true to one's commitments to God.

All of us have had experience of this instability. Sometimes we have great spurts of devotion; we hear a sermon or read a passage in the word of God, and in a moment of religious enthusiasm we undertake great things for the Lord. But it is not long before the first emotion has faded. We are no longer in the mood to carry out our resolution, and so in moments of difficulty we abandon what we have begun. Thus we make little progress in the spiritual life.

The vows of the religious life are an excellent remedy for this human fickleness. We promise by vow that we shall strive ceaselessly for Christian holiness whether we are in the mood for striving or not. We profess that we shall no longer live by mere emotional enthusiasm which comes and goes; we steadfastly bind our will by vow to follow a set program for growth in holiness. Whether our emotions help us or hinder us, we shall live according to our will, consecrated or made firm and stable by vow.

This is what Vatican II means in saying that religious profession is a fuller expression of the baptismal consecration. It is a personal, loving, devoted response to baptismal consecration deepened and strengthened and permanently stabilized by vow, in love's "liberty strengthened by obedience" (*LG* 43).

So that this devotion consecrated by vow will not grow cold, by these same vows we commit ourselves to live according to a regular program—our rule and constitutions—a program of life and spiritual exercises geared to stimulate a daily deepening of devotion and self-giving in the spirit of consecration. Love's willing fidelity to the program one has vowed to live keeps this devotion ever alive and dynamic and growing, and conquers emotion's frequent unwillingness which might have caused us to abandon the pursuit of holiness. Moreover, religious profession brings with it a special consecrating grace which will make the will ever more steadfast in its devotion, in proportion to one's fidelity to the program he has vowed to follow.

We see, then, the urgency of modernizing the regular observances prescribed by the religious rule. Such adaptation to the times will restore our full confidence in these observances as effective means of growing in the devotion and holiness of Christ. The revised constitutions should be a definite, concrete program for holiness which is truly livable in modern conditions.

Consecration of the Faculties

There is a third element in our Lord's consecration which needs to be duplicated in us. It was not enough for Jesus, first, to be consecrated in his very being by the divine Word, and it was not enough for him, secondly, to consecrate his will to the Father in ever living devotion. He had to live out his consecration, expressing it in the actual accomplishment of his mission, using his various human powers in the execution of the Father's work.

Therefore, as the instruments of his consecrated will, all of our Lord's human faculties and powers had to be sanctified by grace for carrying out every good work entrusted to him by his Father. This consecration of our Lord's faculties consisted in the various infused virtues, such as patience and fortitude, humility and mercy, perfecting these human powers by subjecting them totally to his will and orienting them to the service of his Father. Thus all our Lord's human powers of mind and body were completely at the service of his human will in carrying out the salvific will of the Father. This holiness or consecration of all our Lord's human faculties flowed from the Person of the divine Word whose faculties they were; this holiness of his faculties was part of the total holiness of his entire being and action. By the virtues consecrating his faculties, he was equipped for every work of holiness that belonged to his mission.

It was through his virtues that Jesus had complete self-possession, possession of all his human powers so that he could use
them perfectly in the divine service. If, for example, Jesus had
not possessed himself in patience and fortitude—the virtues con-
trolling his sadness and his fears—he could have abandoned the
difficult task assigned to him by the heavenly Father. Only because he had complete self-possession, the virtuous mastery of all
his powers, was he able to give himself totally to the accomplishment of his mission.

So too, we cannot fully give ourselves to God and his work
unless we possess ourselves in virtue. We have mature self-possession only to the extent that we have all the virtues which
regulate the use of our powers. The virtues thus make us apt
instruments of God, "equipped for every good work" (2 Tim.
3:17).

We see, then, that the baptismal consecration is not enough;
neither is our response to it in devotion, not even when this
devotion is stabilized or consecrated by the religious vows. When
we consecrate ourselves by the vows, we have seen, we offer ourselves to God in permanent availability in eager readiness of
will. This loving readiness of will is the very heart of our living
consecration. But more is needed. We need to possess ourselves
in virtue so that what we offer to God will actually be usable by
him. Of what good is it to offer ourselves to his service if we
have so little self-possession that we cannot carry out the tasks
he assigns to us, and indeed, cannot love him fully, because we
are unable to express our love in the works that are pleasing to
him? We need the mastery of our powers through the virtues,
then, so that as God's living instruments we can carry out the
work he has given us.

Our consecration, therefore, has to be steadily perfected by a
growth in self-possession, so that we will be available to God not
merely in readiness of will, but in ever increasing actuality, ever

more fit as Christ's living instruments in carrying on his own mission.

That is why, when we consecrate ourselves to God, making ourselves totally his in poverty, chastity and obedience, existing for him alone, we commit ourselves at the same time to the program of continuing spiritual discipline prescribed by our religious rule. Not only do we stabilize the devotion of our will so that we will forever be the Lord's, but in that same devotion and by those same vows we bind ourselves to live the regular life which will so discipline all our faculties that they will indeed be the Lord's own in perfect virtue; and so that our devotion will not be destroyed by the difficulties of life which cannot be endured except in true virtue.

Consecration to the Holy Spirit

By consecration, we said, we become God's own, we exist in total availability to him for the accomplishment of his purposes. This means availability to the Holy Spirit of God. For the Spirit of the Lord comes upon those whom God chooses for a mission. Thus, when David was anointed with oil by Samuel and consecrated as king, "the spirit of the Lord came upon David from that day forward" (1 Sam. 16:13).

This is supremely true of Christ, the one whom the Father consecrated and sent into the world. "The Spirit of the Lord is upon me, because the Lord has anointed me" (Isa. 61:1). Jesus read these words of Isaia aloud in the synagogue at Nazareth and announced that they were fulfilled in his person (Lk. 4:18f.)

"The Spirit of the Lord shall rest upon him," Isaia had said, "a spirit of wisdom and of understanding, a spirit of counsel and of strength, a spirit of knowledge and of fear of the Lord, and his delight shall be fear of the Lord" (Isa. 11:2–3).

"Fear of the Lord" is religious reverence and submission. Jesus was ever totally in obedient submission to the Father, ever alert to the directives of the Spirit of God. His human nature precisely as human was inadequate for carrying out his divine mission. His human mind needed to be enlightened by the gifts of wisdom and understanding and counsel and knowledge; his human emotions had to be fortified by the gift of fortitude, his human will was surrendered to the Spirit of God in the gift of fear or reverence. St. Luke takes pains to point out that in everything he does, Jesus is led by the Holy Spirit (Lk. 3:22; 4:1; 4:14–22).

So too, we are consecrated by the Holy Spirit. For example, when we are anointed with the oil of chrism in the sacrament of confirmation, the fullness of the Holy Spirit comes upon us so that we will be his own in doing God's work. We are consecrated in our very being as his living instruments. But it is up to us to make ourselves his in *willing* availability, in perpetual alertness to his inspirations, forever holding ourselves in docile attentiveness, in readiness to be moved by the Spirit. The basic attitude to be cultivated is a deep religious reverence and submission to God's saving will.

But, as we have seen, more is required than readiness of will. The Holy Spirit cannot use us very well if we are not self-possessed in virtue. For example, were he to inspire us to carry out a difficult mission for Christ, and we had no courage, no patience in trials, no perseverance, we might abandon the mission and "grieve the Holy Spirit" (Eph. 4:30). Or, when he moves us to a noble task for Christ, if we have no humility, we may spoil the work by our pride and selfishness in working for our own glory.

The undisciplined person, in other words, is unfit for carrying out the works of the Holy Spirit. If Christian and religious consecration is availability to the Holy Spirit, we see why it entails a program of self-discipline which will make our availability actual and not merely a readiness of will. This is why religious profession, as a fuller response to the consecration of baptism and confirmation, entails a more rigorous program of self-discipline, which one vows to follow.

The regular prayer and penance and devoted fidelity of a well-ordered religious life will give and improve and preserve the self-possession in which alone we can be available to God in full actuality and not merely in readiness of will. Only as we thus grow in the self-possession of true virtue does our consecration grow deeper, becoming a fully lived reality, and not merely something we promised to strive for when we first committed ourselves by vow. We are, of course, specially consecrated in our being from the moment we make religious profession. But that consecration has to flow into the holiness of ever more perfect action so that we are not only ready in heart to serve God, but are able to carry out effectively and fruitfully every task he entrusts to us.

Loving fidelity to our vows drives us on to carry out the never ending self-discipline prescribed by our religious rule. For our devotion and our virtues will deteriorate if their strength is not maintained by the continuing discipline of regular observance.

In revising our religious constitutions, then, we must clearly keep in mind the need of specific religious observances which will help us to achieve this goal of continuing self-possession in virtue. We can never claim that we are so mature spiritually that we are no longer in need of daily discipline.

Therefore, the motu proprio *Ecclesiae Sanctae* reasserts the Church's traditional teaching that "religious should devote themselves to works of penance and mortification more than the rest of the faithful" (*ESr* 22). However, it says that these practices should be revised in such a way that they can be effectively carried out in modern circumstances, or new forms of mortification should be adopted from modern conditions of life.

We have given examples showing how lack of self-possession may cause us to fail in missions committed to us by the Holy Spirit. But even more fundamentally, lack of self-possession prevents us from even receiving missions from him, for it interferes with recollection and attentiveness in receiving his inspirations. An undisciplined soul which is ever agitated by anger, or distracted from God by vanity, or burdened down by self-indulgence in food and drink, or scattered abroad by disorderly desires, does not live in consecrated alertness to the inspirations from above.

One's religious consecration, begun in religious profession, must therefore be deepened daily in the practice of self-discipline which is indispensable if we are to have the living, dynamic consecration which is a living availability and alertness to the Spirit of God in recollection. Consecration is perfected only to the extent that we are actually surrendered to God the Holy Spirit, coming ever more fully under the influence of his seven gifts, to be moved by him as he wills.

And only in silence can such alertness to the Holy Spirit be perfected. Silence is necessary for a live consecration; above all, the silence of our emotions—the self-possession, in freedom from agitation, which is the fruit of virtue acquired in self-discipline.

For to be consecrated to the person of Christ and to his work is to be consecrated to the way of the cross. Religious are vowed to walk in this way. Theirs is a vocation to follow Christ precisely as "the one whom the Father has consecrated and sent into the world" (Jn. 10:36). He was sent to be the holocaust offered for our redemption. He responds to this consecration, saying, "For them do I consecrate myself"—that is, I offer myself in sacrifice—"that they also may be consecrated in truth" (Jn. 18:19). All who follow him in this way consecrate themselves as a living offering with him.

14. Dynamic Consecration

The religious makes profession of the evangelical counsels, says Vatican II, "in order to derive more abundant fruit from his baptismal grace" (*LG* 44).

The special consecration of religious, the Council says, "is deeply rooted in their baptismal consecration and expresses it more fully" (*PC* 5). The metaphor "rooted" implies that the religious consecration is one living thing with the baptismal consecration, just as a tree with its fruits is one with its roots. The religious consecration derives its vital energy from the baptismal consecration and grows out of it, expressing it more completely, somewhat in the way that the fruit is the full development and expression of the roots of a tree.

This way of speaking of the religious consecration as a living growth and fruitfulness rooted in baptism implies that the religious consecration is something alive, dynamic, capable of further growth and of becoming ever more intimate. Religious consecration should be an ever living, ever deepening response to the initial consecration of baptism. The Council implies this

114

possibility of growth in the intimacy of consecration when it states that one's consecration is the more perfect the more clearly it expresses by firmer and more stable bonds Christ united to his Bride, the Church.

Christian and religious consecration, then, is a participation in the consecration of the Church to Christ, a sharing in the living bonds uniting God's People to him. What are these living bonds between Christ and his People?

On Christ's part, they are his active presence with them by his sanctifying power and grace, and his permanent claim upon them by reason of the indestructible baptismal character consecrating them as his own. On the part of God's People, the living bonds are faith, hope, and charity. The more alive, the more dynamic, the more actual these three virtues are in a person, so much the more intimately he participates in the Church's union with the divine Bridegroom, and therefore so much the more fully he lives his baptismal consecration. The fullness of consecration as something living and dynamic thus consists in giving to the Lord the fullness of one's love and devotion in living faith. It consists in being ever alive to the Lord, awaiting him in eager expectancy, ever attentive to him in love's living fidelity, ever present to him in total availability that he might accomplish in us and through us the purposes of his saving love.

Dynamic Faith, According to St. Paul

No one has ever expressed these truths more adequately than has St. Paul. In bringing the Gospel to his converts, in forming the life of faith in them, St. Paul says he has espoused them to Christ in faith and undivided devotion: "I betrothed you to one spouse, that I might present you a chaste virgin to Christ. But I fear lest, as the serpent seduced Eve by his guile, so your minds may be corrupted and fall from a single devotion to Christ" (2 Cor. 11:2–3).

A single devotion to Christ. . . .

The apostle is here speaking to the whole Church at Corinth; the whole People of God is bride of Christ in faith. But Paul's words, "single devotion to Christ," are an echo of his earlier words concerning consecrated virgins. Paul had recommended virginity precisely because it facilitated "undivided devotion to the Lord" (1 Cor. 7:35). Christian virginity, in other words, strives to give fullest possible expression to the Church's consecration to the Lord alone in faith and devoted fidelity.

A deep understanding of St. Paul's teaching on faith and fidelity, then, would be of great value in understanding the meaning of religious consecration as a living, dynamic, wholehearted, ever deepening devotion to the Lord.

For St. Paul, faith is first of all an obedience to Christ. Paul tells the Corinthians that the purpose of his apostolic power is "bringing every mind into captivity to the obedience of Christ" (2 Cor. 10:5). And he tells the Romans, "We have received the grace of apostleship to bring about obedience to faith among all the nations for his name's sake" (Rom. 1:5).

Faith is an obedience or submission to the Gospel for the purpose of receiving the justice or holiness which comes from God alone. "For I am not ashamed of the gospel, for it is the power of God unto salvation to everyone who believes, to Jew first and then to Greek. For in it the justice of God is revealed . . ." (Rom. 1:16–17).

The Gospel which one obeys is a power, "the power of God unto salvation" (Rom. 1:16). For it reveals the power of God which is in Christ to bring us the righteousness or holiness which only God can give. For it is "the gospel of God . . . concerning his Son who was born to him according to the flesh of the offspring of David, but constituted Son of God by an act of power in keeping with the holiness of his spirit, by his resurrection from the dead" (Rom. 1:2–4).

Faith is a surrender to this power of Christ, or rather, to Christ himself, in obedience to the purposes of his love; it is a submission to him to receive the gift of justification and sanctification and life everlasting.

Man cannot achieve this holiness by his own work. "To him who does not work, but believes in him who justifies the impious, his faith is credited to him as justice" (Rom. 4:5). In other words, faith is a consenting to the work which God wills to accomplish in us; and this is a continuing work of ever increasing sanctification, ending in life everlasting. One must therefore ever remain in the obedience of faith, in an ever continuing action of surrender to the purposes of divine love. To live one's consecration to the full, then, is to live always in this obedience, this ever continuing openness to Christ.

Faith thus involves also a renouncing of one's self-sufficiency. For one cannot be justified by one's own works. And one cannot be perfected in holiness by one's own efforts alone. St. Paul himself renounced everything that he might live the life of faith. "The things that were gain to me, these, for the sake of Christ, I have counted loss. Nay, more, I count everything loss because of the excelling knowledge of Jesus Christ my Lord" (Phil. 3:7f). Faith is a surrender to Jesus, the Word of God. It brings us a divine light, divine knowledge. But this word of light is a word of life, a word to be lived, a word which gives movement and direction to life.

Therefore, I renounce my own sufficiency in thinking, I renounce my own opinions, to be filled with the excelling knowledge of Jesus Christ my Lord.

One must renounce all self-complacency, all trust in one's own righteousness, one must empty self to be filled with the light and holiness which God works in us by faith. To live one's Christian consecration, then, to be filled with God's life and holiness, one must die with Christ. One dies by faith to live the life of Christ himself. "With Christ I am nailed to the cross. It is now no longer I that live, but Christ lives in me. And the life that I now live in the flesh, I live in the faith of the Son of God, who loved me and gave himself up for me" (Gal. 2:20).

Who loved me. . . .

Faith is thus a living response to Christ's love. Faith expresses itself in a love returning his love. "I live in the faith of the Son of God who loved me" means "I live in the love of the Son of God—in his love for me, in my love for him."

For faith, which is obedience to the purposes of his love, has opened me to receive his Holy Spirit. "The love of God is poured forth into our hearts by his Holy Spirit who is given to us" (Rom. 5:5). The holiness of God, given to us in faith, is thus in reality God's own love in us—his own love pouring itself into our hearts in the giving of the Holy Spirit, begetting us as his children; and our love responding in that same Holy Spirit in the cry, "Abba, Father!" conforming us to the image of the Son that he might be firstborn among many brethren (Rom. 8:29).

The obedience which is faith is therefore a returning to God in the filial obedience of Christ. The Apostle shows that we who had died in the disobedience of Adam are made alive in the obedience of Christ (Rom. 5:17). But we come to life only when by the obedience which is faith we enter into Christ's own obedience and make it our own. By faith and baptism we participate in Christ's obedience, for, says the Apostle, we are baptized into his death, which has its value only because it is the expression of his loving filial obedience to his Father. In his obedience we begin to live to God in a spiritual resurrection (Rom. 6:3–11). Faith is thus a going to the Father in the obedience of Christ as we cry out with Jesus, in the filial love poured into our hearts by the Holy Spirit, "Abba, Father!" Faith thus fashions us in the likeness of Christ, so that he may be the firstborn of many brethren.

All this because, as the Apostle expresses it, we have "obeyed from the heart that form of doctrine into which we have been delivered," the Gospel (Rom. 6:17). In wholehearted love, ever giving ourselves in the obedience of faith, we are ever receiving a deepening of the grace of adoption as sons. The Apostle exhorts us to live true to this obedient faith by giving our whole being and all our members as instruments of obedience: "Do not yield your members to sin as weapons of iniquity, but present your-selves to God as those who have come to life from the dead and your members as weapons of justice for God" (Rom. 6:13).

That is, you are no longer slaves of the tyrant Sin; you are totally available to Christ, in faith and loving obedience, for the advancing of his reign. Such is your Christian consecration. It is a participation in Christ's own consecration and a sharing in his mission as "the one whom the Father has consecrated and sent into the world" (Jn. 10:36). In faith, then, we live our con-secration in ever active readiness for the accomplishment of the divine purposes.

Faith Expressed in Love of Neighbor and in Hope

Because faith is a loving response to Christ who loved me and gave himself up for me, "faith works through charity" (Gal. 5:6). In saying this, the Apostle is speaking specifically of love of neighbor (cf. Gal. 5:13–15). For my loving response to Christ's love in delivering himself up for love of me is my love in giving myself up for neighbor.

This is what St. Paul means when he says "the charity of Christ impels me" (2 Cor. 5:14). Christ's own charity, communicated to me in the obedience of faith, impels me to love with Christ's own love, in the way that Christ loves. In faith I have come to the conclusion that since in love Christ died for all, then I myself in that same love must bring the benefits of that love to all.

If faith is an obedience to the power of Christ, a submission to the purpose of his loving, saving will, it necessarily gives rise to hope: "Justified by faith . . . we exult in the hope of the glory of the sons of God" (Rom. 5:1–3). The Gospel word which we obey in faith is a word of promise, and in hope we rely confidently on God's steadfast fidelity to his word. In faith, then, we consider God trustworthy, and base our whole life upon him as upon our solid rock. Especially, our life is based upon faith in his love for us: "the life I now live in the flesh, I live in the faith of the Son of God who loved me and gave himself up for me."

Faith thus expressed in hope becomes confidence, trust in God, finding one's sufficiency in him alone, renouncing self-sufficiency and the sufficiency one might have sought in created things. Faith and hope therefore involve Christian poverty, emptying self of trust in created goods in order to be filled with God. "The faith I love best, says God, is hope" (Péguy). God loves Christian hope so much because it is a refusal to find one's sufficiency anywhere but in God, and therefore it opens us to the purpose of his love. Inseparable from hope, then, is poverty of spirit, in which one relies upon God alone. In this poverty, we live in wonderful receptivity to the inpouring of God himself and his holiness. Christian consecration, then, as an expression of living hope, is a permanent openness to the workings of the Holy Spirit.

Finally, faith expresses itself in love's steadfast fidelity. Our faith and hope are based upon God's steadfast love and fidelity toward us; such love deserves only steadfast fidelity in return. St. Paul, espousing his converts like chaste virgins to Christ in faith, considered fidelity or undivided devotion as an essential quality of this Christian faith, so much so that when he saw the fidelity of the Corinthians threatened by false teachers, he was enflamed with God's own jealousy for his bride, the Church. If faith expresses itself in love for the Christ who loved us and gave himself up for us, it is true faith and love only when it is characterized by constancy and fidelity.

The Special Consecration of the Religious

If eager devotion of will is the heart of Christian love and consecration, steadfast fidelity is its backbone. As Vatican II states it, "consecration is the more perfect when, by firmer and more stable bonds, it better expresses Christ united with his bride, the Church" (*LG* 44). There again we see why there is something special about the consecration of a religious. By religious profession one's love and devotion for Christ is given the added stability of vows, it is permanently sealed by vows.

A vow, by its very nature, is sacred, inviolable, and always implies unshakable fidelity, for what is vowed is God's own in such a way that no one else can touch it, not even the one who gave it. No one can appropriate to self what belongs to God. What is vowed truly partakes of God's own inviolability and sacredness. Whatever belongs to him in a special way is to be reverenced as he himself is reverenced.

By the grace of religious consecration, God communicates something of his own sacredness or transcendence to the consecrated person. Consecration, rendering something sacred, we said, is more the work of God than it is the work of the person making the vows. God's very acceptance of the religious vows brings a consecrating grace which gives a deeper participation in God's holiness. All Christian belonging to God is more than an extrinsic label on the outside of our being, saying, "This is God's." Consecration is intrinsic, it is a participation in God's own life as his children. His life in us, penetrating our very being, consecrates us from within. It is God's presence in us which consecrates us as his temples.

Therefore, religious consecration, as a deepening of the baptismal consecration, obviously brings an interior grace deepening this belonging to God, this participation in his own life and holiness. It brings a dynamic ability to enter more profoundly into the living bonds uniting Christ and his Church. This is the truth behind the traditional doctrine that religious profession is like a second baptism, bringing one more intimately into God's own life and holiness, in proportion to one's sincerity and faith in making the profession, and in proportion to one's fidelity in living it in dynamic faith, hope and charity.

We see, then, how the religious, no matter how much he or she is present in the world and open to the world, is not of the world, but participates deeply in the otherness of God's own life and holiness. What a responsibility this brings! One must remain ever open to God, ever alert to him in living faith, in active receptivity to the holiness which he wills to deepen progressively in those who are his own. Dynamic, living consecration requires something on our part, and something on God's part. On our part, it has to be this ever active availability to God in faith, hope and loving fidelity. On God's part, it is the ever continuing activity of his consecrating grace progressively deepening his holiness in us.

To live our consecration, then, is to live ever in that obedience which is faith, that perpetual openness to and cooperation with the purposes of divine love and holiness which are worked in us by the Son of God in power of sanctification (cf. Rom. 1:4).

We see, then, why religious should be taught to live their consecration in hope. The added stability and firmness given to the baptismal consecration by the religious vows comes primarily from God, whose acceptance of the vows, we said, is a consecrating grace which will always be at work in the faithful religious. God will not abandon his own. If a vow is a will to give something inviolably to God, God's accepting grace keeps it inviolable. Fidelity to the vow requires trust in God's rock-like fidelity. God alone can make it possible for one to live God's holiness. God must always be communicating his holiness to his own people, their spirit of consecration must be an ever living openness to receive holiness from him.

Dynamic Consecration and the Vows

If the fullness of Christian and religious consecration is dynamic alertness to God and availability to him in living faith, steadfast hope and loving fidelity, why is religious consecration expressed in terms of chastity, poverty and obedience?

Chastity, poverty and obedience are really incomprehensible apart from the living charity, hope and faith to which respectively they correspond. We should take care to understand this relationship between the counsels and the theological virtues.

The purpose of the evangelical counsels is to facilitate one's undivided, ever actual attention to the Lord and his work in faith, hope and charity. St. Paul states this explicitly in regard to virginity, whose purpose, he says, is "to make it possible for you to attend to the Lord with undivided devotion" (1 Cor. 7:34–35), to be concerned with the things of the Lord—his kingdom of love in self and in others.

In poverty, too, according to Jesus, we sell all else to follow Christ more closely. Poverty, we said, corresponds to hope, for our true treasure is eschatological, heavenly. God, not possessions, is the hope upon whom we found our life.

And religious obedience is a very concrete, down-to-earth expression of faith, the faith which is all-embracing obedience to the divine purpose. Obedience to the Church, represented to us in our superiors, is an excellent practical way of living in total surrender to the faith, in complete submission to the power of the Gospel working in the Church. "Under the influence of the Holy Spirit," says Vatican II, "religious submit themselves to their superiors whom faith presents as God's representatives, and through whom they are guided into the service of all their brothers in Christ" (*PC* 14).

We see, then, why religious consecration is such a deepening of the baptismal consecration, bringing us more intimately into the living bonds of faith, hope and charity uniting the Church to

Christ, opening us more fully to Christ's consecrating, sanctifying presence. The purpose of the three vows is to make faith, hope and charity as dynamic as possible, so that one can be always alive to the Lord, fully attentive to him in single devotion, awake and receptive to the sanctifying purposes of his love, fully available to him at every moment for his work of advancing his kingdom of holiness in ourselves and in the world.

The baptismal consecration incorporates us into the Church, the living temple of God's holiness. But we are fully temples of God only when we are fully alive to the God who dwells in us, and this can only be when faith, hope and charity are alive. Lively faith and living love are the arms in which we consciously embrace the living God who dwells in us. Faith opens the door and brings God in: "Christ dwelling through faith in your hearts; so that, being rooted and grounded in love . . . you may be filled unto all the fullness of God" (Eph. 3:17).

When God fully lives in us in this way, when we are living temples of his holiness, then indeed we will be making Christ present in the world. We will be the open doors through which his holiness will invade the world in which we live.

15. Religious Consecration and Eucharistic Participation

The words of Elizabeth to Mary—"Blessed is she who has believed, for the things spoken to her by the Lord shall be accomplished"—ring true of everyone who makes religious profession sincerely and prudently. The person who makes religious profession has heard a very personal message from Christ which she has believed, she has heard an interior word of God spoken in her heart, to which she responds in faith and love by the act of religious profession.

And just what word has Christ spoken to her? Is the word too personal, too intimate, to be discussed publicly? She who has rightly made profession has indeed heard a message which is intensely personal and intimate, the Lord truly has called her by name and has spoken his message to her heart. The response he called for is the total gift of self, the consecration of her whole being, to belong exclusively to him, and to him forever.

And yet, the content of this intimate personal message is the same as the content of the message which is addressed to all mankind from the cross of Calvary. It is God's message of love

125

spoken in his crucified Son. It was expressed from the cross not so much in words from the lips of Jesus, but rather, his whole crucified being cries out to our hearts, "God so loved the world that he gave his only-begotten Son" (Jn. 3:16).

But the night before he died, Jesus did put into words the meaning of his sacrifice on the cross; and not only into words, but into deeds and sacramental action. Taking bread into his holy and venerable hands, he blessed and broke it, saying, "Take and eat, for this is my Body, which is delivered up for *you*—for you Twelve here present—and for many others. Do this in remembrance of me."

Every time the apostles and their successors, the priests of the Church, do this in remembrance of Jesus, Jesus himself is doing it again in the action of his priests. The action of Jesus, delivering himself up in sacrifice, is made sacramentally present in the consecrating action of the priest, so that through the priest Jesus himself takes bread and wine into his holy and venerable hands, and gives it to those participating in the Mass, saying, "This is my Body which is delivered up for *you*—for you who are here present—and for many others. This is the chalice of my Blood, which is being shed for *you*—for you who are here partaking— and for many others."

Those who are truly alive to Christ in living faith as they participate in the Mass, hearing these words of Jesus spoken to them personally, hearing them in the intimacy of their hearts, say in response, as Paul the Apostle once said, "Christ loved *me*, me personally, and delivered himself up for me!" Perhaps one does not think to express it in quite these words, but that is the unmistakable impression which fervent and frequent eucharistic participation leaves in one's heart. Through repeated, sincere participation, one becomes ever more thoroughly convinced that Christ is indeed his personal savior; and in response, he can say in all truth with St. Paul, "The life that I now live in the flesh,

I live in the faith of the Son of God, who loved *me* and gave himself up for me" (Gal. 2:20).

We can hardly doubt that Christ communicates his most intimate messages to the fervent Christian either in actual eucharistic participation, or in graces which are the flowering of the sacramental graces of the Eucharist. It is chiefly through his personal presence and action in the liturgy that Christ impresses his word upon a Christian's heart; but it is a word so surpassing all spoken words that the Christian himself cannot reexpress in words what he has heard in the deepest reaches of his being. In fact, the word is so interior and so spiritual that sometimes he hardly even realizes that God has truly spoken to him, that God has manifested to him his personal love for him. God has so loved this Christian that he has given his only-begotten Son not only *for* him on Calvary, but *to* him here and now in the Eucharist. What word could be more eloquent than this, our Lord's eucharistic action in handing over his own body and blood to him?

Though the person may not have fully reflected upon the divine message of love which has been thus impressed upon his heart, the way he thenceforth lives, the way he thenceforth loves God and neighbor more truly, will reveal that he has received the message.

To receive such a message in eucharistic participation, of course, one has to be spiritually attuned to Christ in living faith. In the actual eucharistic participation, we said, the interior word can make a spiritual impression too deep to be understood in the form of ideas or in words, and so the person may not be aware of how deeply and effectively God has spoken to his heart. Only gradually does he realize the full significance of the message Christ has impressed in him in this eucharistic grace. This full awareness comes only in additional prayer and meditation. In recollection, in mental prayer, the Holy Spirit leads one into the full meaning of what Christ has impressed in the heart in the

Eucharist, so that gradually the person is able to articulate it in his mind, becoming aware of its full implications.

It is for these reasons that the motu proprio *Ecclesiae Sanctae* reminds religious that mental prayer is necessary for the full fruitfulness of participation in the Eucharist and in the liturgical office. In giving directives for the renewal of the prayer life of religious institutes, the motu proprio says:

> In order that religious may participate more profoundly and more fruitfully in the most holy mystery of the Eucharist and in the public prayer of the Church, and that their whole spiritual life may be nourished more abundantly, greater prominence should be given to mental prayer instead of a multitude of prayers, retaining nevertheless the pious exercises commonly accepted in the Church, and giving due care that the members are instructed diligently in leading a spiritual life (*ESr* 21).

Mental prayer, then, is necessary for more fruitful eucharistic and liturgical participation.

The history of St. Dominic and his first brethren tells how their contemplative prayer was the blossoming forth of their liturgical participation. We are told how, after the termination of the official public liturgy, they would prolong their personal prayer, sometimes at great length. The seed of the word planted in the liturgical readings and the inner grace impressed in their hearts in the Eucharist bore its rich fruits in their silent recollection. Here we find the deepest reason for silence in religious houses.

But to return to our main theme. A religious vocation, that intimate personal word of grace, calling to religious profession— who can doubt it—is normally spoken in the profoundest depths of the heart in eucharistic participation, in that intimate spiritual way which surpasses all words. It is a message of love which is too big for words. And so, of course, one does not necessarily become aware immediately that he has received the message; one does not always understand its full implications at first; it is not immediately articulated in thoughts, in clear concepts or words.

It is not surprising that the interior word of religious vocation is spoken in one's heart in the eucharistic renewal of the Sacrifice of the Cross. For a religious vocation is the word of Calvary, it is the call of divine love spoken by the whole being and action of Jesus on the cross, but now impressing itself on a heart in a personal way, drawing forth from that heart a gift of self in the likeness of that same divine love which is speaking from the cross. The eucharistic action is Christ's preferred way of impressing this message of love on one's heart and calling forth the total response in love. For, as we have said, the Eucharistic Sacrifice is the very action of Christ on the cross here and now made present to us sacramentally. Therefore, it reveals and bestows the same divine love of Calvary. It reveals and bestows it as an intimate personal love for those who are present and alive to Christ in true participation in faith and love. And so it draws forth from such hearts the response to Christ on the cross which God desires.

Religious consecration can be fully understood only in terms of such a response. In repeated eucharistic participation, a person becomes more and more aware of the divine love for him personally, and more and more clearly realizes that such love calls for a return of love. It dawns on him that somehow he has to give himself up totally to Christ, just as Christ has given himself up totally to him. His love for Christ has to be in the likeness of Christ's love for him, his gift of self has to be in the likeness of Christ's gift to him. "Christ loved *me,* and gave himself up for *me;* I love Christ and give myself up to him, totally, in the likeness of his sacrifice on the cross."

Such is the meaning of genuine religious consecration. It is the total sacrificial giving of self in response to Christ's sacrificial giving of himself. If religious profession does not somehow mean this to the one making it, then he is not making it as he ought.

And if it is in eucharistic participation that Christ gives himself in the most intimate and personal way possible in this life, it is also in eucharistic participation that one's response is perfected; religious profession is not fully lived unless it is daily deepened in eucharistic participation.

Christ's word of love, we said, is too big for words. Christ himself is the word; and his divine love for mankind is revealed in his action of self-giving on the cross. His personal love for this person or that person is revealed to the person in his action of self-giving to that person in the Eucharist. So too, one's love in response is too big for mere words, and can be expressed only in the action of total self-giving in return, and has to be not only in the likeness of Christ's self-giving, but within Christ's own self-giving, in a sacrificial action which is a participation in Christ's sacrificial action. One's self-giving has to be taken into our Lord's self-giving, which is sacramentally made present to us in the action of the Eucharistic Sacrifice.

It is, then, in eucharistic participation itself or in the flowering of the graces granted in the Eucharist that Christ speaks the intimate word calling one to the total gift of self to him in religious consecration. Consequently, throughout one's life, in repeated eucharistic participation, that word, that call of love, impresses itself ever more deeply in a heart—if the the person takes care to keep his heart ever pure and open to these divine communications of love. And therefore, this daily deepening of the word of Christ's personal love in one's heart draws forth a daily deepening response, a daily perfecting of the self-giving of one's religious profession.

Each day, as I accept again Christ's offer, "Take and eat, this is my Body," he gives himself anew to me personally, more profoundly than before. Each time he says to me again, in this intimate way, "This is my Body which is given for you—you personally," he speaks anew to me of his love for me, his wordless message of love is impressed more deeply in my heart—if I have kept my heart open and pure.

And this makes possible my ever more perfect gift of myself in response. For this word of love imprinted in my heart is a creative word, calling forth new love from me, creating in me the grace and charity in which I can now respond on a deeper level than ever before.

If I am a professed religious, my profession is perfected and deepened in that eucharistic participation, because Christ's delivering himself up to me personally impresses its likeness upon my love so that I love in the same way in response, and deliver myself up for him and to him; and not just in the moment of participation, but in all of my living. I give myself to him as a fullness of his own sacrifice, "filling up what is wanting to his sacrifice, for his body, the Church."

For one gives self to Christ, that through him and in him and with him one might give self to the Father as he did, and for one's fellowmen as he did. If Christ's eucharistic gift of himself to me impresses the likeness of his own love and sacrifice upon me, I give myself in response in the way he gave himself—for the same motives and purposes.

For every really Christian self-giving is truly a participation in Christ's own self-giving on the cross, so that the sacrifice of the Head is continued in the sacrifice of the member. Therefore, religious profession, too, has its truest, fullest meaning only to the extent that it is in the likeness of Christ's own self-giving, inspired by the same love, and for the same purposes.

Vatican II makes it clear, we have seen, that for religious, as for all Christians, the supreme rule is the following of Christ as presented in the Gospel. To live the Gospel is to live the life of Christ and to strive for the ever more complete likeness of Christ, the likeness of Christ in his supreme characteristic, his charity in making his self-offering for the salvation of mankind, his consecration as sacrificial victim. For this he came into the world, this made him what he is; he is described as "the one whom the Father has consecrated and sent into the world" (Jn. 10:36). He was consecrated as the victim for our salvation. "For them I consecrate myself that they also may be consecrated in truth" (Jn. 17:19).

The supreme rule of the religious life, the following of Christ, is meaningless if it does not mean that, if it does not mean that one is to follow Christ in his sacrificial self-giving in love. For everything Christ did on earth, every virtue in his life, points to the cross, in which it finds its completion. For what is his poverty at Nazareth, his obedience to Mary and Joseph, his humility in the carpenter shop, his works of mercy in helping his needy fellowmen, but a part of that supreme sacrificial poverty and obedience and humility and mercy expressed on the Cross of Calvary? Whatever he did on earth is meaningless apart from Calvary, the whole of his life is part of his mission to redeem mankind by his obedience to the Father, his going to the Father in filial, obedient love. "In coming into the world he says, 'Behold I come to do thy will, O God!' " (Heb. 10:5–9). The entirety of his life is a self-giving for us, begun at the instant of his entry into the world and perfected in his leaving the world in that same loving obedience.

Our response to such love needs to take on the likeness of such love. One's whole being needs to be given to him in a completion and "filling up" of his self-giving for the salvation of the world.

But even before it is a giving for the world, it is a giving to the Father. If he gave himself up in love for me—and for many —even more fundamentally he gave himself up to the Father, in love for the Father, in zeal for his glory. One's giving of self in religious profession, too, is a going to the Father in the obedience and sacrifice of Christ.

And so, too, it is the perfect participation in the life of the Holy Trinity. For it is the likeness of Christ's union with the

Father in the Holy Spirit. The Son who is eternally one with the Father in the love which is the Holy Spirit, the Son who is forever giving himself to the Father in the Holy Spirit of love, in every moment of his life as man goes to the Father in that love, gives his humanity totally to the Father in that love.

In that same Holy Spirit, we too cry, "Abba, Father!" In Christ, we too offer self in sacrifice to the Father, for the same motives and purposes. Our religious life is a holocaust, a total self-offering, in response to the Word of the Cross, the divine word of love impressed in our hearts in the Holy Sacrifice of the Mass.

Religious profession, and a life in fidelity to it, is meaningless if it does not mean all of this. It is called "religious" for that very reason—it is a total participation in Christ's supreme religious act, the Sacrifice of the Cross.

How can we deepen our understanding and our living of this fact? Christ will have to speak his word of love ever more clearly in our souls, if it is to win precisely this word of response. And where and how does he so speak it, if not chiefly in eucharistic participation, and in the continuing mental prayer in which we receive the fuller fruits of the Eucharist?

We should therefore strive daily to see our eucharistic participation precisely in this relationship to our religious profession, which was our response to the call of the divine love of Calvary, impressed personally on our hearts by Christ in the Eucharistic Sacrifice. Let us daily at Mass see Jesus in action in the action of the priest, saying, "This is my Body which is given for you; this is my Blood which is shed for you—you personally." Daily we should be able to cry out with St. Paul in renewed awareness: "The religious life I now live in the flesh, I live in the faith of the Son of God who loved me—me personally—and gave himself up for me!"

16. "There I Am in the Midst of Them"

We read in *Perfectae Caritatis*: "Thanks to God's love poured into their hearts by the Holy Spirit, a religious community is a true family gathered together in the Lord's name and rejoicing in his presence (Matt. 18:20)" (*PC* 15).

"Rejoicing in his presence . . . ."

What sort of a presence of Christ is this? Is it a mere moral presence? If we read in a superficial way the words of St. Matthew's Gospel which are here echoed by the Council, perhaps we might think that Christ's presence among us is a mere moral presence, manifest in our unity of wills. Our Blessed Lord says, in Matthew: "When any two of you are in agreement here on earth regarding anything they ask for, their prayer will be granted by my Father in heaven. For where two or three are assembled in my name, there I am in the midst of them" (Matt. 18:19–20).

Is this agreement which is required for obtaining our petitions a mere union of wills concerning something we ask for? And to be assembled in his Name—is that also a mere moral union of

wills? We can never be content with so superficial an interpretation of these words of Matthew once we have meditated on the
same concepts as expressed more fully and on a deeper level in
the Gospel according to John.

There we learn that the agreement among ourselves which wins
the answer to our petitions is no mere agreement concerning this
favor or that favor which we ask of God. No! It is rather a deep-
down unity in hearts, a unity in charity, a unity of life, a unity in
the Holy Trinity. For our Blessed Lord petitions his Father to
give us a unity which is a participation in the unity in which he
and the Father are one: "That all may be one, even as thou
Father in me and I in thee, that they also may be one in us. . . .
I in them and thou in me, that they may be perfected in unity"
(Jn. 17:21, 23).

"I *in* them." This is a real indwelling of Jesus in those who believe in him. "Abide in me, and I in you," he had said a little
while earlier. "If you abide in me, and if my words abide in you,
ask whatever you will and it shall be done to you" (Jn. 15:4, 7).
There we have the deeper explanation of the agreement which
is required if the things we ask for are to be granted. If we abide
in Jesus in faith and in loving obedience to his word, he dwells
in us. "If anyone love me, he will keep my word, and my Father
will love him, and we will come to him and make our abode with
him" (Jn. 14:23).

And because Jesus is *in* us, and the Father is in Jesus, we are
perfected in unity. This unity in the life and love of the
Father and the Son is the unity which wins for us whatever we
ask of God. How wonderfully powerful, then, are our prayers
for ourselves and for our apostolate when we are truly one in
charity, when we are united in Christ who is in our midst—in
our midst not in a mere moral presence, but as One who dwells
in our hearts in full reality.

Christ dwells in us through the action of the Holy Spirit in
us. The words of Vatican II with which we began tell us that "a

religious community is a true family thanks to God's love poured into their hearts by the Holy Spirit." But where the Spirit is, there is Christ. For all action of the Holy Spirit in the Church is the action of Christ Jesus, the Head of the Church, who acts in his members by bestowing on them the Holy Spirit and all his graces. Where the Holy Spirit is present, Jesus Christ is himself present, bestowing the divine life and love—"the glory."

"Father, the glory that thou hast given me, I have given to them, that they may be one even as we are one." The glory of Jesus is his glory as only Son coming from the Father. "We saw his glory—glory as of the only-begotten of the Father" (Jn. 1:14). His glory is his divinity which he receives from his Father eternally, and which he received into his humanity at the instant of the Incarnation—to bestow it upon us! "Of his fullness we have all received" (Jn. 1:16).

When he says, then, that he has given his glory to us, he is saying that he has given us a participation in his own divine sonship, so that we are called, and are, sons of God—a true family of God's children. For to as many as received him—by believing in his Name, his Name "Son of God"—he gave them to be sons of God (Jn. 1:12).

The true sons of God are one even as the Father and his only Son are one. Christian unity in charity is the proof of this sonship, and thereby it is the revelation to the world that God has sent his eternal Son: "That they also may be one in us, that the world may believe that thou hast sent me" (Jn. 17:21). They could not be sons of God unless the Father had sent his only-begotten. Their unity in charity, then, proving that they are sons of God, proves that God has sent his Son. Commenting on the words of Jesus, "that the world may believe that thou hast sent me," St. Thomas Aquinas says that the greatest proof of the truth of the Gospel is the charity of the faithful.

Unity in charity is proof not merely that the Father has sent the Son, but that the Son has remained with us, that he is present among us and dwelling in us. Thus our charity for one another is truly a living presence of Christ, it is a revelation of Christ to the world: "that the world may know that thou hast sent me."

The whole Church, of course, has this mission to be a revelation of the good news by its unity in love. But religious are called to give, by their community life, a still more vivid expression of that unity in charity. Such is the role of a religious community in the Church. As "a true family gathered together in the Lord's name and rejoicing in his presence" (*PC* 15), they manifest to the world that God has sent his Son to bestow divine sonship upon all who believe in him. "The religious state," says Vatican II, "clearly shows all men the unsurpassed breadth of the sway of Christ the King and the infinite power of the Holy Spirit marvelously working in the Church" (*LG* 44).

How, then, are religious to deepen this unity in love for one another which reveals to others Christ's presence among them, that all may be drawn to him?

Certainly religious should cultivate an awareness of Christ living in one another. The deep brotherly or sisterly reverence for one another existing in religious communities is due to an awareness of the dignity of one another as brothers or sisters of Christ and as sons or daughters of the Father.

In truth, however, this awareness of Christ in one another can only be as deep as our awareness of Christ himself, Christ in his own Person. No one can recognize Christ in neighbor unless he has recognized Christ himself. One can recognize a likeness only if he has seen the original.

In these days it is important to appreciate this truth, for many writers of the "God-is-dead" variety are de-emphasizing the need of religion, and tell us that God is to be found only in neighbor, only in the community, only in the world about us, and that the seeing Christ in him. The more intimately Christ lives in our treat this point more fully in the following two chapters.

If, then, there is any weakness of charity among us, if we are not recognizing Christ in one another, if we are not reverencing Christ by our actions toward one another, no doubt it is because we are not adequately recognizing Christ as he is in himself. We are not recognizing Christ vividly enough in living faith—at Mass and in prayer and in continuing recollection. We have failed to deepen daily our consciousness of Christ in his own Person, and that is why our ability to reverence him in others has grown dull.

Or, to put it again in a positive way: The vividness of our reverence and charity for neighbor is in proportion to the vividness of our direct encounter with Christ in living faith each day at Mass and in prayer and all day long in prayerful recollection. If we have vividly met Christ today at Mass, if Christ is alive in our consciousness most of the time, then we will recognize Christ in everyone, not necessarily in the sense that we will think explicitly of Christ each time we deal with neighbor, but in the sense that we will treat neighbor with the same kindness and respect that we would give him were we here and now vividly seeing Christ in him. The more intimately Christ lives in our consciousness, the more spontaneously we will act toward neighbor as we would act toward Christ himself.

We must cultivate, then, this twofold consciousness—an awareness of Christ in his own Person, and an awareness of Christ in our neighbor. The two awarenesses will mutually sharpen one another. The more consciously we reverence Christ in neighbor, the easier it will be to be alive to Christ in prayer and recollection, and above all, in the eucharistic celebration. Likewise, the more we are aware, in recollection, of Christ's presence in our hearts, the more certainly we will reverence him in others.

Our community life in charity thus deepened in this way will be a great source of apostolic power. For the more perfect our community love, the more efficaciously Christ will be in our midst, and so the more effectively he can use our institute in his work of salvation. A religious institute is apostolically effective only to the degree that it is one in charity, only to the degree that Christ is in its midst. The community sends forth its members on their apostolate, the community works through them; and they are effective only to the extent that they abide in the communinty in true obedience and community charity. Even though we may be scattered physically in many different religious houses, we must continue to maintain the spiritual bonds of strong community solidarity in charity and mutual concern.

Only thus will our religious institute be an efficacious presence of Christ in a world to be saved.

"Abide in me and I in you," he says. If we abide deeply in him, in him we will be able to be one with all others.

17. Religious Consecration and Openness to the World

One of the hopeful signs of the times is the Church's renewed awareness that she is the community of God's People, present in the world, open to the world, involved in the world, one with the whole human community. The Holy Spirit seems intent upon breaking down all barriers between the Church and the rest of the human race. This phenomenon is manifesting itself also in the religious life, where there is a wholesome tendency to remove as much as possible the walls of separation between religious and the rest of the Church and the world.

However, if religious have to be in some sense like the world, present in the world, and open to it, even more they have to be like God, open to him, present with him. If they need to break down the barriers between themselves and the world, even more they need to break down the barriers between themselves and God, so that they may be filled with his transcendent holiness, and thus bring his holiness into the world. They have to be God's open door to the world.

140

Not only religious but all Christians are faced with the problem of how to be present in the world and like the world, and yet
at the same time unlike the world in the way that Jesus wills that
his People be unlike the world. "They are in the world," he
says, "but not of the world" (Jn. 17:11, 16). The Christian is
profoundly different from the non-Christian even though he
strives to be like his fellowmen in all the good and truly human
values which he shares with all mankind.

Forgetfulness of how the Christian is essentially different defeats our very purpose in wanting to be like our fellowmen, with
them, and open to them. We are to be different by being like
God, filled with his holiness. God is completely transcendent.
That is, he is forever infinitely different from his creatures, he is
infinitely surpassing, infinitely other. This otherness or transcendence is his holiness, his sacredness.

But God's "otherness" is not necessarily "apartness." For God
is intimately present to all things. This is his immanence. The
Scriptures declare that God fills all things (Jer. 23:24); he is "all
in all" (Sir. 43:28). These two attributes of God, transcendence
and immanence, are not at all contradictory. God's holiness or
transcendence is not apartness.

The Christian is not of the world because he shares in the
transcendence, the "otherness," the holiness of God himself. And
yet, this sharing in God's transcendence does not necessarily set
the Christian apart from his fellowmen, any more than God's
transcendence destroys *his* presence or immanence in the world.
Certainly the Christian's holiness, which is a participation in
God's transcendence, does not necessarily require physical apartness.

There is a widespread tendency at present to try to destroy, as
it were, the transcendence of God, and to break down all distinction between the sacred and the profane, between the consecrated and the secular. Such, for example, is the meaning of

much of the "God-is-dead" theology. In his book, *The Gospel of Christian Atheism,* Thomas J. J. Altizer,[1] insisting on the immanence of God, denies his transcendence. The transcendent God, the God above all creation, Altizer claims, "emptied himself" of his transcendence when he became immanent (that is, completely embedded) in the man Jesus. And when Jesus died, says Altizer, this immanent God began a long evolutionary process of embedding himself deeper into the very fabric of the profane universe. The true Christian must therefore reject the resurrection of Jesus, says the professor, since resurrection implies that God somehow regained his aloof transcendence by "jumping back up into heaven."[2]

But according to the Holy Scriptures, the immanence and transcendence of God are in no way contradictory. In fact, when Jesus returned to the Father in his resurrection and ascension, and sent the Holy Spirit to "fill all things" (Eph. 4:10), God became more intimately immanent in his creatures than ever before; and when the work of Jesus and the Holy Spirit is finished, then God will be truly "all in all" (1 Cor. 15:28).

And yet God, no matter how intimately present he becomes in his creatures, will ever remain infinitely transcendent.

If the "God-is-dead" theology, in its laudable desire to bring God closer to the world, has attempted to destroy the transcendence of God, certain movements in the Church, in the same desire, have tended to break down all distinction between the consecrated and the secular. For example, as we have seen, in eagerness to accomplish the Church's work of "consecration of the world," some have denied the value of the consecration of religious. They have claimed that this special consecration sets

[1] Thomas J. J. Altizer, *The Gospel of Christian Atheism* (Philadelphia: Westminster Press, 1966).

[2] This brief summary of Altizer's position is adapted from *Newsweek,* April 11, 1966, p. 76.

the religious apart like the Pharisees, building up a wall between the religious and the rest of mankind.

These people are right, of course, in insisting that religious must avoid everything that gives the impression that they consider themselves a people apart from the rest of men. But at the same time, in these days when God's transcendence or sacredness is being very much de-emphasized, religious must bear witness to it, they must be filled with the holiness of God, so that they can make it more perfectly immanent in the world. Religious, then, have to reconcile the good tendency to break down barriers between themselves and the world with the necessity of retaining a strong sense of the sacred.

In truth, the Church's new openness to the world, inspired by the Holy Spirit, is not a desire to destroy what is holy by removing all barriers between the sacred and the profane, but a desire to bring holiness into what is profane, "that God may be all in all" (1 Cor. 15:28). For this purpose, many barriers do need to be removed, so that holiness can overflow into all things. However, it is not a case of profaning the sacred, but of sanctifying the profane. The Church does indeed need to be in the world, to sanctify the world.

Salvation history shows God himself at work breaking down the barriers between the sacred and the profane, as he ever more completely invades mankind with his own holiness. And so too, in the living of their consecration, religious should emphasize, not apartness from the world, but rather being filled with the holiness of God, so that through them God may continue his work of invading all mankind with his holiness.

The Concept of the Sacred

God led his People by degrees to an understanding of sacredness or holiness. The history of the concept of the sacred shows that originally one of its root elements was apartness. The sacred was that which was set apart from the profane and consecrated to God as his own. The sacred is therefore inviolable, for it is the Lord's personal property. Thus God's people Israel is described as "sacred to the Lord" (Jer. 3:2), and the Lord threatens evil to anyone who would presume to lay hands upon it (Ps. 104:15).

Moreover, in the Scriptures whatever is sacred takes on something of God's own transcendence or "otherness." This participation in God's holiness is more essential to the concept of consecration than is the idea of apartness or separation. As the New Testament showed clearly, a sacred person can share in God's transcendence or holiness and still be present in the midst of the profane. "They are in the world," says Jesus of his disciples, but "they are not of the world, even as I am not of the world" (Jn. 17:11, 16).

The history of salvation shows that God set his chosen People apart as sacred and filled them with his own holiness, precisely so that through them he might make himself present in the world, filling the world with his own life and glory, invading the world with his own holiness through this sacred People. His People are God's open door to the world.

And yet, no matter how widely this holiness of God penetrates mankind and becomes immanent in the world, it nevertheless remains ever transcendent. God's holiness ever infinitely surpasses all that it fills, untainted by anything it touches. As the rays of the sun are untainted by the filth they touch, but rather purify it, so God's holiness purifies, heals, sanctifies whatever it penetrates.

Salvation history, then, reveals a progressive breaking down of the barriers between the sacred and the profane, so that the divine holiness can be more present to men. But, as we said, this process is never a profaning of the sacred; it is always a sanctifying of the profane.

For example, in ancient Israel, the most sacred of all places was the Holy of Holies in the temple, a place set apart from all others so that God might fill it with his presence and thus dwell among his People. On the day of dedication of the temple by Solomon, God had filled the temple with his majesty and glory as the sign of his acceptance of this house, which was to be his dwelling among his chosen ones and his meeting place with them. His throne room was the Holy of Holies, his throne was the outstretched wings of the cherubim over the Ark of the Covenant. But his presence there was ever a veiled one, for no one except the Highpriest, and he only once a year after offering a sacrifice of atonement, could penetrate behind the veils setting this apart as an inviolable sacred place.

But one day, when Isaia was praying in the temple, suddenly before his eyes God seemed to break forth from the sacred limits of the Holy of Holies, so that all the earth was filled with his glory, not just the narrow confines of that sacred spot (Isa. 6:1–4). All the earth became his dwelling. It was as though the veil of the Holy of Holies existed no more.

St. Paul shows how this vision is fulfilled in Christ. In his own flesh on the cross, says St. Paul, Jesus "has broken down the intervening wall of the enclosure" (Eph. 2:14). There was a wall in the temple at Jerusalem beyond which the Gentiles, as profane persons, could not pass under pain of death. God dwelt behind that wall among his sacred People. Though his was a deeply veiled presence, nevertheless he was truly with them and they were a holy people precisely because of his presence among them. The Gentiles, on the contrary, says the Apostle, were "without God in the world" (Eph. 2:13).

But Christ on the cross broke down that separating wall, and God, as it were, burst forth from the Holy of Holies and made all the nations his living temple. The Gentiles, once "strangers and foreigners" are now fellow-citizens with the saints, that is, with the holy people of Israel, and together with them are consecrated by the Holy Spirit as "a temple holy in the Lord," with Christ himself as the chief cornerstone. All the nations "are being built together into a dwelling place for God in the Spirit" (Eph. 2:22). All mankind is thus called to become "sacred to the Lord," his holy dwelling place.

The Ever Transcendent God

In Ephesians 1:23(d), the Church is called the fullness of Christ "who fills all in all." The words "all in all" are an echo of Sirach 43:28, in which God is said to be "all in all." Sirach, however, was speaking only of God's creative and upholding omnipresence. According to Sirach, God not only fills all things, but as it were spills over in an infinite way, in what theology calls his attribute of immensity: "and greater is he than all his works" (Sir. 43:29). Though God fills all things, giving them their perfections, he cannot be contained by them; he is infinitely transcendent, infinitely surpassing, infinitely other.

But when St. Paul speaks of Christ filling all in all, he is no longer speaking of the natural filling of all things by the omnipresence of the divine creative power, but of the supernatural filling of creatures with God's own life and holiness by the giving of the Holy Spirit. When Christ fills all in all by filling the Church with his Holy Spirit, Christ too remains infinitely transcendent, greater than all the fullness he communicates to his People, greater than his Mystical Body. For even when the Church has reached her final perfection, when she has grown up to "the mature measure of the fullness of Christ" (Eph. 4:13) and has been "filled unto all the fullness of God" (Eph. 3:19), Christ and God and the Spirit will remain infinitely transcendent. Although God will be filling his People with his own divine life and personal presence, nevertheless he will still be infinitely other, infinitely surpassing.

As St. Paul expresses it, even when God is all in all, dwelling in the fully perfected living temple, the Church, he is still "above all"—"One God and Father of all, who is above all, and throughout all, and in us all" (Eph. 4:6). For Christianity is not pantheism. God and his People, God and his creation, never become identical, even when the People of God are fully united to God in transforming union, and completely glorified by the full indwelling of the Holy Trinity.

The Direct Encounter with God

We must beware, then, of those current exaggerations which claim that we are to find God, not in himself, not in prayer or in worship, but only in the Christian community with which he has identified himself. The truth is, we must repeatedly encounter God in his own Person, and not merely in his members. We must meet God in frequent contemplation of the three divine Persons who dwell in us.

The fellowman in whom we encounter Christ is a sign leading us to find God in himself. For example, if we see Christ in the poor and needy, we see him in them in the sense that their condition reminds us of the suffering Christ whom we have already met, Christ who suffered for all of us. We gratefully express our faith in what he has done for all of us when we were poor and needy in sin, by serving him in serving the neighbor with whose miseries he has identified himself in his sufferings. But to recognize Christ in his members whom we serve presupposes that we have first recognized Christ in his own Person, meeting him in living faith, in prayer and in the sacraments.

Thus, we who feed the hungry and clothe the naked and instruct the ignorant, and recognize Christ in them, do so because we have first met Christ in Person in the eucharistic liturgy, and in the strength of that eucharistic food we go forth to meet him and serve him in his members. Thus our union with his Eucharistic Body is perfected in union with his Mystical Body. But our union with one another in the Mystical Body is a union with one another in God. It is because we are directly united to God in faith, hope and charity—with God who dwells in us—that we are united to one another. As Vatican II expresses it, the Church is "a people made one in the unity of the Father and of the Son and of the Holy Spirit" (*LG* 4).

And even when we reverence Christ in neighbor because neighbor is already Christ's living member, participating in Christ's life in the Holy Spirit, our meeting with Christ in neighbor is still only an indirect meeting with Christ. A direct meeting with Christ can take place only within us, in living faith and charity. Neighbor is a sign of Christ, eliciting from us an act of faith and charity when we serve him for the sake of Christ. But every act of faith and charity unites us directly to Christ. This encounter with Christ in faith and charity really takes place within us, in the temple of our living faith and love, in our living consciousness of the God for whose sake we serve neighbor, the God who is directly present to us because he is dwelling within us by grace.

Furthermore, if we are Christ to our needy fellowman, it is only as instruments of the divine love which is manifest and somehow at work in our charity. Our presence to neighbor is only an actual grace for neighbor, a transient grace alerting him to the God whom he must find as he is in himself. The neighbor who has seen in us a sign of God's love for him will encounter God directly only in sanctifying grace; that is, only when God invades his very person with sanctifying grace and his indwelling presence. When we are Christ to our neighbor, our neighbor only indirectly encounters Christ in us; he directly encounters Christ when Christ dwells within him by grace and he is alive to Christ in living faith and love.

The indirect encounter with God in neighbor or in nature,

therefore, is not enough. Neighbor or nature is only a sign of God, alerting us to God, leading us to the God who wills to dwell within our very being and in our living consciousness by grace, where we are directly united to him.

If God's People go forth into the world to meet their fellow-men, and if our fellowmen somehow encounter God in us, this preliminary encounter with God whom they see in us is not enough. Neighbor or nature is only a sign of God, alerting us to him. Our fellowman must be brought to God through the liturgy where he will directly encounter God in the sacraments, and above all in the Eucharist. That is why Vatican II says that all the Church's activity flows from the liturgy and leads back to it (*SC* 10). God's People meet him directly in the eucharistic liturgy and in prayer, and then go out to find him and serve him in their fellowman, bringing fellowman back to the Eucharistic Sacrifice that there he too may meet God directly.

These are some of the truths we are trying to convey in saying that God remains ever transcendent, infinitely surpassing all creatures. He can be encountered only imperfectly through the medium of creatures, and only indirectly. The creatures through whom we meet God are at best only sacraments.

Nature can be called a sacrament of God only in the very widest sense of the term. Nature is only a sign of God, stimulating us to seek him as he is in himself. But God is more hidden than manifest in nature. "Greater is he than all his works. . . . Beyond these, many things lie hid; only a few of his works have we seen" (Sir. 43:29, 34).

The Church is a sacrament of God in a much stricter sense. God's People are not only sign, but also instrument of the supernatural presence of God by grace. And still, as sign, the Church alerts us to the transcendent God who infinitely surpasses all signs, and as instrument brings us to him, or rather him to us, so that by the grace given to us in the Church, we may be united directly to him in living faith and love.

We must not think, then, that God can be found only in our fellowman, and in no more perfect way than that.

We shall resume the theme of this chapter after the solution of certain difficulties which no doubt have arisen in the minds of some of our readers.

18. Answers to Difficulties

When the foregoing chapter was originally presented as a lecture, one questioner asked, in the discussion which followed: "If we can approach the reality of God without the image, what was the point of the Incarnation? Don't we go to the reality through the image?"

In the lecture itself, it was not denied that we encounter God in Christ, the Image of the invisible God (Col. 1:15); it was maintained, however, that we recognize Christ in others only if we have recognized Christ himself.

When Christ, the Image, first came among men, he himself was recognized for what he truly was only by those who had already met God in their hearts. Jesus explains to his opponents why they cannot recognize him: it is because they do not really know God, and do not love him. "The Father himself, who has sent me, has borne witness to me. But you have never heard his voice, or seen his face. . . . I know that you have not the love of God in you. I have come in the name of my Father, and you do not receive me" (Jn. 5:37, 42). . . . "If God were your Father,

151

you would surely love me. . . . The reason why you do not hear is that you are not of God" (Jn. 8:42, 47).

Moreover, no one recognizes Christ, the revelation of God, without an interior experience of God, an interior grace: "No one can come to me unless the Father who sent me draw him. . . . 'They all shall be taught of God.' Everyone who has listened to the Father, and has learned, comes to me" (Jn. 6:44–45).

If even Christ himself could be recognized only by those who had an interior light from God, an interior recognition of God, how much more is this interior light necessary if we are to recognize the lesser revelation of God in the rest of our fellowmen.

Father Schillebeeckx, in *Christ the Sacrament of the Encounter with God,* explains how the pagan recognizes God in nature only because he has first had an interior experience of God through grace:

> All humanity receives that inward word of God calling men to a communion in grace with himself. This obscure call causes those among the heathen who listen to it in uprightness of heart dimly to suspect that there is a redeeming God who is occupying himself personally with their salvation. Such an inward religious experience produced by grace does not yet encounter the visible embodiment of that grace . . . [i.e., Christ].
>
> Nevertheless, life in this created world gains a new and deeper meaning when man lives in the world as one who has received this call from God in his inmost being. . . . Life itself in the world then belongs to the very content of God's inner word to us. It interprets dimly at least something of that which God personally, by the attraction of his grace, is whispering in our hearts. . . . creation begins to speak to us the language of salvation . . . creation becomes a sign of higher realities. The course of nature, human life in the world and with the world, tells us more because of God

speaking within us than ever it could of itself. . . . Thus in paganism, too, the inward grace achieves a certain visible manifestation.[1]

Another question from the audience was this: "When you say that we must see God in himself in order to recognize him in others, how do you explain these words of Teilhard de Chardin: 'The light of heaven becomes tangible and attainable to the Christian through the crystal of creatures'?"

De Chardin saw so much of God in nature because he was already so deeply spiritual a man, because he had deeply experienced God in prayer. The inner grace of God is too great to be expressed in ideas or in words. Only gradually, with the help of the signs of God he finds in nature, in the Scriptures, and above all in Christ and his Church, does man articulate or interpret for himself the inner experience of grace. The signs and words and symbols are meaningful to the extent that they verify, as it were, and help make articulate what a person is experiencing or has experienced through an inner grace. This is what our Lord means in saying that only those who are interiorly taught by God can come to him.

This same interior experience of God in the gift of faith which is necessary if we are to recognize even Christ in himself is certainly presupposed if we are to recognize Christ in our fellowmen. The recognition of God in our fellowmen or in nature, in turn, is a deepening and strengthening of the original recognition, and is, as it were, a required exterior articulation of the inner experience.

Articulating Our Ineffable Interior Graces

These truths are corroborated by the testimony of effective preachers of the word of God, who ever so often receive the

[1] Pp. 7–8.

overjoyed reaction of their hearers: "You said exactly what was in my heart!" Most priests find it difficult to preach to religious women because they are convinced that some deeper, more profound religious message will have to be conveyed to these professional seekers of God, and they fear that they will have nothing to say which these holy people do not already know.

But after some experience in preaching to such persons and to other holy people, the preacher discovers that holy people most *want* to hear the things they already know, and that the most effective sermon is the one which strikes a chord which is already vibrating in the listeners.

Holy people most want to hear what they already know through the inner grace of God at work in their hearts, for they are seeking a confirmation of the divine truths and experiences which have been theirs; they want a verification of realities which they are already dimly beginning to grasp. They are seeking a brightening of the light that has already dawned in them. The genuine inner graces impressed by God in a heart, we said, are too big for words, too big to be grasped in concepts, and so the one who receives them is often not fully aware that he has received them. At first, these graces seem to be more darkness than light, and the soul gropes for the deeper meaning contained in his experience.

And that is why, when a preacher expresses clearly, strikingly, and with conviction something his hearers have already experienced at least in a vague way, the hearers are overjoyed. The outward sign—the word of the preacher—is a confirmation and a deepening of their inward grace, and helps the hearers to interpret more clearly, and to make effective in their lives, the work of grace which God has already begun in them.

Frequently, then, a preacher or a confessor is told, "You said exactly what was in my heart!" The preached word or the word of counsel is joyfully accepted as a seal of divine approval, a new sign from God that their hopeful and fearful groping has been in the right direction. "How did God reveal to you my heart?" said St. Albert the Great to Blessed Jordan of Saxony after a sermon by Jordan touching on the very vocational problems with which St. Albert was then wrestling. The inner thoughts or gropings plus the verifying witness of others (preacher or fellow Christian) are, as it were, one same presence of the God who is "all in all."

The charismatic word of preaching, or counsel, or exhortation or admonition, strikes a note which makes the soul vibrate like a tuning fork, but only because the soul is already, in greater or lesser degree, in tune with God; or, at least, not hardened against God by past rejections of divine invitations.

Ordinarily, then, the souls who are most accustomed to listening interiorly to God are the ones who are most receptive and most impressed and most delighted with the word of God brought to them by others. So, too, Christian community living is deepest where the members are deeply in tune with God, and therefore wonderfully open to a mutual influence of grace from one another.

This mutual influence of grace among the members of the community is an indispensable articulation and expression of the ineffable graces planted by God in their hearts, which necessarily have to be interpreted in terms of the Christian living of the children of God. Because—often without fully realizing it—they have had some inner experience of God the Holy, they are able to recognize the sacredness of their fellowmen and of all things, and reverence them accordingly. Fellowmen and God's other creatures thus become signs of the God who "is not far from any one of us, for in him we live and move and have our being" (Acts 17:27). The ineffable inner grace and divine light and love in our hearts are, as it were, reflected back to us by our fellow creatures and broken down as in a prism, so that they can be grasped and understood. But only because the light is already within us can we recognize its reflection in others. For, by reason of the psychological workings of human nature, man normally interprets his fellowman in the light of his view of himself. As a man is, so he judges everything else. Two men walking out of a door together can have opposite reactions to the weather: one says it is chilly; the other says no, it is warm. The diverse judgments result from the diverse bodily conditions of the two men.

Thus a lustful man is likely to see his fellowman in terms of lust; in looking at a woman, he does not see Christ in her, he sees her only as a possible aid to his lust. It is the holy man, who already experiences himself as the image of Christ, who most spontaneously sees neighbor also as the likeness of Christ. We tend to judge everything in the light of our subjective condition; and so we need some personal experience of Christ, some recognition of Christ himself, before we can recognize him in others, before we can know what it really means to find God in neighbor. He who has never experienced Christ will scarcely know how to find him in neighbor.

As we are, then, so we judge. So that we will be successful in consistently seeing Christ in our fellowmen, we must take care to encounter him frequently in himself. Serving him in fellowman is, of course, a necessary expression and deepening of the original personal encounter with Christ, and is a predisposition for renewed and still more profound meetings with Christ in prayer.

When we are vibrating in tune with God, hearts who are seeking God will vibrate in tune with us. We find in neighbor and neighbor finds in us, only what God has put there, only what God is vibrating there.

Our primary task always, whether as apostle or as recipient from an apostle, is to be in tune with God in simplicity of heart, with a keen religious sense, a sense of the sacred. The whole purpose of every apostle and of every spiritual direction and every spiritual conversation is to teach others to be attentive to God who speaks in hearts. The person who aspires to be Christ to his fellowman must learn that, like John the Baptist, he is only a voice crying in the wilderness, which must decrease to the extent that the inner voice of God in his listeners' hearts is being perceived.

A written question from the audience called attention to the necessity of encountering God in "the signs of the times." "God," wrote the questioner, "is revealed *now* through his Spirit in the workings of men. How can we know God except through men? Could you explain your statement that we must first know God and then only can we discover him in men?"

Unknown to the questioner, the answer she was seeking was already expressed in her question: "God is revealed now *through his Spirit* in the workings of men." The inner light of the Spirit makes it possible to recognize God in the "signs of the times." Openness to the Holy Spirit is a prerequisite for this recognition. Vatican II explains that God can be accurately found in the signs of the times only in the light of the Gospel (and it is to be noted that this is not a case of meeting God in person, or directly, but only of discerning his workings). The scrutiny of the signs of the times and their evaluation in the light of the Gospel require that one be led by the Spirit of God and have the light of faith, that light which is already a grace and experience of God himself.[2]

In response to all the questions we have been considering, the following words of Vatican II are again apropos:

> Only by the light of faith and by meditation on the word of God can one always and everywhere recognize God "in whom we live and move and have our being" (Acts 17:28), seek his will in every event, see Christ in everyone whether he be a relative or a stranger, and judge correctly the true

[2] See *GS* 11, quoted on p. i of the Introduction.

meaning and value of temporal things both in themselves and in their true relation to man's final goal (*AA* 4).

To sum up, then: the necessity of finding Christ in our fellow-men, and of finding God in his workings in nature and in contemporary salvation history, does not abolish but presupposes the need of finding God as he is in himself. It is not enough for man to find God in his effects, in his creatures, in his workings in the world and in the Church; man needs to experience God as he is in himself; and he needs to verify, interpret, elaborate, articulate, express and deepen this ineffable experience with the help of the signs of God in nature, in the Scriptures, and in God's People.

It is exceedingly important, then, that we never lose the idea of God's infinite transcendence. The contemporary desire to break down all barriers between God and the world sometimes goes so far as to lose all sense of the sacred and of God's infinite transcendence. The infinite God can never be inserted into a finite cosmos, nor even into the Mystical Body of Christ.

Consecration of the World

If, then, God so infinitely transcends the entire created cosmos, and even the Mystical Body of Christ, what is the task of the Church in the secular world? This task, often referred to as "consecration of the world," is, said Cardinal Montini, "to permeate the vast realm of the profane world with Christian principles and powerful natural and supernatural virtues."[3] It is the task of building the temporal world according to the true will of God, making it a more human place to live in, and an ideal soil for receiving the word of God and the divine life and holiness which God wills to plant in it (*LG* 36). The secular or profane world

[3] Cardinal Montini, quoted in *Osservatore Romano*, March 23, 1962.

has its own autonomous values which must be respected and
guaranteed, and never vitiated by an unconsidered attempt to
replace them with sacred values. "For it must be admitted that
the temporal sphere is governed by its own principles, since it is
rightly concerned with the interests of this world. But that omi-
nous doctrine which attempts to build a society with no regard
whatever for religion . . . is rightly to be rejected" (*LG* 36).

God wills to communicate to this profane world, rebuilt according to Christian principles, his own transcendent holiness by
filling the hearts of men with his Holy Spirit and his own indwelling. Such a well-ordered world is necessary if the divine life
is to thrive in the hearts of men.

Religious by their holiness are called to bear witness in a
striking way to these transcendent realities with which God
wishes to fill the world. For, says Vatican II, "by their state in
life, religious give splendid and striking testimony that the world
cannot be transformed and offered to God without the spirit of
the beatitudes" (*LG* 31). By their poverty, chastity and obedience,
which are a striking, concrete, effective way of living the beatitudes, religious empty themselves of all else so that they may be
filled with the holiness of God, and thus bear witness to the holiness which God wishes to pour forth into the hearts of all men.

That is what the Council means in saying that religious are
to be eschatological signs, bearing witness that the heavenly
realities are already at work among men. By the spirit of the
beatitudes, lived strikingly in poverty, chastity, and obedience,
they manifest that although the Church is in the world, it is not
of the world. The Church can never be absorbed by the secular
city, and so, of course, neither should religious be absorbed by
it, no matter what their mission in the world. In fact, their
fundamental mission in the world, their chief sign value, is by
their "otherness" to bear witness to the transcendent world.

Therefore, even while we labor to make God ever more immanent in mankind, helping to build up the Church as the living

temple of God, we must ever keep alive the sacred sense of the divine transcendence and infinite holiness. Without ever giving the impression of separateness or of being cut off from the world, religious must nevertheless bear witness to the otherness, the sacredness of God. Though this divine holiness will forever remain infinitely transcendent, it nonetheless desires to be present in all things.

The otherness of religious, their sacredness, must consist precisely in their being as filled as much as possible with the holiness of God, thus bearing witness that on the Cross of Christ the divine holiness has broken down the barriers between heaven and earth and wills to fill all things with the sanctifying Spirit, so that God may be all in all. The divine holiness can break into the realm of the profane with the help of religious only to the extent that religious themselves are filled with that holiness, showing forth by their lives that, in the last analysis, there is only one reality, one goal, toward which all men must tend—the possession of God. One can bear witness to the divine holiness, and make it present in the world, only by living it. Religious, then, should be truly living temples of the Holy Trinity, glowing as it were with the divine presence, which they must make vividly manifest by their faith, their charity, their joy in hope, their being "knit together in love" (Col. 2:2, s).

Like the Church herself, religious are to be present in the world, open to the world, involved in the world, but only for the sake of making God's holiness present in the world. By reason of God's holiness in them, they are definitely not of the world. They are unlike the world, for they participate in God's own otherness. They have to have the courage to live this otherness, the courage to be different from the world, and thus bear witness to the transcendent God, the holy God, and draw all things to the beauty of his holiness.

They have to be filled with God. And that is why they have to be emptied of all else. The religious must learn above all to break down the barriers between himself and God. And when God's holiness has thus found easy access into him, he in turn can be God's open door to the world.

If a religious neglects to cultivate openness to God and strives only to be open to the world and only to be present to the world, instead of God's holiness invading the world through him, he will be invaded by whatever is perverse in the spirit of the fallen world.

Therefore, even if, in all the true human values, religious have to be like the people they are trying to save, and present with them and open to them, even more they have to be like God, open to him, present with him, so filled with his presence and holiness that they make him present in the world. Through his holy People, as through an open door, God's holiness invades the world and transforms it in his own likeness, so that at last God will be all in all.

19. The Apostolic Value of Religious Consecration

In its pastoral approach to divine revelation, Vatican II presents God's word not in abstract terms and principles, but in a concrete way. It shows the word at work in man, and man responding to the word, becoming involved in salvation history. This, we have seen, is how the Council presents Mary, and this is how it presents the religious life. Religious are described in their intimate involvement in the Church's work of salvation. The ecclesial-apostolic dimension of their life is clearly brought out.

Since *Ecclesiae Sanctae* requires that revised constitutions should express the union of the religious life with the Church, let us further examine what Vatican II has to say on this point.

We have seen that the Council presents religious profession as a firmer, more stable, more intimate participation in the Church's indissoluble bond with the divine Bridegroom, and that this bond was first actualized and perfected in the person of Mary. Consenting to the word of God, "embracing God's

162

saving will with a full heart . . . Mary consecrated herself totally as servant of the Lord to the person and work of her Son" (*LG* 56).

In these same terms, Vatican II describes the commitment of the religious life. To consecrate self to Christ is to consecrate self to his Person and to his work as continued in the Church. "Impelled by the love which the Holy Spirit has poured into their hearts, they live more and more for Christ and for his body which is the Church. Therefore, the more fervently they are united to Christ by this total, life-long giving of themselves, the richer the life of the Church becomes, and the more vigorous and fruitful its apostolate" (*PC* 1).

In other words, one cannot give self to Christ without simultaneously giving self to his mission of salvation, which is the whole reason for his own existence as man. "The one whom the Father has consecrated and sent into the world" (Jn. 10:36) is practically a proper name of Jesus in St. John's Gospel, expressing his very nature as Savior. In giving themselves to the Person of Christ, then, religious give themselves at the same time to his work of salvation.

Or, to put it the other way around: one cannot consecrate self to the *work* of Christ except by consecrating self to his *Person*. For every apostolate in the Church is necessarily rooted in the very Person of Jesus.

Vatican II capitalizes on this truth to bring out the extraordinary apostolic power of the religious life. Precisely because religious are so intimately consecrated to Christ alone, they are endowed with great apostolic power. This power is theirs, or rather the Church's, in proportion to how intimately they live this consecration. Consecration, we have said, should be living, dynamic, daily growing in intimacy. This growth in the perfection of one's consecration, with the consequent increase in one's apostolic power, is expressed by the Council in this way:

Impelled by the love which the Holy Spirit has poured into their hearts, they live more and more for Christ and for his body which is the Church. Therefore, the more fervently they are united to Christ by this total, life-long giving of themselves, the richer the life of the Church becomes, and the more vigorous and fruitful its apostolate (*PC* 1).

The fruitfulness of the apostolate, in other words, is in proportion to the intimacy of one's union with Christ. The real key to the understanding of the apostolic fruitfulness of religious consecration is the words "God alone," which occur at least six times, like a regular refrain, in the Council's words concerning the religious life (*LG* 42c; *PC* 5a, d, e; 6; 7). Religious are so valuable to the Church and to the world precisely because they are consecrated to God alone. Given totally to Christ in undivided devotion (*LG* 42), they are totally available to him and his salvation work. As *Perfectae Caritatis* states it:

Members of every kind of religious community must bear specially in mind that the profession of the evangelical counsels was their response to God's call, so that they might not only be dead to sin, but also renounce the world and live for God alone. They have made over the whole of their lives to his service, and this is a special type of consecration, deeply rooted in that of baptism and expressing it more fully (*PC* 5a).

Elsewhere, the Council brings out the apostolic value of the religious life by describing the apostolate in its very source and showing how religious should live at this source. From the life hidden with Christ in God springs forth the urgency of their apostolic life and labor for neighbor. "Those who profess the evangelical counsels should above all else seek and love God who first loved us. In every circumstance they should nourish the life hidden with Christ in God, from which flows and is impelled the love of neighbor for the salvation of the world and the building up of the Church" *(PC 6)*.

"And so members of every religious institute must seek God alone and above all else; they should combine contemplation, by which they become united to him in mind and heart, with apostolic love, by which they strive to join in the work of the redemption and spread the kingdom of God" *(PC 5e)*.

The one only source of both contemplation and apostolic love is Christ: "Religious, therefore, loyal to their profession, leaving all things for Christ, must follow him as the one thing necessary, hearing his words and making his work their concern" *(PC 5d)*— "hearing his words" in contemplation, "making his work their concern" in apostolic love.

Since apostolic love receives its impelling power from the life hidden with Christ in God, "for this reason members of religious institutes must zealously cultivate prayer and the spirit of prayer, equipping themselves from the authentic sources of Christian spirituality" *(PC 6b)*. At this point, the Council prescribes the Scriptures and the liturgy as the great sources both of the interior life and of love of neighbor and dedication to the Church and her mission.

If the extraordinary apostolic power of the religious life flows precisely from the religious consecration to God alone, it follows that the religious life is fully relevant to the life of the Church and her apostolate to the extent that it remains the way of the evangelical counsels, and not modified to such an extent that it is no longer different from secular life. The more a religious is a religious, the more valuable he is to the Church. Such is the thought of the Council in saying: "The more fervently they are united to Christ by this total life-long self-giving, the richer the life of the Church becomes and the more vigorous and fruitful its apostolate" *(PC 1)*.

In unmistakable terms, then, the Council has told us that the religious life is relevant to the Church and its mission in the world today in direct proportion to how well religious live the inner mystery of the Church: her indissoluble union with Christ who is the source of all holiness and of all apostolic power. Adaptation in externals will be fruitless without the revitalizing of these bonds of union with God alone:

> Since the prime purpose of the religious life is to enable the members to follow Christ and become united with God through the profession of the evangelical counsels, the fact must be honestly faced that even the best adaptations to the needs of our time will fail of their purpose unless a renewal of spirit gives life to them. Indeed, the interior renewal must always be given first place even in promoting external works *(PC* 2e).

Section Eight of *Perfectae Caritatis* develops in more detail how the inner spirit must ever permeate external works. Or more than that, it shows the inseparability of the religious spirit and the apostolic spirit which must animate both the internal life of the religious community and all its apostolic activity:

> In these institutes (the ones dedicated to the apostolic life) apostolic and charitable works belong to the very nature of the religious life, because they are a sacred ministry and special work of charity which the Church has commissioned them to do and which are to be carried out in its name. Therefore, the whole religious life of the members should be inspired with the apostolic spirit and the whole apostolic action should be animated by the religious spirit *(PC* 8).

The religious spirit which must permeate all their apostolic activity is the spirit of total consecration, the spirit of total life-long giving of self to Christ alone in ever greater intimacy, as a total holocaust in union with his own self-surrender for the salvation of mankind. This spirit is expressed in the "practice of virtue, in particular the virtues of humility and obedience, fortitude and chastity, by which they share in Christ's emptying of himself and participate in his life in the Spirit" (*PC* 5).

Since consecration to Christ is necessarily consecration also to his mission of salvation, the apostolic spirit should penetrate not merely the actual apostolic works but the entire religious life of those engaged in them, just as the religious spirit, the spirit of consecration, should animate the entire apostolate. The apostolate is a continuation and expression of the inner sacrificial self-giving of the religious, and so is an essential part of one's ever living consecration. Likewise, one's self-giving within the community life, and in its religious observances, should be offered in an apostolic spirit. The perfection of this self-offering in living the community life will vitalize the apostolate of the community.

Thus, one's interior spiritual life and one's apostolic activity are intimately united as one total offering to God which bears abundant apostolic fruit. Blending of the interior life and the apostolate, blending contemplation and action, is less of a problem to the degree that one is thoroughly penetrated with the spirit of consecration, "the religious spirit" (*PC* 8). The spirit of consecration to God alone in dynamic faith, hope and charity is a living prayer. When one has this spirit, one prays always, one is a living liturgy, a continuing worship of God, in everything one does.

This spirit of consecration, this living consecration, includes love of the Cross. The labors and frustrations of the apostolate are accepted in the spirit of consecration as a participation in Christ's mission to be a redemptive sacrifice. When one has this spirit, one's fidelity is not easily shaken by the difficulties of one's life and labors. And in such consecrated labors, Christ is made present in his sacrificial self-giving.

It is clear, then, that the religious life is relevant to the mission of the Church in the world today only to the extent that religious are really religious—really what Christ expects religious to be. If religious modify their life to such an extent that they no longer differ from the laity, then they are no longer relevant to the Church: they are not fulfilling their special role as religious in the Church. They may as well stop calling themselves Jesuits, Franciscans, Dominicans and the like, and get married.

If they were to do this, however, they would be rejecting God's special call. Religious profession, "a special type of consecration," says the Council, is made in response to a special call from God "to renounce the world and live for God alone" (*PC* 5). By reason of this call and grace, religious have a different role from that of the laity, and so are relevant to the life of the Church only by being different from the laity, not by being just like them. They are relevant only to the extent that they are truly poor, totally chaste, really obedient.

And they are relevant to the Church and to the world because their apostolic works are "a sacred ministry," a holy service which the Church has commissioned them to do, the special service which the Church therefore expects of them for the forwarding of her own mission to the world. Their total consecration has made them totally available to Christ and to his Church. Therefore, they can be and are entrusted with the Church's own work, and carry out her office and responsibility. In proportion to the perfection of their spirit of consecration, of self-giving, in this work, the Church is fruitful in their ministry. Their consecration to Christ alone—to his Person and to his work—is the source of their special apostolic power as religious. "In order, therefore, that members may respond to their call to follow Christ above all and to serve Christ himself in his members, their apostolic activities must stem from an intimate union with him" (*PC* 8).

Their living, dynamic consecration to Christ alone in lively faith, hope and charity should be daily deepened, in self-sacrificing dedication to the Cross. "Let all religious therefore spread throughout the whole world the good news of Christ by the integrity of their faith, their love for God and neighbor, their devotion to the Cross, and their hope of future glory. Thus will their witness be seen by all, and our Father in heaven will be glorified" (*PC* 25).

20. Contemplation Joined with Apostolic Love

It is remarkable how Vatican II, primarily concerned about the Church's pastoral and apostolic mission, has so emphatically reasserted the role of contemplation in the Christian and apostolic life. It has shown clearly how the whole apostolate of the Church flows from an intimate union with Christ, a union achieved in listening to his word and responding to it in love. It is only to the extent that we go to Christ and enter more deeply into him that we can succeed in bringing him to the world.

We are told in the Constitution on the Liturgy that the Church is both contemplative and active: "It is of the essence of the Church that she be . . . eager to act and yet intent on contemplation, present in this world and yet not at home in it" (*SC* 2).

Already in 1956, Pope Pius XII had described religious priests engaged in the active apostolate as they "whose chief duty it is, by seeking God alone and uniting themselves to him, to contemplate divine things and to transmit them to others."[1]

[1] Pius XII, *Sedes Sapientiae*, 27, in G. Courtois, ed., *The States of Per-*

Vatican II proposes the same pattern not only for religious priests but for all priests: "They should ever nourish and strengthen their action from an abundance of contemplation, doing all this for the comfort of the entire Church of God" (*LG* 41).

And in the decree on the religious life, all religious without exception, clerical and lay, men and women, are told to "join contemplation with apostolic love." It does not say, "add contemplation to the apostolate," meaning, "season your apostolate with a little prayer," nor does it say, "add the apostolate to your prayer," meaning, "dilute your contemplation with a bit of apostolic action."

No, contemplation and apostolic love have to be inseparable companions in everyone's religious life, as two manifestations of one same life and love. Indeed, every Christian life has to be a balanced blend of prayer and action, with the proportions of the mixture varying from individual to individual and from community to community.[2]

The Council does not say, "join contemplation with apostolic *action*," but with "apostolic *love*." For even cloistered religious who have no external apostolic works do and must have apostolic love, a burning thirst for souls giving rise to prayer and sacrifice, benefiting the apostolate of the whole Church in a hidden but very effective way. Moreover, so-called apostolic action is not Christian nor religious nor apostolic unless it is enflamed through and through with apostolic love, which, says the Council, "is the soul of the entire apostolate" (*AA* 3).

The apostolate of the laity, too, the Council tells us, must flow from meditation of the mystery of Christ. "Since Christ, sent by

---

fection According to the Teaching of the Church (Westminster: Newman, 1961), p. 279, #607.

[2] We have treated in some detail the problem of blending contemplation and action in the Christian life in our book *Like the Word* (St. Louis: Herder, 1965), Chapter 22, and especially Chapter 23.

the Father, is the wellspring and origin of the whole apostolate of the Church, it is evident that the success of the lay apostolate depends upon the laity's living union with Christ, according to the Lord's words, 'He who abides in me and I in him, bears much fruit, for without me you can do nothing' . . . Only by the light of faith and by meditation on the word of God can one always and everywhere recognize God 'in whom we live and move and have our being' (Acts 17:28), seek his will in every event, see Christ in everyone whether he be a relative or a stranger, and judge correctly about the true meaning and value of temporal things both in themselves and in their true relation to man's final goal" (*AA* 4).

There we have a tremendously important truth (worth repeating here, although we have considered it before)—we can recognize Christ in neighbor and in the world and in the affairs about us only if we have recognized him in his own Person. We need to see clearly that contemplative love and apostolic love and apostolic activity are only different movements or expressions of one same charity for God and for neighbor. Charity is one. We love neighbor in the same love in which we love God. We express love for God in prayer, and we express love for God in love for neighbor, and love for neighbor chiefly in service of neighbor.

The Council's documents repeatedly insist that all the faithful must participate in Christ's prophetic mission, his bearing witness to the truth. But our witness is not true unless we witness to what we have really seen and experienced and lived. Jesus, "the faithful and true witness" (Apoc. 3:14), declared, "We speak of what we know, and we bear witness to what we have seen" (Jn. 3:11). He says this in the plural, because he is referring also to his People, who are witnesses with him. One has to see, one has to contemplate, before one can bear witness.

But just how does one contemplate?

Christian charity by its very nature desires contemplation, for ardent love always desires the presence of the beloved. If anyone loves Christ ardently enough, and is impelled by this love to want to contemplate him, he will be taught by God how to do so. "They all shall be taught of God" (Jn. 6:45). A lover reveals himself fully only to one who loves in return. If one is intent upon Christ, alive to him in love, and patiently, perseveringly seeks him, he will reveal himself in due time.

But in this persevering search, are there any clues we must follow? Although only God, by the inner grace in which he draws us, can teach us to contemplate, we do know the things to which we should direct our attention. We should contemplate above all the Mystery of Christ, in which alone God fully reveals himself. And especially, we should contemplate that supreme word of love—Christ crucified!

In heaven, the object contemplated will be the divine essence, the very being and life of God, the life of the three divine Persons; and also the fullness of God as communicated to the perfected Mystical Body of Christ, the Church. But on earth, the object to be contemplated is God precisely as he has revealed himself to men; not God as we might like him to be so that he will suit our own desires, but as he has truly made himself known in revelation.

We know a thing by the way it acts. A thing's action is a revelation of its being. So too, God has revealed himself in salvation history, in his divine action in saving his People. The supremely perfect revelation of God, the supreme word of revelation, therefore, is Jesus Christ, in whom and through whom God's saving work is completed, Jesus Christ who is God in Person, in action among us for our salvation. "He who sees me sees also the Father" (Jn. 14:9).

If, then, in contemplation we are to look at God as he has revealed himself, on earth the chief object contemplated is Jesus

Christ, the Word Incarnate, perfect revelation of God, manifesting God as actively present to save us. "No one has at any time
seen God. The only-begotten Son, who is in the bosom of the
Father, he has revealed him" (Jn. 1:18).

The Living Book of Charity

The Christian, therefore, ever keeps his eyes on the Lord Jesus.
On his preaching journeys, every now and then St. Dominic
would say to his travelling companions, "You walk on ahead a
little bit, or drop behind a few paces, and let us meditate on the
Savior." Once when a certain priest asked St. Dominic the source
of his effective preaching and where he got his learning, Dominic
answered, "I have made my chief study in the book of charity,
which teaches everything."

By "book of charity" Dominic meant Christ crucified, opened
wide on the cross, revealing to all mankind that God is love and
salvation; and not only Christ on the cross centuries ago, but
Christ crucified present to Dominic's faith here and now, Christ
alive to Dominic in the liturgy and in his mental prayer and in
his meditative reading of the Scriptures. Those who watched St.
Dominic at prayer tell us that it was his custom, after listening
to the word of God in the refectory or in choir and being filled
with the devotion he drew from these words, to withdraw to a
solitary place and be recollected in the presence of God. Perhaps
then he would open the Scriptures and read a bit. But very
shortly he would seem to be in a lively face-to-face conversation
with Someone. He was in the living presence of the Lord whose
words were before him in the written page.

Dominic's book was truly the living book of Christ's life—not
just Christ's life as lived centuries ago, but Christ who is here and
now alive in our faith, Christ who is opening himself as a book
to our love which seeks him so ardently, Christ who reveals him-

self in contemplative grace to those who are open to him in love's burning desire.

The chief object of Christian contemplation, then, is the Mystery of Christ: God present among men in Christ, God communicating himself to men in Christ. We use the word "mystery" in the sense in which St. Paul used it so frequently: that is, a revelation of the hidden purposes of divine love, a love and purpose infinitely too large to be expressed in mere human words, and which can therefore be revealed only in the very action in which God communicates to us the riches of this love. This is especially his action in giving his Son to us in the Incarnation, and in delivering him up for us on the cross (Rom. 5:8; 8:32; Jn. 3:16). Every detail of God's action among us in Christ is called a mystery inasmuch as it is a symbol or sign, revealing God himself and the purposes of his love, and inasmuch as through the very symbol he accomplishes in us these purposes of his love.

That is why we find St. Dominic forever contemplating and lovingly savoring the mysteries of our Lord's life, or rather the Mystery, for it is one perfect revelation and communication of divine love. With Dominic, our eyes should be ever upon the Lord Jesus in action among us, our heart should be ever pondering with Mary the things Jesus said and did, for only thus can we penetrate to the deep revelation of God's heart which these things contain. The divine love manifest in the mystery cannot fail to win a response of love. As we ponder the mysteries, we too, like Dominic, will soon be in the living presence of Christ, in lively faith, hope and charity—provided that we are living a well-disciplined life, putting into practice the indispensable principles of Christian asceticism. Contemplative love and apostolic love are not given to us on a silver platter. We have to labor for them in the way of the cross. They do not spring from mere human emotion.

The Cross: Summa of Salvation

"I have made my chief study in the book of charity which teaches everything." It teaches everything, for in Christ crucified the entire revelation of the Old Testament salvation history is summed up and perfected in one concrete saving act of God: "God so loved the world that he gave his only-begotten Son!" The *Summa* of all truth is the crucifix, symbol of our Lord's whole life as a "going to the Father." St. Paul said, and Dominic with him, "I determined not to know anything among you, except Jesus Christ and him crucified" (1 Cor. 2:2), and "I count everything loss because of the excelling knowledge of Jesus Christ, my Lord" (Phil. 3:8).

St. Thomas Aquinas, too, learned at the cross all that he knew about God, all that he put into his *Summa*. It was from the cross that Jesus said to him, in a living presence, "Thomas, you have written well of me."

All the rest of salvation history finds its meaning only in the Paschal Mystery, the Mystery of Jesus, the Sacrificed Lamb. Through the words of Jeremia and Ezechiel, for example, God had revealed himself as a Shepherd who would personally gather together his sheep who had been scattered abroad because of the negligence of false shepherds. This revelation was completed in the deeds of Jesus. "Seeing the crowds, he was moved with compassion for them, because they were bewildered and dejected, like sheep without a shepherd" (Matt. 9:36).

In the open book of the cross, we must see with St. Dominic the compassionate Shepherd giving his life, stretching his arms out wide "that he might gather into one the children of God who were scattered abroad" (Jn. 11:52). In the same contemplative vision in which we see the Shepherd giving his life, we see the sheep for whom he gave it. In one same movement of contemplative love, our heart embraces both the crucified Shepherd and the ransomed sheep. It is impossible for Christian contemplation to be selfish, for one cannot see Christ crucified without seeing all those for whom he shed his precious Blood, and consequently seeing self as an offering with Christ for their salvation.

That is why the mere sight of a city would move St. Dominic to tears of compassion for its inhabitants, who were bewildered and dejected like sheep without a shepherd. Dominic had already seen all these bewildered sheep in gazing on Christ crucified. In the same movement of contemplative love in which he had embraced the Lord, he had poured himself out for their salvation. He had contemplated himself as nailed to the cross with Jesus, as one living sacrifice with him, filling up by his apostolic labors what was wanting to the sufferings and labors of Jesus for his body, the Church.

We know that this is how it was with Dominic, for Blessed Jordan writes that even when Dominic was a youth, apostolic love already flamed forth from his contemplative love, urging him to offer his whole being for the salvation of his fellowmen. This, says Jordan, was Dominic's most frequent petition in those early days: "That a true love might be his, to help effectively in the saving of souls; for only then did he consider himself a true member of Christ's body, when he could spend himself and be spent, even as the Lord had spent himself for us on the cross." This prayer for apostolic love sprang spontaneously from his contemplation of Christ on the cross.

With Dominic, we too contemplate the mystery as described by St. Paul—the eternal purpose of divine love to bring all things under the headship of Christ (Eph. 1:10), to reconcile all mankind "in one body to God by the cross" (Eph. 2:16), "in his body of flesh through his death" (Col. 1:22). Understanding this mystery with St. Paul and St. Dominic, we see ourselves as part of it, as taken into it, and ardently desire to be incorporated into it ever more fully.

Such are the fruits af Christian contemplation: an ardent desire to be one body with Christ on the cross for the salvation of all, a burning charity which pours itself out as a sacrifice for souls. Only charity like this gives Christ's own effectiveness to the word one preaches or the lesson one teaches or the witness one lives.

For God is love, and charity alone can reveal him—his charity in action in Christ crucified, his charity in action in his members who spend themselves and are spent in the divine love poured forth from the pierced side of Christ, poured forth into their hearts by the Holy Spirit who is given to them. Words cannot express God, only his own divine love in action in Christ and in his members can reveal him, the love which can be read only in the open, living book of the cross, which teaches everything.

And where is that book most alive, most truly present to us? In the Holy Sacrifice of the Mass. The Mass, his ancient biographers tell us, was St. Dominic's chief devotion. There the full mystery of Christ is present in the living action of God in the liturgy, working to gather together the members of the Mystical Body. The Eucharistic Sacrifice is the revelation of divine love here and now active among us in all its redeeming power.

At the Mass, St. Dominic the contemplative was at his best. Copious tears poured down his face as he offered the Holy Sacrifice, but especially at the Pater Noster. For he would come to the altar in the full consciousness of all the dejected and bewildered sheep he was trying to save, and moved to deep compassion like Jesus, he would shed tears for them. His only relief from his sorrow over their misery was to offer his own life and service with Christ in the Eucharistic Sacrifice.

But the infinite saving love of God, present in the Lamb of God on the altar before him, would turn Dominic's tears of sorrow into tears of joy. His more abundant tears at the Pater Noster came no doubt from his joy in the reconciliation with the Father obtained for the sheep in the Blood of the Lamb.

Dominic could joyously say "Our Father" with all the sheep who were about to be fed by the Good Shepherd giving them his own Body and Blood. And he could say it joyously in the name of those other sheep not yet of the fold, but whom, by the power of this sacrifice, he would be able to bring into the fold for this nourishment, whenever he went out to preach.

Such is the pattern of Christian contemplation, plain to see in the open book of charity. Before your eyes "Jesus Christ has been depicted crucified" (Gal. 3:1). Such contemplation infallibly bears fruit in apostolic love.

21. Consecrated Chastity— "God Alone!": the Theologal, Eschatological Value

In his body on the cross our Lord Jesus Christ broke down the wall of separation between Jews and Gentiles; with the shedding of Christ's blood, God broke through the walls of his sacred place in the temple and began to fill all mankind with his presence. St. Paul applies this truth repeatedly in the seventh chapter of First Corinthians, the one in which he speaks explicitly of consecrated virginity. A persistent refrain sounds throughout the chapter: "let every man remain in the calling in which he was called" (7:20); "in the state in which he was when called, let every man remain with God" (7:24); "as the Lord has allotted to each, as when God has called each, so let him walk" (7:17; cf. also 7:26).

The eminent Scripture scholar Father Lyonnet[1] explains this refrain in terms of the wall of separation broken down by the cross of Jesus. In pre-Christian days, when a pagan was converted

[1] I. de la Potterie, S. Lyonnet, *La Vie selon l'Esprit* (Paris: Cerf, 1965), pp. 239–241.

180

to the Jewish religion, it was often necessary that he completely abandon his former manner of living, lest he, a member of God's holy people, should be contaminated by the profane world from which he had been converted. For it was exceedingly difficult for a Jew to avoid contact with the unholy things and persons in the pagan world about him which would make him ritually impure, unholy. To maintain his sacred status, he had to live practically in a world apart.

But St. Paul lays down the principle that it is not necessary for converts to Christianity to set themselves apart. They need not abandon their former way of life; all they have to abandon is sin. "Let each man remain in the calling in which he was called." No way of life is to be considered unholy, for the Lord has sanctified all things by his cross. "Wast thou a slave when called? Let it not trouble thee. . . . For a slave who has been called in the Lord, is a freedman of the Lord; just as a freeman who has been called is a slave of Christ"(7:21–22). What does it matter whether you are a slave or free? The one thing necessary is the fact that you are "in the Lord," you belong totally to him, and you can live in the presence of God: "Brethren, in the state in which he was when called, let every man remain *with God*" (7:24). Remain with God! The Lord has power to sanctify every state in life, every human occupation, and indeed the whole world. The Christian need not depart from the world in which he lives, for he is "in the Lord," and the Lord's power to sanctify both him and the world is at work in him. All things can be sanctified by Christ's power, all peoples can be made holy by his spirit.

The walls of separation, then, are broken down; the holiness of God is invading the world to make all things holy. No more need of religious segregation, no more need of cutting oneself off from others. Apartness is no longer of the essence of sacredness. The essence of holiness is to be "with God," "in the Lord." "In the state in which he was when called, let every man remain with God."

Holiness, the Apostle tells the Romans, is not a matter of what foods we eat or do not eat, what days we observe or do not observe. Holiness is belonging to the Lord. "For none of us lives to himself, and none dies to himself; for if we live, we live to the Lord, or if we die, we die to the Lord. Therefore, whether we live or die, we are the Lord's" (Rom. 14:7–8).

Since this thought is the framework of the whole chapter in which St. Paul treats of Christian virginity (1 Cor. 7), we can hardly say that St. Paul considered virginity as primarily a segregation, an apartness, in the sense of cutting oneself off from the rest of the Church and mankind. Primarily, virginity is for the sake of being the Lord's own, of being filled with his holiness, of being entirely devoted to him, wherever one is. If a slave should not let it bother him that he is a slave, because he is a freedman of the Lord, if every Christian, no matter what his status in life, is the slave of Christ and should remain with God, this too must be the all-important thing in Christian virginity. The celibate remains as he or she is so that he or she can give undivided attention to the very essence of Christianity—namely, belonging to the Lord, remaining with him, becoming more and more filled with his divine holiness, ever more penetrated by his Holy Spirit:

> He who adheres to the Lord is one spirit with him. . . . Do you not know that your members are the temple of the Holy Spirit, who is in you, whom you have from God, and that you are not your own? . . . The virgin thinks about the things of the Lord, that she may be holy in body and in spirit. . . . I say this for your benefit, not to put a halter upon you, but to promote what is proper, and to make it

possible for you to attend to the Lord with undivided devotion (1 Cor. 6:17, 19; 7:34–35).

The essence of virginity and celibacy, then, is to be the Lord's own: to be devoted to God alone with undivided heart. For this reason, says Vatican II, chastity or celibacy holds the preeminent place among the evangelical counsels:

> The holiness of the Church is fostered in a special way by the many counsels whose observance the Lord proposed in the Gospel to his disciples. Among these, the eminent place is held by the precious gift of divine grace given by the Father to some so that in virginity, or in celibacy, they may more easily devote themselves to God alone with an undivided heart (1 Cor. 7:32–34) (*LG* 42).

When the Council Fathers were debating the schema on religious life, they argued over the order in which the three vows should be treated. The schema had them in this order: obedience, chastity, poverty. Some objected to this, saying that the traditional order should have been kept: poverty, chastity, obedience. Still others insisted that chastity should be first, then poverty, then obedience, for this is the order in which the vows are treated in *Lumen Gentium*. This last group won out, and in the decree on the religious life as finally promulgated, the order of treatment is chastity, poverty, obedience (*PC* 12–14).

We may wonder why so august a body as an ecumenical council should discuss what may seem to be a matter of little importance. The more we reflect upon it, however, the more we realize that the Holy Spirit was at work in this discussion, calling our attention to the profound theological significance in the order in which the vows are treated in *Lumen Gentium*.

There, as we have just seen, we are told that virginity and

celibacy are preeminent among the counsels because they enable
one to devote self to God alone, with undivided heart. This is
the theologal value of religious consecration. The vow of chastity fosters in a wonderful way the direct vital personal relationship with God in faith, hope and charity.

The idea of being consecrated to God alone has been a
stumbling block for some of our contemporaries. Unable to fit
their idea of apostolate into the concept of belonging to God
alone, thinking that the two are contradictory, they claim that it
is selfish to want to be devoted to God alone, and almost mock-
ingly they brand such consecration as "me and Jesus" spirituality.

If the desire to be devoted to God alone in celibacy or virginity
is selfish, then St. Paul and Jesus Christ advocate selfishness, for
the Council quotes them in saying that being devoted to God
alone is the purpose of consecrated chastity. Far from being
selfish, the gift of self to God alone to belong entirely to him as
his most special possession is a special source of spiritual apostolic
fruitfulness. "This perfect continence for the sake of the kingdom
of heaven," says *Lumen Gentium*, "has always been held in
special honor in the Church, as a sign of charity and a stimulus
to it, and as a special source of spiritual fecundity in the world"
(*LG* 42).

This idea is further developed in *Perfectae Caritatis*, which
shows how chastity leads to charity; and genuine charity of its
very nature is unselfish:

> The chastity "for the sake of the kingdom of heaven"
> (Matt. 19:12) which religious profess is to be valued as an
> outstanding gift of grace. For it liberates the heart of man
> in a singular way (1 Cor. 7:32–33) so that it may be more
> enflamed with charity for God and for all men. And there-
> fore it is not only a special sign of the heavenly goods, but
> also is the most apt means by which religious dedicate

themselves with undivided heart to the service of God and the works of the apostolate (*PC* 12).

Like any document, the Council's words will stand out in clearer meaning if we recall the signs of the times, the contemporary mentality in response to which the words sprang forth. In the second-last revision of the schema on religious, in the paragraph just quoted, there was a word which the final version deleted. We could wish that it had not been deleted, considering the difficulty some of our contemporaries are having in grasping the true nature of Christian celibacy. The deleted word was "transcendence." Consecrated chastity, said the older schema, "is a special sign of the transcendence of heavenly goods." If one has an accurate concept of heavenly goods, he knows they are transcendent, for transcendence is an essential note in the concept "heavenly goods." And so no doubt the word "transcendence" was deleted because it seemed redundant, since "heavenly goods" would seem to express the idea adequately. At any rate, the passage now reads, "chastity is a special sign of the heavenly goods."

The word "transcendence" was originally put into the schema to counteract contemporary man's excessive preoccupation with the temporal, the relative, the situational, the existential. In much modern thinking there are no transcendent, eternal values, no absolute values, but only relative values which change with each new situation.

This sort of thinking has invaded even religious life, and explains, for example, why a religious will say, "Things have changed; and so my conscience tells me I am no longer bound by my constitutions." Her next step will be to say, "The situation has changed, so I am no longer bound by my vows." People like this have lost all concept of the sacred, the inviolable, the transcendent, the eternal. When one lives by a philosophy like that, he is "tossed to and fro and carried about by every wind of doctrine devised in the wickedness of men" (Eph. 4:14). Such people "will not endure sound doctrine, but having itching ears, will heap up to themselves teachers according to their own lusts" (2 Tim. 4:3).

Every error is close to being a truth, and it usually masquerades as this truth. The contemporary preoccupation with the merely situational would no longer be an error if it were rightly coordinated with the truth of eternal values. And that is why the Church's current concern for aggiornamento, its desire to adapt itself to the modern situation, is not mere existential relativism, but is rather the effort to bring the eternal light of the Gospel to shine on the contemporary scene, and to rebuild the temporal world in that light.

So too in the decree on religious, even while the Council lays down principles for the adaptation of religious life to the contemporary situation, it carefully insists that each religious be deeply rooted in the transcendent, eternal, eschatological values, and be a sign to the world of these values. This is principally accomplished by consecrated chastity. The precise reason for consecrated chastity, according to Paul, is freedom from the passing things of the world so that one might be devoted with undivided heart to the Lord alone, who alone is utterly transcendent:

> I tell you, brothers, time is running out . . . for the world as we see it is passing away. I want you to be without worries. The unmarried man is busy with the Lord's affairs, concerned with pleasing the Lord. But the married man is busy with the cares of this world, concerned with pleasing his wife. So he is divided. The unmarried woman, like the virgin, is concerned with the things of the Lord, that she may be holy in body as well as in spirit (1 Cor. 7:29–34).

These are the words the Council refers to in saying that the celibate seeks the Lord alone, with undivided heart. Christ the Lord is the eternal one who, in becoming man, introduced eter-

nity into time for the salvation of mankind. Our mastering of the
temporal and sanctifying it and making it meaningful depends
upon our relationship to Christ, who alone gives eternal value to
the temporal elements in human life. The eternal Christ remains
present in time through his Bride the Church; and the consecrated virgin is called to bear witness by her whole being to this
one thing necessary, this union with Christ through which he
communicates eternal salvation to the world. Without this union
with Christ, the Church would be helpless to save the world; and
her members are helpless in salvation work to the extent that
they fail to achieve the intimacy of this union.

We see, then, why among all the counsels given in the Gospel
to promote holiness—and holiness is intimate union with the
Trinity in Christ—the Council Fathers give the first place to
virginity or celibacy, for its whole purpose is to enable the consecrated one to live in full reality the intimacy of the Church's
bridal union with Christ, which makes her the fruitful mother
of mankind. The virgin is espoused to the transcendent Lord,
thus bringing eternity into time, with all its saving power. The
more the celibate is empty of self, and of everything else, in the
spiritual virginity which is purity of heart, purity of self-seeking,
the more he or she can be filled with Christ, and the more effectively make him present in the world to save others.

Chastity is not only a special sign of the heavenly goods,
but also is the most apt means by which religious dedicate
themselves with undivided heart to the service of God and
the works of the apostolate. In this way they recall to the
minds of all the faithful that wondrous marriage decreed by
God—to be revealed fully in the future age—in which the
Church takes Christ as its only Spouse (PC 12).

Christ is the only Spouse also of the virgin, and of the celibate,
and that is why they are signs of the Church as Bride of Christ,

and that is why virginity and celibacy, when rightly lived, are so marvelously fruitful spiritually in the salvation of others. Although in the physical order one can be a mother without love, without giving self in wholehearted genuine love to a husband, this is not so in the spiritual order. One is spiritually fruitful in bringing others to God only in proportion to one's wholehearted gift of self to Christ, only in proportion to the intimacy of one's loving spiritual union with Christ, the Bridegroom of his Church. In chastity, religious are called precisely to live this bridal union with Christ in fullest possible reality, to be spiritually espoused to him alone, with undivided heart, in ardent charity. Just as bridal union is presupposed to lawful earthly maternity, so intimate union with Christ in charity is presupposed to apostolic fruitfulness.

And therefore in the paragraph entitled, "Concerning Religious Institutes Dedicated to the Apostolic Life," *Perfectae Caritatis* says: "So that the members may respond first of all to their vocation to follow Christ, and serve Christ himself in his members, their apostolic action must proceed from intimate union with him" (*PC* 8). In these words the Council is merely applying an undeniable truth of the spiritual, Christian life: one's spiritual impact in saving others is always in proportion to the closeness of one's union with God in Christ. For did not Christ say, "As the branch cannot bear fruit of itself unless it remain on the vine, so neither can you unless you abide in me . . . He who abides in me, and I in him, he bears much fruit; for without me you can do nothing" (Jn. 15:4–5).

In consecrated chastity, one strives to live in fullest possible reality St. Paul's description of Christian life as having Christ dwelling in our hearts through faith, and being rooted and grounded in love (Eph. 3:17), and adhering to the Lord so intimately that we become one spirit with him. As man and woman become one body in marriage, so, says the Apostle, "he who cleaves to the Lord is one spirit with him" (1 Cor. 6:17), living one life with him in his Holy Spirit. "It is now no longer I that live, but Christ lives in me" (Gal. 2:20). The precious grace of consecrated chastity gives one a wonderful freedom for living these Christian realities. But one must cooperate with this grace and strive for an ever more complete emptying of self, to be ever more perfectly filled with God alone, that one might become another Christ, making *him* present in the world, not self.

The apostolic value of one's consecrated chastity, we have seen, is in direct proportion to the intimacy of union with Christ which one achieves in this effort for perfect love. That is why *Perfectae Caritatis*, whose purpose is to give principles for adaptation to the modern situation, puts so much emphasis on the interior life, saying, for example, "It is necessary that the members of every community, seeking God alone and before everything else, should join contemplation, by which they fix their minds and hearts on him, with apostolic love, by which they strive to be associated with the work of redemption, and to spread the kingdom of God" (PC 5). In other words, one must be deeply rooted in the transcendent God whenever one attempts to redeem this changing, passing world. "Let them strive," says the Council, "to foster, in all circumstances, a life hidden with Christ in God" (PC 6). No changing situational circumstances can shake the stability of one so firmly united to God with undivided heart. This adhering to the Lord alone in steadfast love is so intimately a thing of the interior depths of the soul that it is the one thing in religious life least touched by the vicissitudes of time. We see then why consecrated chastity is the deepest foundation and highest summit of religious life, and holds first place among the three vows, "for it liberates the heart of man in a singular way, so that it may be more enflamed with charity for God and for all men" (PC 12).

22. Eschatological Desire

The whole being of every acorn desires to be an oak tree, just as the whole being of an infant desires to become a man. God has built a desire for fulfillment into each thing he has made. We can call this "ontological" desire, from the Greek word *onta*, meaning "being," since such desire is built into the very being of each thing.

But no acorn, no matter how much it grows, no matter how closely it approaches the maturity of oak tree, ever becomes aware of that desire of its being. An acorn's desire never becomes conscious and personal. But it is different with a child. A child can become ever more aware of the true nature of his being, and so eventually he can desire, with an explicit, conscious, personal desire, the perfection which his nature desires ontologically. In fact, by reason of his rational, personal nature, he never will attain the fulfillment which his being desires unless a conscious personal desire drives him to seek and choose all that will bring him to true fulfillment. Especially, a Christian must become aware of and explicitly desire all the supernatural fulfillment ontologically desired by the life of grace poured into him at baptism. For sanctifying grace, of its very nature, is like a divine seed desiring full growth and fruitfulness.

So too the whole being of religious life cries out for something. Religious life has a supernatural ontological desire built into its very nature. What *does* religious life desire by its very nature? Religious have to know this, so that they can be aware of it and desire it explicitly, with all the conscious personal desire they can muster, for only by personal desire and choice can they reach this fulfillment.

The ontological desire of religious life is identical with the ontological desire of Holy Church, the virgin bride of Christ. This follows from the Council's teaching that religious profession is a special consecration, deeply rooted in that of baptism and, by firmer and more stable bonds, expressing more perfectly Christ indissolubly united to his bride, the Church. Thus the religious life is the living image of the Church as bride of Christ. That is why we say that the ontological desire of religious life is identical with the ontological desire of the Church as virgin bride of Christ. Therefore it is the function of religious in the Church to give the most explicit expression possible to the ontological desire of the whole People of God. Religious must give striking expression to what the Church desires by her very nature, by her whole being.

As long as the Church is on earth, she is in a sense groping her way—somewhat like an acorn buried in the earth, blindly reaching for new life in a green shoot, and then in branches, finally in leaves and in fruit. For, says St. John, "it has not yet appeared what we shall be" (1 Jn. 3:2). And, says St. Paul, "We do not know what we should pray for as we ought, but the Spirit himself pleads for us with unutterable groanings. And he who searches the hearts knows what the Spirit desires" (Rom. 8:26).

If then it has not entered into the hearts of the great ones of the Church even to begin to imagine "what things God has pre-

pared for those who love him" (1 Cor. 2:9), what about the
average man in the Church? Many members of the Church
scarcely know where they are going.

And therefore the Church has appointed her religious to strive
to live the Christian life in all its perfection, to strive to live it
in the greatest fullness possible on earth, and thereby be, for the
rest of God's People, a living image of the goal towards which
all should be striving. This is the eschatological function of the
religious life, what Pope Paul has called the chief "sign value"
of religious.

Contemporary theology puts much emphasis on eschatology—
the theology of the last things, the things to come. Vatican II has
much to say about the eschatological value of the religious life.
By their whole being, religious bear witness to the heavenly
realities:

> The People of God have no lasting city here below, but
> look forward to one that is to come. Since this is so, the re-
> ligious state, whose purpose is to free its members from
> earthly cares, more fully manifests to all believers the pres-
> ence of heavenly goods already possessed here below. Fur-
> thermore, it not only witnesses to the fact of a new and
> eternal life acquired by the redemption of Christ, but it fore-
> tells the future resurrection and the glory of the heavenly
> kingdom (*LG* 44).

Religious, then, in their whole being and way of life are to be
a living image or prefiguring of the last perfection of the Christian life, the heavenly life. They are, as it were, to live heaven on
earth.

However, even though the life of grace is the life of heavenly
glory already begun, on earth we live heaven chiefly in desire.
And therefore religious are to desire, with personal desire, as explicitly and as ardently as possible, what the whole being of the

Church desires ontologically.

All the desire of the Church's very being is summed up by St. John in the Apocalypse in one word—the last word of the Bible, summing up the whole Bible—"Come, Lord Jesus!" (Apoc. 22:20). Everything, both in the external structure and in the interior life of the Church, is ordered by its very nature towards one thing: perfect union with the divine Bridegroom. Her whole being ever cries out: "Come, Lord Jesus!"

The vow of chastity, says *Perfectae Caritatis*, in a very special way expresses the life to come. "Chastity . . . is a special sign of the heavenly gifts. . . . Religious . . . recall to the minds of all the faithful that wondrous marriage decreed by God—to be fully revealed in the future age—in which the Church takes Christ as its only Spouse" (*PC* 12).

In her profound essence, the Church, the People of God, may be defined as communion of men with God in Christ Jesus. By communion we mean participation in God's own life. St. John calls it "fellowship with the Father and with his Son Jesus Christ" (1 Jn. 1:3). But just as the life of the acorn desires the full life of the oak tree, so too the lesser degrees of communion with God which we have by grace in this life of their very nature desire the consummate union with God in heaven, the perfect union with the Holy Trinity, in Christ, the divine Bridegroom. Grace in us is ever crying out, "Come, Lord Jesus!" Grace is ever thirsty for God, thirsty for the living waters, God himself.

If the life of grace in us of its very nature desires the life of glory, the more consciously aware of this we are, the more explicitly and ardently we desire God with a personal desire, crying out with the bride in the Apocalypse for the speedy coming of the Bridegroom.

All else in the Church—faith, teaching power, liturgy and governing authority—is but the instrument used by Christ the Head in communicating the fellowship in divine life ever more fully to his members. That is why we say that everything in the Church's structure and in her life cries out by its very being, "Come, Lord Jesus!" But that desire, that cry, must be changed from mere ontological desire to explicit personal desire. Since so many in the Church are so blind concerning this *one thing necessary,* and are so cold in desiring it, religious are appointed and consecrated by the Church to cultivate this desire in its full consciousness and ardor, and thus by the witness of their whole life to instruct and inspire others to the same fervent desire.

Or to put it all in terms of the love of the bride for the divine Bridegroom: The religious is engaged by vow to strive without cease for the maximum love of God. This explains the title of the decree on the religious life: *Perfectae Caritatis*: Perfect Charity. But love too has its ontological desire; love by its very nature seeks and desires the presence and the full possession of the beloved. Even though now, in the darkness of faith, charity already embraces God himself, charity cannot be satisfied with this obscure union; it aspires to the fullness of vision, without veil and without termination. Fervent charity strives even now to contemplate the Beloved to the full extent of earthly possibility, to the full extent in which he wills to reveal himself. Therefore Christian charity by its nature is contemplative, for charity—like any love—of its very nature has an ontological desire for the presence and enjoyment of the beloved. That is why the Constitution on the Sacred Liturgy declares that the Church, though eager to act, is yet ever intent on contemplation (*SC* 2). The Church cannot live without contemplation of her Lord.

Religious, as living images of the Church, are called to live this aspect of the Church's life in all its intensity. Prayer and contemplation enflame in our hearts the ardent desire for God which cries, "Come, Lord Jesus!"

But that same charity which so ardently desires God and union with him ardently desires also to serve neighbor and bring him also to God. Like St. Paul, the People of God, when they are truly ardent in charity, are torn between two desires—the desire to be with God, and the desire to be at the service of neighbor: "For me to live is Christ and to die is gain. . . . Indeed I am hard pressed from both sides—desiring to depart and to be with Christ, a lot by far the better; yet to stay on in the flesh is necessary for your sake" (Phil. 1:21, 23).

Perfectae Caritatis urges both these desires upon religious, saying, "They are to join contemplation . . . with apostolic love" (*PC* 5). Like the Church, "though eager to act" they are to be "ever intent upon contemplation" (*SC* 2). As signs of the heavenly things to come, religious, above all else, must cultivate that ardent desire for the divine Bridegroom.

This desire for the presence and full possession of the beloved can be called charity's eschatological tension, or stretching toward final fulfillment. Just as the acorn in its whole being desires to be an oak tree, charity in its whole being desires its full perfection, its eschatological or last perfection; namely the ceaseless contemplation of and perfect union with the divine Bridegroom.

Religious life—whether in its active or in its contemplative phases—by its nature as ceaseless struggle for the perfection of charity, necessarily and explicitly includes love's eschatological desire. Charity is entirely orientated toward the speedy, definitive union with the divine Bridegroom. The function of religious life in the Church is to cry out explicitly, without cease, "Come, Lord"—"*marana tha*"—the cry which fills the whole space between our Lord's resurrection and his parousia or coming in glory (1 Cor. 16:22). The ceaseless cry of the Virgin Church is expressed above all from the hearts of religious, whose whole life is summed up in that one word of the Apocalypse which gives meaning to all human life and history: "Come, Lord Jesus!"

If this is the desire of the whole being of the Church and of everything in its life and structure, and if, unfortunately, this desire is still only implicit or even unconscious in the hearts of so many of her members, in the hearts of religious it has to be ever as explicit and personal, as conscious and ardent, as possible. It is the basic mission of religious in the Church always to be giving explicit expression to the Church's deepest desire for the divine Bridegroom, for chastity, espousal to the Lord alone, is the preeminent evangelical counsel.

Since this explicit desire can be inspired only by the Holy Spirit—"the Spirit and the Bride say, Come!" (Apoc. 22:17)—the religious must strive to be always docile and attentive to all the Spirit's inspirations. His or her basic attitude of life must be one of listening to the Spirit in recollection, in order to stir up ardent eschatological desire, the desire for the consummate union with the Bridegroom.

But though all religious ever ardently desire the presence of the divine Bridegroom and eagerly await his coming, they must be content meanwhile to find him in neighbor. In fact, they will not find him in himself, at his second coming, if they have not found him day by day in the least of his brethren. For at his coming he will say, "Come, blessed of my Father" (Matt. 25:34), only to the ones to whom he can say also: "I was hungry and you gave me to eat, naked and you clothed me, sick and you nursed me, ignorant and you instructed me; I needed to learn arithmetic and you taught me." For only in these does he recognize his true bride, only in these who have loved him in his members.

Desire for the divine Bridegroom is never authentic unless it desires him also for all his members, unless it desires to bring all mankind into union with him. The cry of the Virgin Church, "Come, Lord Jesus," is a cry on behalf of all her children and of all mankind, for she desires the Lord for all. If the religious must bear this desire of the Church ever explicitly in her heart, she must desire Christ ardently for all her fellowmen. She gathers the ontological desire of all human hearts into her own heart, and there makes this desire explicit and personal, and offers it to God for fulfillment in his final union with all of redeemed mankind.

Such is the basic eschatological function of each religious in the Church. Not like an acorn which only unconsciously, impersonally gropes for fulfillment, but rather, in full awareness, eagerly, joyously, she runs to meet her Bridegroom to conduct him into her own heart, and into the hearts of all the People of God.

> "The Spirit and the Bride say, Come!
> And let him who hears, say, Come!"
> (Apoc. 22:17).

23. Religious Chastity
and Personal Fulfillment

In *Perfectae Caritatis*, the "signs of the times" shine through to us. This is as it should be in a document whose purpose is renewal and adaptation. Like the Council's other documents, this one will convey its full meaning to us only if we are aware of the contemporary thinking to which it is a response.

The philosophy of the times is personalistic, preoccupied with personal fulfillment. The Council was aware of those religious who do not integrate the good insights of this philosophy into the immeasurably broader perspectives of their divine life of grace, but try to fit their religious existence into the narrow confines of a mere naturalistic personalism, and talk and act as though their whole goal in life were mere personal fulfillment. This is too self-centered an approach for a Christian.

The Gospel does not put the emphasis on personal fulfillment. It speaks rather of getting out of self, or dying to self to be alive to God, of losing one's life to find it, of emptying self to be filled with God, of living a life hidden with Christ in God and therefore killing what is earthly in one's members, of being

198

nailed with Christ to the cross if one wishes to find fulfillment
in his resurrection.

Religious who put all the emphasis on personal fulfillment
soon begin to say, "Religious obedience and religious chastity
are too restrictive; they hamper my personal development. Only
in the intimate personal relationship of marriage can I find my
full personality." We are beginning to hear American religious
say these things; Europeans were saying them twenty years ago.

These are the false doctrines referred to in the paragraph on
chastity of *Perfectae Caritatis* (*PC* 12). Pope Pius XII had repeatedly spoken against these errors. In 1952, he attributed the
disastrous drop in the number of religious vocations in Europe
largely to those who extol marriage at the expense of virginity.
"They go so far," he said, "as to present marriage as the sole
means capable of ensuring the due development and natural perfection of the human personality."[1]

But celibacy also, says Vatican II, helps develop the human
personality:

> Religious should not only be warned against the dangers
> to chastity which they meet, but they should be so instructed
> as to be able to undertake the celibacy which binds them
> to God in a way which will benefit their entire personality
> (*PC* 12).

Celibacy, then, can benefit the entire personality. The Council
thus reaffirms the doctrine of Pius XII, whose fuller treatment
of the subject makes an excellent commentary on these words of
the Council. The approach of Pope Pius to this question is magnificently supernatural. This is very important in an era of exaggerated reliance on a naturalistic and merely psychological
approach to love and personality, with these findings of psychol-

[1] Courtois, *op. cit.*, p. 215, par. 477.

ogy inadequately integrated into the doctrine on Christian grace and charity.

With sorrow [writes Pope Pius] we recently had to censure the opinion of those who go so far as to maintain that marriage is the only means of ensuring the natural development and due perfection of human personality. . . . It cannot be held, as some maintain, that the "mutual assistance" which the partners seek in Christian marriage is a more perfect aid to the acquisition of personal sanctity than the so-called "loneliness of heart" of virgins and celibates. For even though it is true that all those who have embraced the state of perfect chastity have renounced this form of human love, it cannot be asserted in consequence that this privation involves a diminution and impoverishment of their human personality, because they receive from God, the giver of heavenly gifts, a spiritual aid which is vastly superior to the "mutual assistance" rendered by husband and wife to one another. By giving themselves completely to him who is the source of their existence and who shares his divine life with them, far from diminishing their personality, they enrich it immensely. For who has a better right than virgins to apply to themselves the wonderful words of the Apostle Paul: "I live, now not I, but Christ lives in me" (Gal. 2:20).[2]

These words of Pope Pius deserve profound meditation. Is the divine Spouse going to be of less help to his virgin bride than an earthly husband is to his wife? The Lord communicates his own divine life to her so that she finds a divine fulfillment in him. In the summer of 1965, Dr. Baars, a practising American psychiatrist, gave a convincing lecture on priestly celibacy. All that he said applies also to consecrated chastity in religious life.

2 Encyclical, "Holy Virginity," in Courtois, *op. cit.,* pp. 236–237, pars. 519–520.

Dr. Baars shows that consecrated celibacy inspired by motives of divine charity can more quickly bring one to personal maturity than does Christian marriage. Psychological studies, he points out, have shown that the average man usually does not take the spiritual life with fullest seriousness until late middle age, after he has had much experience of the transient nature and the emptiness of the things which he has been enjoying, and has begun to experience at times an intense loneliness in the face of life's approaching end. He finds that there is a space in his soul which even all his loved ones on earth cannot begin to fill.

In contrast to this picture of the average man stands that of the celibate who did not choose to wait until the passing of time would direct him to a more spiritual outlook on life. In one magnificent gesture he devoted himself to the attainment of spiritual values to which the average man does not feel attracted until much later in life, preoccupied as he is for so many years with material goals and temporal affairs. Already in the early stages of maturity the celibate decides to forego the possession of these material goods in the realization of their changeable and temporary nature as compared with the enduring and unchanging values of the spiritual life.

Viewed in this light, the celibate life is an inner anticipation of a mental attitude which ordinarily does not develop until a much later stage in life. When this state of life is voluntarily self-imposed for the proper motive and under suitable conditions, it is difficult to see how it could be considered an obstacle to human maturity and fulfillment. Of course, God's grace is an absolute necessity in this process of anticipation of a maturity which ordinarily is attained only by way of a gradual psychological process.[3]

[3] C. W. Baars, "Love, Sexuality and Celibacy," in Augustine Rock, O.P., ed., *Sex, Love and the Life of the Spirit* (Chicago: Priory Press, 1966), p. 66.

Dr. Baars' reference to the role of grace in the celibate's more speedy progress to full maturity brings us back to the words of Pius XII: "Virgins and celibates receive from God a spiritual aid which is vastly superior to the mutual assistance rendered by husband and wife to one another." What is this spiritual aid? Above all, it is the grace which is at the very heart of the vocation to religious chastity: it is a grace of spiritual bridal union with God himself. Vatican II teaches that religious profession, as a special consecration, expresses strikingly the indissoluble union of Christ with his bride the Church. Celibacy and virginity are a participation in the Church's bridal union, they are a striving to live it in fullest possible reality. The Church is espoused to Christ the Word, in faith. The spouse of the religious is this same Eternal Word. He is a spiritual Word; theirs is a purely spiritual union with him. That is why the decree on religious insists that all religious without exception must listen to his words, like Mary, Martha's sister: "Faithful to their profession, and leaving all things for the sake of Christ, religious are to follow him as the one thing necessary, listening to his words and solicitous for the things that are his" (*PC* 5).

Dr. Baars spoke of "an intense loneliness in the face of life's approaching end," a loneliness which the average man occasionally experiences when he approaches late middle age. This makes him take the spiritual life more seriously. It teaches him to open himself more to God to be filled with him, for only in God can any man find his true fulfillment. "There is always some hidden place in the sanctuary of the soul where God alone dwells. Both husband and wife need to respect this in each other."[4]

The celibate or virgin experiences this loneliness, this emptiness, much earlier in life, for he or she sacrifices the joys of human companionship in marriage in order to seek the divine Bridegroom directly. The very grace of her vocation to seek God alone impels her to strip herself of everything which could be an

4 C. Heris, *Spirituality of Love* (St. Louis: Herder, 1965), p. 229.

obstacle to the possession of the Lord. For in possessing him, one must be content to possess nothing else, not even one's own self. This is the ultimate of giving; but it is also the ultimate of receiving. It demands a great void, too big to be filled by anyone or anything but God alone. Vatican II speaks of the necessity of religious sharing in Christ's emptying of himself so that they may share in his life in the Spirit; and this emptying is accomplished especially in humility, obedience, fortitude, chastity (*PC* 5).

This emptying of self requires the greatest of sacrifice, the complete renunciation of all that human nature clings to and desires so ardently, the fulfillment of the self. This emptying must be accomplished in a "dark night" of loneliness and aloneness. This is not merely the loneliness which the religious should expect to experience occasionally because of the renunciation of the joys of marriage. Even more, it must be the emptying of self of all vanity, of unworthy ambition, of pride of any sort, of riches, of self-indulgence. This is the purity of heart, the virginity of heart, necessary for espousal to God.

When this aloneness or emptying of self has been achieved, then God moves in in all his fullness, and suddenly the virginal heart realizes that in having him she has all else. She has been filled—fulfilled—not in her own self, but in him; not in her own personality (although she retains that) but in his Person. St. Thomas Aquinas expressed it so accurately when he said to our Lord, "I want nothing but yourself, Lord," for he realized that here was true possession, true riches. At the end of his life, when he had emptied himself completely and was completely filled with God, even his great theological genius seemed to Thomas to be only so much straw.

"It is not good for man to be alone." These words of the Creator concerning the institution of marriage lead us also to the most profound meaning of consecrated chastity. "It is not good for man to be alone," for no man or woman can find fulfillment in self. The virgin in purity of heart empties self of everything, but precisely so that she may be filled with God, fulfilled in him.

Precisely because it is not good for any man or woman to be alone, the celibate needs a strong and active union with God in living faith and charity if she is to remain pure and if she is to perfect her purity of heart. If she is not filled with God, then the vacuum will fill up with petty selfishness of one kind or another.

That is why a deep life of prayer in ever increasing faith, hope and charity is essential to a celibate life. The celibate is the spouse of the Word and must be in continuing communion with him—he is the sole reason for her celibate existence. Nothing short of him can justify celibacy as a special consecration, since the celibate has renounced all right to be possessed by any human being.

Since, then, it is not good for man to be alone, since man cannot live without love, the virgin needs a very lively faith in God's love for her personally. Since God is Spirit, and her bond of union with him is spiritual, his love for her will not always have the reverberations in her emotional being which she might wish. And therefore at times she will experience a loneliness and emptiness. But certainly in proportion to her real need, the Lord will manifest his presence to her by spiritual graces when necessary, and at times she will experience joy in her whole being, and not merely in the so-called "fine-point" of her soul. But these encouraging experiences are only an invitation to seek the fuller spiritual possession of him which is possible only after a more complete emptying of self, and an ever increasing concern for the things which please him.

To live this sacrificial life which necessarily involves the willing foregoing of many emotional joys, God's grace and a firm faith are required. The virgin lives by this faith. In faith she is espoused to the Eternal Word; she eagerly looks forward to his full revelation of himself which is to come.

But daily she does experience his love for her when she is

united to him in holy communion, even though sometimes it may be in the dryness of sheer faith. What more perfect pledge of his love could he give than holy communion?

Before she is strong enough to live entirely by pure faith, she must be upheld by a community life in which the genuine charity of her fellow religious, expressed in true concern for her welfare, will also be a sign of God's love for her. That is why Vatican II says: "Let all, especially superiors, remember that chastity is guarded more securely when true brotherly love flourishes in the common life of the community" (*PC* 12). Here the Council is recognizing man's psychological need for tangible signs of love. The divine charity in our hearts, expressed in mutual thoughtful concern for one another in community life, is truly a sign and presence of God's own love upholding us.

When, in this way, the religious is humanly upheld in receiving true charity from others, she learns to find personal fulfillment in giving herself in turn in the same unselfish thoughtfulness and service inspired by charity; and thus she herself becomes a sign of divine love to others. This giving of self in helping others is a giving of self to God, for whatever she does to the least of his brethren, she does to him.

For the full maturity of this self-giving in service of others, she must take care really to put her heart into it; and by heart we mean her genuine interest, her sincere concern. Only a consciousness of God will guarantee that this genuine, active concern for neighbor will always be there, so that her charity will be universal, not discriminatory; that is, so that she will ever be ready and willing to serve anyone and everyone, each one according to his need, not limiting herself to helping only those to whom she is naturally attracted. Even the pagans love those who love them, says Jesus. Only this universal, non-discriminating charity is the mark of the mature Christian person.

Love as genuine as that will infallibly manifest itself through her whole being. She will not have to worry about whether or not her love is warm, she will not have to force any artificial affection. Warmth and humanness will be manifest in her sincere thoughtfulness for others, it will show in her unstinting generosity, in her forgetfulness of self. She will need no artificial emotional manifestation of a love which is more genuinely manifest in the sincerity of her voice, in her ability to listen, in her kind consideration, in her patience, in her self-sacrificing service. The purity of a virginal heart, free of all selfishness, can love spontaneously—with a charity which expresses itself sincerely in her whole being, for her whole attitude clearly manifests that in love she is completely at the service of anyone who needs her.

Thus she finds true fulfillment in coming out of herself, in forgetting self, and giving self to God alone by giving self to all her neighbors, for they all belong to God.

If, then, we ever feel lonely in our consecrated life, let us remember that this loneliness is a necessary stage in the working of the grace of celibacy. In this loneliness we must reject promptly the temptation to day-dream of the joys of earthly marriage. A consecrated person has no right to indulge in such dreams, which must be sacrificed as promptly as one renounces a temptation to anger or to impurity or to murder. The act of rejecting a temptation even to think of abandoning one's consecration is an act of giving oneself anew to the divine Spouse, and so is a deepening of one's vowed union with him. Let us not forget, then, that before the religious can be completely filled with God, she has to experience, and even cultivate, emptiness, aloneness, so that she can be filled with God; and so that, consequently, she can love neighbor all the more generously and unrestrictedly and warmly. For, as St. Francis says, "It is in dying that we live!"

24. The Church of the Poor: Sign of the Times

Among the hopeful signs of the times is the Church's reawakening to the Gospel message concerning poverty. "Nowadays," says Pope Paul, "people often speak of 'the Church of the Poor.'" This is an aspect of the religious society founded by Christ that is full of meaning. When it is properly understood, it carries us back to the Gospel origins of the Church, to the very plan of God for the salvation of the world, to the unforgettable and incontestable example of Christ who was poor himself, and who announced his good news to the poor. . . .

"This revindication of poverty as the Church's own very special treasure opens up for us a vein of the richest and loftiest spirituality that seems destined to spread in the consciences of the Christians of our time."[1]

The Holy Spirit himself is inspiring a growing desire in the Church to bring Christ's poverty into our daily lives, he is arous-

[1] Address to St. Vincent de Paul Society, *The Pope Speaks,* X (1965), pp. 161–162.

ing zeal for the spirit of poverty in men of good will everywhere, because the needs of the times truly require this. The sure sign, then, that we have responded to the Holy Spirit and are in the mainstream of the Church's current spiritual renewal is the sincerity and the degree of our zeal for poverty.

What are these conditions of the times to which the Holy Spirit is responding by stirring up love of Christian poverty? They are what Pope John XXIII called the disgrace of destitution—not just poverty here and there, but downright misery and abject privation on an ever increasing scale—a material destitution which breeds a spiritual destitution and hopelessness, entailing the loss of many souls.

In the material destitution of which Pope John was speaking, man is degraded to a subhuman level; he does not have the material resources necessary for living in accordance with his human dignity. In this condition he cannot live a life of virtue without a miracle of grace. It would take unheard-of heroism for him to react in a holy manner to such a condition. This destitution is distinguished from ordinary poverty by an utter hopelessness of spirit.

Unfortunately, the disorders in the present workings of human society are such that destitution is increasing at an unprecedented rate. This is the disgrace of our times, that in human society so many are forced to live at a subhuman level, without the indispensable natural supports for human dignity and the life of grace.

This material and spiritual destitution of great masses of mankind in our times is a voice of God crying out to us, it is Christ crying out to anyone who has ears to hear: "I am hungry and naked; feed and clothe me. I am spiritually ignorant and morally bankrupt; enlighten and inspire me."

In answer to these signs of the times, this material and spiritual destitution of the masses, the Holy Spirit is inspiring a new outlook on Christian poverty, and he is giving a new orientation to the poverty of religious. His answer to destitution is the figure of Christ as Servant of Yahweh, who emptied himself in poverty and became the servant of all. In the current spiritual renewal in the Church, everything is being geared towards humble service of our fellowmen in love—everything, whether it be authority or obedience, poverty or possessions, virginity and celibacy, marriage or lay apostolate, charisms or personal interior life. Everything must take on the likeness of Christ the humble Servant who emptied himself for love of all.

Lumen Gentium presents to us a sketchy portrait of "the Church of the Poor," the rediscovered Gospel image of God's People, which, says Pope Paul, is a sign of the times. The Church is described in the likeness of Christ, as being poor herself, and laboring to relieve material and spiritual poverty wherever she finds it:

> Just as Christ carried out the work of redemption in poverty and under oppression, so the Church is called to follow the same path in communicating to men the fruits of salvation. Christ Jesus, "though he was by nature God, emptied himself, taking the nature of a slave" (Phil. 2:6), and "being rich, he became poor" (2 Cor. 8:9) for our sakes. Thus, although the Church needs human resources to carry out her mission, she is not set up to seek earthly glory, but to proclaim humility and self-sacrifice, even by her own example.

> Christ was sent by the Father "to bring good news to the poor, to heal the contrite of heart" (Lk. 4:18), "to seek and to save what was lost" (Lk. 19:10). Similarly, the Church encompasses with love all those who are afflicted with human weakness. Indeed, she recognizes in the poor and the suffering the likeness of her poor and suffering Founder. She does

all she can to relieve their need and in them she strives
to serve Christ (*LG* 8).

The Church, then, is beginning to see herself once again as the
poor servant of the poor.

In the light of this new emphasis, one is tempted to say that the
essence of Christian and religious poverty is service of the poor
in love: "Go, sell what thou hast, and give to the poor" (Matt.
19:21). Be yourself totally at their service. One is evangelically
poor like Jesus when he keeps nothing for himself and consecrates all he has and all he is to the spiritual and corporal needs
of others. Whatever one possesses, whether spiritual or material
riches, is looked upon as belonging to the poor, for everything is
held in stewardship, in responsibility, to be administered entirely
in the service of one's needy fellowman and the kingdom of God.

But there is much more to Gospel poverty than that. Evangelical poverty is hope in God before it is service of neighbor in love.
For in relationship to God, all of us are ever poor and needy, and
especially, in need of mercy and forgiveness. All of us ever need
to look to God in hope.

But in gratitude to Christ, who became poor for our sakes that
by his poverty we might become rich, we in turn empty ourselves,
keeping nothing back in greed, serving Christ whom we see in his
poor ones. The poor are always with us as a reminder of Christ
in the poverty and sufferings which he endured for our sakes, and
we make a return to him by serving him in them. At the same
time that the poor remind us of Christ in his poverty, they remind us of our own poverty before God. The poor are thus signs
of Christ, and they are signs of our own neediness before God.

When we see the poor in the first way, as signs of the needy
Christ, we respond with the poverty of service, the poverty of
giving, of keeping nothing for self. When we see the poor in the
second way, as reminders of our own neediness before God, we

respond to God with the poverty of spirit expressed in hope, the poverty of receptiveness from God.

According to the Scriptures, the ideal poor man, the poor man whose poverty is a spiritual value, is he who has nothing superfluous, and is fully content with his status. He is free of all greed and inordinate possessiveness, for God is his true treasure, God is his hope. "Give me neither poverty nor riches," he prays, "provide me only with the food I need" (Prov. 30:8). And whatever he has over and above his own needs, he is ever ready to give to others who are in need. For the Scriptures never look upon physical want or poverty as something good; on the contrary, they who do not rush to the aid of those in need are condemned. The Scriptures desire that no one should be allowed to remain in need; everyone should have the necessities of life. Those who have superfluous goods must use them in helping others.

It is clear, then, that Christian poverty, evangelical poverty, is never a matter of mere economics. It is not measured primarily by how much or how little one possesses. As a spiritual value, poverty consists first of all in relationships with God and in relationships with fellowmen. With regard to God, our poverty is our acknowledged neediness before him, our helplessness without him; and it expresses itself as hope in him, as an openness to receive all things from him as from our Father. It bears witness to the transcendent divine realities we await from him. With regard to neighbor, Christian poverty expresses itself as a readiness to give all things, as a becoming poor that needy neighbor might become rich.

In relationship to God, then, we are ever poor ones receiving, and spiritual poverty is hope of receiving; in relationship to neighbor we should ever be giving, and poverty is love's service in giving.

In response to the signs of the times, Vatican II in the decree on the religious life has made it clear that all religious must be poor in fact as well as in spirit (*PC* 13). Religious poverty has a sign value; it must bear witness to the Church of the poor, and to all that this means. If necessary, religious must find new forms in which to express their poverty in keeping with the special needs of the times. What these new forms will be, the Council Fathers did not say. Though the Holy Spirit is stirring up in the Church a true desire for poverty, he has not yet guided us into the precise ways of fully implementing that desire. The next move is up to us. We must give serious thought and experimentation to the matter.

Pope Paul says that we all find difficulty in practising the poverty of the Gospel, and he called upon the bishops of the world to help him draw up concrete directives for the whole Church in this matter.[2] It will not be easy to bring our new zeal for poverty into practical everyday living. But bring it we must. Otherwise we will not be in the mainstream of the spiritual renewal which is taking place in the Church. New forms of poverty will be worthless unless they express the authentic Gospel message. We must therefore study the theology of poverty—the precise meaning of evangelical poverty in itself and specifically for our times.

One thing is certain: considering the signs of the times, "the Church of the poor"—the poor Church at the service of the poor —should be manifest above all in religious. Religious must strive to make it strikingly clear to everyone that everything they possess is totally at the service of God's People. It is entrusted to them by God as a stewardship. But this consecration of all their resources, both spiritual and material, to whosoever needs them will be manifest above all in the self-sacrificing love with which they use all things, and not only things, but their time, their talents, their whole being. They are poor for the sake of promoting the kingdom of God. The apostolic love motivating every fibre of their being and every element of their religious life must declare to all who need their help: "It is you I want, not your

2 "Ecclesiam Suam," *The Pope Speaks*, X (1965), p. 273.

possessions. . . . I am perfectly willing to spend what I have, and to be expended, in the interests of your souls, even if, loving you the more, I must be loved the less" (2 Cor. 12:15, j). "Remember how generous the Lord Jesus was: he was rich, but he became poor for your sake, to make you rich out of his poverty" (2 Cor. 8:9, j).

25. The Four Values of Poverty

Poverty's Ecclesial-Apostolic Value

"She laid him in a manger, because there was no room for them in the inn" (Lk. 2:7). Only one other sentence in the Gospels rivals this one in expressing graphically the poverty of Jesus. The other sentence is our Lord's words to the man who wanted to join him in his apostolate: "The foxes have dens, and the birds of the air have nests, but the Son of Man has nowhere to lay his head" (Lk. 9:58). From the very moment of his birth Jesus was poor, with no place to lay his head except a stranger's manger. Every apostle has to be poor like Jesus.

St. Paul also has a sentence which makes a strong bid for first prize for speaking well of our Lord's poverty: "Being rich, he became poor for your sakes, that by his poverty you might become rich" (2 Cor. 8:9).

The Second Vatican Council, in speaking of religious poverty, chose this text along with another one from St. Paul, namely: "he emptied himself" (Phil. 2:7). Thus we are given to understand that Jesus became poor, above all, by emptying himself in humility, becoming obedient unto death. His poverty is supremely manifest on the cross, where he stripped himself of everything, even life itself, that we might become rich. It is the mystery of the cross which reveals to us the poverty of Christ in its total reality. Using these two texts from St. Paul, the Council strongly emphasizes the charity for us which motivated the poverty and obedience of Jesus, and thus shows forth the charity which should motivate the poverty and obedience of religious:

> The Church continues to ponder the warning of the Apostle who in urging the faithful to charity exhorts them to have in themselves the mind which was in Christ Jesus, who emptied himself, taking the form of a slave . . . becoming obedient unto death, and who "when he was rich, became poor" for our sakes. Since it is always necessary that the disciples imitate this charity and humility of Christ and bear witness to it, Mother Church rejoices to find in her bosom many men and women who more closely follow the Savior's emptying of himself and more clearly manifest it, by embracing poverty in the freedom of the sons of God, and by renouncing their own wills . . . in obedience (*LG* 42).

The primary motive of religious poverty and obedience, then, is charity like Christ's own, along with humility, its correlative. Thus Vatican II emphasizes the ecclesial value of poverty: its value in the Church as an expression of love of neighbor. In the desire to become like Christ in his charity for all, the religious empties self of possessions to be at the service of all. "He became poor, that by his poverty you might become rich" (2 Cor. 8:9). The religious too becomes poor that he might be free to serve, that he might enrich others. "As poor yet enriching many," says St. Paul in his description of a true apostle (2 Cor. 6:10).

Vatican Council II is quite insistent that the Church must imitate more closely than ever the poverty of Christ. If the

Gospel is to be preached effectively to the poor, then the Church must become like the poor Christ. Religious, moreover, must "diligently practise . . . that voluntary poverty which is highly esteemed especially in our day as a sign of the following of Christ" (*PC* 13).

We have already noted some reasons why voluntary poverty should be highly esteemed in our day. Our Blessed Lord, however, has always wanted his apostles to be poor, as he himself was. Poverty is to be the sign that his followers are completely unselfish in their mission, motivated entirely by divine love for mankind. They do not labor for what they themselves can get out of it, but only for what they can give. "Freely you have received," said Jesus to them, "freely give" (Matt. 10:8). Religious poverty, then, should be the sign of burning love which desires only to serve, not to be served.

And thus it is a sign of the divine love and mercy of Jesus who sent us. Religious poverty should be a witness to God's love and concern for mankind. It should speak the good news that God does care for the poor and the afflicted and the sinner. In becoming poor with the poor, the apostle shows that he has not come to exploit them, but only to serve them; "for the Son of Man also has not come to be served but to serve, and to give his life as a ransom for many" (Mk. 10:45). Such a manifestation of divine love will win a return of love.

In this twentieth century, the poor seem to think that the Church has no love for them. In most places, the working classes have tended to identify the Church with the rich and powerful. Today more than ever, then, the Church must find ways of bearing witness to the divine love which is truly hers. The only effective way of doing this seems to be voluntary poverty, self-sacrifice on behalf of the poor and afflicted, service in the likeness of Christ the Suffering Servant.

The Gospels certainly bring out this aspect of voluntary poverty as a service of the poor. "Go sell what you have and give to the poor" (Matt. 19:21). Vatican II directs religious to take these words seriously. Religious institutes, it says, "must strive to offer as it were a collective witness to poverty and gladly use their own goods for other needs of the Church and for the support of the poor, whom all religious should love in the heart of Christ" (*PC* 13).

A few lines before, the Council had said, "With regard to religious poverty, it is not enough to use goods in a way subject to the superior's will, but members must be poor in fact and in spirit, having their treasures in heaven (Matt. 6:20)." In other words, religious can no longer justify the abundance of their possessions by saying, "They are community property; I have nothing I can call my own personally; I am truly detached, for I use things only by permission." A religious may indeed be truly detached in poverty of spirit, but that is no longer enough. Conditions in the world today require that poverty really shine forth as a true witness to the Church's concern for the poor. That is why the Council says that individual poverty is not enough, but religious institutes as such must offer a collective witness to poverty; and recommends as one way of doing this the willing use of community goods for other needs of the Church and for the support of the poor.

Religious constitutions should therefore be adapted to bring out more clearly this ecclesial-apostolic aspect of poverty, which good religious, of course, have always understood and tried to live.

Theologal-Eschatological Value of Poverty

If religious should share their material possessions with others, they must never forget that it is chiefly spiritual riches that religious poverty brings to the Church and to the world. By voluntary poverty they not only bear witness to their sympathy and active concern for the poor, and to the reality of their love for them, they also bear witness to the reality of divine things, to the divine love which has heavenly riches in store for them. They show that the kingdom of God is not of this world. When Jesus said to the man who wanted to follow him, "The foxes have dens, the birds have nests, but the Son of Man has no place to lay his head" (Lk. 9:58), he was already on his steadfast journey up to Jerusalem (Lk. 10:51): he was going to the heavenly Jerusalem by way of the earthly Jerusalem where he would be despised and put to death. He had no place to lay his head because his kingdom is not of this world.

Religious poverty must especially bear witness to these heavenly realities. As Pope Paul VI expressed it, "This seems to us to be the most urgent and up-to-date 'sign' value that religious life is called upon to offer the community of the faithful."[1] This lesson is very especially needed in the midst of the current materialism. Rich and poor alike are greedy for material pleasures and comforts.

Therefore even while we bear witness to God's love for the poor by our selfless efforts to better their lot, at the same time by our own willing poverty we must reveal to the poor that the better material situation which we help them achieve is not an end in itself, but provides, rather, suitable growing conditions for the grace of God planted in us as a seed growing up into life eternal.

Thus, even while the Church labors to better the social condition of all the poor, so that they may live a life in keeping with their human dignity and their dignity as children of God, at the same time by her own poverty she must bear witness to the heavenly realities, and she does this in an especially striking way in her truly poor religious.

If this message concerning the heavenly realities is truly to shine forth, it is not enough for religious not to possess the goods of this world. Their poverty must not be something merely nega-

---

[1] "Aggiornamento and the Religious Life," *The Pope Speaks,* X (1965), p. 332.

tive, it should not be the mere absence of possessions, nor merely detachment from these possessions. For there have been even pagan philosophers who renounced and despised material possessions. This pagan voluntary poverty, however, was not religious poverty, it was not the poverty of a follower of Christ.

What, then, is the very positive element which makes voluntary poverty specifically Christian? Our Lord gives the answer. "Where your treasure is, there also your heart will be" (Matt. 6:21). If the Christian is poor in spirit, if his heart is completely detached from material possessions, it is because his heart is so firmly attached to God, who is his only true treasure. In love for God he cuts himself off from involvement in acquiring the things of this world, so that he may possess God all the more efficaciously.

It is this burning love for God which must shine forth to the world in the poverty of the apostle, bearing witness to how lovable that God must really be when one sacrifices all things to possess him, the pearl of great price, and gives all one's energies to help others love him, by showing them how much God loves them. Poverty is worthless as an apostolic value if it is not glowing with love of God, a love which makes the apostle give up all things so that he can bring neighbor also to this God whom he loves so ardently.

Christian poverty, consequently, is an expression not only of love for God but also of hope in him. In the Bible, the "poor ones of Yahweh," the poor in spirit, are they who trust in God alone. They have learned from long experience their helplessness, their neediness, their emptiness without God their Savior. They are spiritually poor in the sense that they recognize the full truth of their creaturely nothingness, and the futility of trusting in mere created things; they are convinced that God is their only hope. They cut themselves off from trust in mere created things so that they may rely on God in pure hope.

This confident hope in God must shine forth to the world in

the voluntary poverty of the religious, bearing witness to the truth that God alone is our hope of salvation and happiness. We should hope in other persons or things only insofar as somehow they help us to God. Voluntary poverty should be the shining expression of total and joyous dependence on the heavenly Father, who feeds the birds of the air and clothes the lilies of the fields, and knows the needs of his children who seek first his kingdom. Vatican II says: "While they procure (by their labor) what is required for their sustenance and works, religious should banish all undue solicitude and trust themselves to the provident care of their Father in heaven" (*PC* 13).

Such love of the Father above all things and hope in him alone presupposes an enlightened faith which has learned to see all the good things of creation as signs of a loving Father, who himself is more lovable than all his gifts, and who alone is to be loved and sought sheerly for his own sake.

"Where your treasure is, there also your heart will be." In voluntary poverty, it must be unmistakably evident that one's heart is firmly, ardently with God. Religious poverty must glow with divine love. Only when it is so shining with love does it have real apostolic value, for only then does it effectively bear witness to the divine treasures which have captivated our hearts.

It is obvious, then, that the apostolic value of religious poverty presupposes the theologal value. The theologal value of the three vows, we have seen, is their power to unite us firmly to God in faith, hope, and charity.

Ascetical Value of Poverty

But this, in turn, entails the ascetical value of the vows. The more ardently and firmly one wishes to be attached to God in love, the more he experiences the need of being completely freed from anything and everything which could in any way impede the swiftness of his flight to God. The desire for poverty in the heart of a lover of God is the expression of this deep-seated need for freedom to love unimpeded by any attachment which could hinder the spontaneous rise of the mind and heart to God, our only treasure.

However, as long as we are on this earth, it is difficult perpetually to maintain our love for God at full fervor. If we are surrounded by the comforts of the world and are using them regularly, little by little we become attached to them again, and the fervor of our charity imperceptibly cools. Experience of this fact shows that it is not enough to claim that we are poor in spirit, that we are not really attached to these material things which we have in such abundance. We have to be poor in reality as well as in spirit. They who are poor in fact, for love of God, are more likely to maintain the fervor of their charity perpetually, for they are not tempted to relax in the enjoyment of their material abundance.

The ardent lover of God, then, experiences the need of daily deliberate self-denial in the use of food and other material things. Only such self-denial, inspired by love of God, will maintain that level of fervor in his faith, hope and charity which will give them true apostolic value in bearing witness to the divine realities. We are deceiving ourselves if we think we are great apostles merely because we are doing apostolic works, when we do not have the intimate union with God in faith, hope and charity which has to shine forth in everything we do.

We see then why the Decree on the Adaptation and Renewal of Religious Life, even while it calls for an adjustment of our life to the apostolic and ecclesial values of the vows, insists at the same time that the theological and ascetical values of the vows must be maintained at full strength. The apostolic witness of poverty is sincere and efficacious only when it is truly theological and ascetical; that is, the expression of a genuine union with God in living faith, hope and charity, manifest in the genuine asceticism of real poverty.

And all these values, we have seen, are united in the christological value, their value in living the life of Christ and making him present in the world. "This state more closely imitates the manner of life which God's Son accepted when he entered the world to do his Father's will, the manner which he proposed to his followers, the disciples; and it continually represents this manner of life in the Church" (*LG* 44). Every true lover experiences a profound need to be like the beloved. In a special way the lover of Christ, called by him to follow him in the way of the counsels, experiences a deep need to be poor just as he was poor, and for the reasons that he was poor—to help him enrich the world with heavenly things. The lover of Christ feels impelled to empty self of all things for his sake, in order to be filled with him and his heavenly graces, and in turn to pour forth these treasures to neighbor also.

As St. Paul expressed it in his description of the true apostle: "As poor, yet enriching many, as having nothing, yet possessing all things" (2 Cor. 6:10).

26. "The Poor You Have Always with You"

Poverty, precisely as poverty or physical want, is never presented by the Scriptures as something good or desirable in itself. On the contrary, both in the Old and in the New Testament it is presented as something actually disgraceful to any human society in which its existence is allowed to continue. Christ condemns those who do not take steps to remove physical want: "Depart from me, accursed ones. . . . For I was hungry and you did not give me to eat . . . naked and you did not clothe me . . ." (Matt. 25:41 f).

In the Old Testament, too, we are taught that poverty must not be allowed to continue. In Deuteronomy, the Lord guarantees that if the Israelite community does his will, the community as a whole will always have such an abundance "that there should be no one of you in need" (Deut. 15:4). There will always be enough to go around. This does not mean that there will be no poor Israelites; on the contrary, as the same passage goes on to state, the poor will always be with you: "The needy will never be lacking in the land; that is why I command you to open

223

your hand to your poor and needy kinsman in your country"
(15:11). Since God gives such an abundance to the community,
"there should be no one of you in need." Those who have must
give to those who have not.

There will always be the poor among you, for a variety of
causes: a man will die, his widow and orphans will be in want.
A man's house will burn down, or a storm will wipe out his
crop. But the want must be cared for promptly.

Everyone should have the necessities of life, the things he needs
for living, in keeping with his human dignity, at more or less the
same level as those about him. To be deprived of these things is
not considered by the Scriptures as good. Far from wishing for a
state of privation, the Christian prays in the liturgy that God
will preserve him from it: "Give me neither poverty nor riches;
provide me only with the food I need" (Prov. 30:8). In incorpo-
rating these words of Proverbs into the Divine Office (Matins
Response, August), the Church accepts as her own an Old Testament viewpoint. The words present the fundamental Christian
attitude towards possessions: I want neither too much nor too
little, but just enough.

Thus we are provided with a kind of basic working definition
of scriptural poverty, the poverty which is a help towards God.
The scriptural poor man is he who has nothing superfluous, and
is content with his state. He is free of all greed and inordinate
possessiveness. Whatever he has over and above his own needs, he
is ever ready to give to others who are in need.

In the Scriptures, therefore, we can distinguish three states in
relationship to possessions: (1) destitution or misery, in which
one is deprived of necessities; (2) scriptural poverty, in which one
has, and is content with, the necessities of life in keeping with
his state; and (3) riches, in which one possesses a superfluity, of
which he must give, so that misery and privation will disappear
as much as possible from the earthly city of God, according to
the teaching of the Acts of the Apostles: "Nor was there anyone

among them in want" (Acts 4:34). The primitive Christian community thus fulfilled the command of Deuteronomy: "There should be no one of you in need" (Deut. 14:4).

If then neither the Old nor the New Testament looks upon privation of the necessities of life as something good, in what sense was Christ poor? It seems that he always had the necessities of life, though no doubt he and Joseph had to work hard for them in the simple workshop at Nazareth. And when our Lord went forth on his public mission, a group of women soon began to follow him, along with his apostles, "to provide for them out of their means" (Lk. 8:3). These women were rich in the sense that they had means to help others, they were poor in the sense that they did not hoard these means, but dispossessed themselves to help the poor Christ.

Moreover, the community of Christ and his apostles had a common purse, in the charge of Judas, from which they provided for their needs. While Jesus rested at Jacob's well, his disciples went off "into the town to buy food" (Jn. 4:8). Certainly this same pattern has almost always been maintained in religious life. All things are held in common, and from the common substance each one is given according to his need so that no one is in want.

In accepting the necessities of life from others, in humility, was Jesus a poor man merely in that *minimum* meaning of one who is content to have enough and nothing superfluous? What right had he to accept alms when he could have been using his carpenter's hammer and earning his living?

He could receive alms because he was a poor man in the *maximum* sense of keeping nothing for himself, of giving all that he had and all that he was in the service of others, of being totally dedicated to relieving the spiritual and material destitution of all mankind. He could rightfully encourage these women to join him in this total dedication.

God is infinitely poor. Charles Ranwez has written:

God has nothing. To have is to hold on to, it is to retain, it is to keep for oneself, it is to be dependent, it is to be possessed by something.

God has nothing, because he has retained nothing for himself, he has kept nothing for himself, not even himself, and especially himself.

For he has given everything, and himself first of all. What is he, if not gift and abandon?

To give himself, why that is his very essence . . .[1]

The Father gives his whole being in eternally begetting the Son. Father and Son give themselves totally to one another in that giving which is the Person of the Holy Spirit—whose proper name is Gift. "God so loved the world that he gave his only-begotten Son" (Jn. 3:16). "Christ loved me, and delivered himself up for me" (Gal. 2:20).

To be poor, then, in the Christian sense, in Christ's way, is to keep nothing for self, to consecrate all that one has and is to the needy, taking care of one's personal needs only to be more fit to give fully of self to others.

That is why sometimes religious communities have great material resources, large buildings, modern facilities, technological advances, and still can live religious poverty. But they live poverty only if in full reality all that they are and all that they have is genuinely consecrated to the spiritually or materially needy. They honestly see everything they have as belonging in some sense to the needy, as held in stewardship for them: and in fact they do administer everything wisely to the best possible advantage of the Mystical Body. Only thus are they living their poverty. Whatever goods religious retain over and above their own necessities of life in keeping with their dignity as children of God are retained in trust for some need of the Mystical Body.

[1] "Bienheureux les Pauvres," *La Vie Spirituelle*, 511 (December 1964), p. 696.

Religious retain these things because they have a task to perform in that Body and these things are necessary in rendering that service.

The real problem is to make it plainly seen by all that this is really so. And it will be truly so only to the extent that the charity of the religious truly is selfless. They have to be sure that their love for mankind, and therefore God's love for mankind, shines forth in the way they use all these things.

Jesus, then, was justified in accepting alms, so that he could be free to devote himself entirely to his work of salvation. But there is another reason why Jesus accepted the necessities of life from those women who followed him. He wished to sanction the teaching of Deuteronomy that no one should be allowed to remain in want, and he desired to bring this doctrine to a new, more sublimely divine, meaning. He wanted to show that care of the needy is service rendered to himself.

When Judas complained because Mary wasted three hundred denarii's worth of precious ointment on the feet of Jesus instead of giving it to the poor, Jesus said, "The poor you have always with you" (Jn. 12:8).

This statement has been much misinterpreted, and even twisted to a meaning directly opposite of what our Lord intended to say. Some, for example, quiet their conscience over widespread poverty, saying, "It is a hopeless task to remove want from human society, so let's not be too disturbed about it. Didn't Jesus say that poverty would never be conquered—the poor you have always with you. Let the poor suffer for Jesus."

This interpretation ignores the fact that Jesus was quoting Deuteronomy and reaffirming and deepening its meaning, not contradicting it. Deuteronomy really said, "There will always be some poor among you to care for. So get busy and care for them. Remove the disgrace of the neglected poor. No one among you should be allowed to remain in need. There will be enough to go around. If you do my will in this regard, I will see to it that there is enough to go around." The modern world in its approach to the population explosion and the resulting poverty should pay more attention to this scriptural key to the problem and God's promise of abundance for all of human society when we keep his commandment of love. Through the labors of our love he will provide the abundance. Man should see his labors as cooperation with the provident God himself.

"The poor you always have with you, but you do not always have me." In saying this, Jesus was identifying all the poor with himself: What Mary has done for me now in my own person, all of you will always be able to do for me in my needy members when I have withdrawn my physical presence. "Let her be—that she may keep it for the day of my burial" (Jn. 12:7). Let her keep her good deed till she realizes that in my sufferings and death and burial I have made myself one with all of God's poor, and am the suffering Servant of Yahweh who have taken upon myself the sufferings of all. "It was our infirmities that he bore, our sufferings that he endured. . . . When he was cut off from the land of the living, and smitten for the sin of his people, a grave was assigned him among the wicked, and a burial place with evildoers" (Isa. 53:4, 8).

Surely the first Christians easily saw this meaning in our Lord's words, for they were so deeply conscious of Jesus as this suffering Servant who had made himself one with all mankind in its poverty before God. They saw that henceforth whatever we do for the poor with whom he had identified himself we would be doing for him. "The Lord prophesied the presence of the poor till the end of the world so that they might be sacraments of his own emptying of himself, so that they might perpetuate among us his own agony. He directed toward the poor the compassion symbolized by the anointing by Mary."[2]

Thus Jesus gives a divine meaning to the almsgiving which

2 P. R. Régamey, "La Pauvreté depuis Vingt Ans," *La Vie Spirituelle,* 487 (October 1962), p. 423.

Judas claimed to want for the poor. Anoint me as Mary did: that is, honor my death and burial endured for your sake by honoring my needy members in the service you render them. For the alert Christian, every act of service of neighbor is a profession of faith in the Lord of all who became servant of all. This is the "faith which works through charity" (Gal. 5:6). Charity towards neighbor professes our faith in the Lord who exercised charity for us to the point of laying down his life in our service. St. Paul equates neglect of the needy with denial of the faith: "If anyone does not take care of his own, and especially of his household, he has denied the faith and is worse than an unbeliever" (1 Tim. 5:8). Charity begins at home, in the community, in the household.

If the poor are like a sacrament in whom we are to see the suffering Christ and find grace in serving him, in turn the one who thus serves is a sacrament to the one served, a sign and presence of Christ who became servant of all. Even when we have removed the disgrace of destitution from human society, the poor will be always with us, for always someone will be needy—in need of the arithmetic we teach, the food we cook, the clothing we mend, the medicine we administer, the sermons we preach, the example we give. We must update our religious poverty, making sure it is a self-giving in love and a keeping of nothing for self, in the likeness of the Servant of Yahweh who kept nothing for himself. Let us be sure that we are doing this first of all within our own household, as the Apostle says we should, and it is bound to shine forth to the world as well, in everything we do for them.

The poor will always be with us, because we need them for the perfecting of our love. Pope Paul VI explains it in these words:

> The person who is Christ's disciple in his hard school of poverty comes to see a wonderful relationship between poverty and charity; you might call them complementary.

This is not just because poverty needs that free, spontaneous and kind help that we call generous giving . . . but also because anyone who loves is in search of someone upon whom to bestow the signs and gifts of his love. What this means is that charity needs poverty in order to develop its characteristic energy for good.[3]

Charity is poor, for it keeps nothing for itself, It therefore needs someone to whom it can give, someone on whom it can use its energy for good, and thus show that it is truly divine. For God "has kept nothing for himself, not even himself, and especially himself."

[3] "Private Charity and the Poor," *The Pope Speaks*, X (1965), p. 163.

27. Christian Poverty and the Values of This World

Christian spirituality is sometimes accused of having no concern at all about this life and living only in hope of a world to come. Instead of caring for the poor and the economically oppressed and bringing social justice to them, it is claimed that the Christian is content to preach heaven to them, saying, "Be patient, suffer with Christ, and someday all will be well with you in eternal life." As Karl Marx put it, religion is the opiate of the masses. It puts them into a stupor so that they are unaware that they are being oppressed.

Obviously, this is a one-sided interpretation of Christian doctrine, ignoring the truth that Christ identified himself with the poor and condemned those who neglect them. But the scandal of widespread destitution which has been allowed to continue even in Christian countries seems to justify the accusation that Christianity has no concern for the "secular city," and preaches its doctrine about heaven as an opiate for the oppressed.

Pope Paul VI has reminded us that the religious life is an eschatological sign, bearing witness to the heavenly realities, showing that the things of this world are not an end in themselves:

> Man's hope must not be avidly and greedily rooted in time; instead, the transcendent hope of the ultimate end must be pursued, in search of that which remains definitively above and beyond the frail and perishable things that pass away.
> This seems to us to be the most urgent and up-to-date "sign" value that religious life is called upon to offer the community of the faithful . . . (Religious) ought to shine forth before their brethren for their total detachment from earthly realities.[1]

One might respond to the Pope by saying, "But isn't that letting us wide open to that accusaion that we have no concern for the poor and for the true values of this world?"

The problem therefore is: How are religious to be eschatological witnesses by their poverty, signs of the heavenly realities, without at the same time giving the false impression that the Church is unconcerned about human well-being in this life? Only too often the spirituality of the religious life has been accused of despising this world, as though marriage and possessions and everything material were somehow evil, or at least something less perfect, something good enough for second-class Christians. If religious really did despise the world in this sense, of course the poor and underprivileged would be right in thinking that religious have no concern about bettering the human lot.

The genuine spirituality of the religious life, of course, has never really despised the world in that sense. In justice to the religious of the past, we should interpret their sayings about despising the world in the whole context of their doctrine and

[1] "Religious Life and Aggiornamento," August 30, 1965, *The Pope Speaks,* X (1965), p. 332.

life. Certainly the history of the religious life in every century presents a glorious record of concern for the needy and of encouraging and building a true human culture and Christian civilization in keeping with the human dignity of the sons of God.

In our day, the "despising of the world" attributed to religious is accused of impoverishing the world at a time when mankind should be getting the most out of all its material resources, in order to provide the necessities of life for a world population which is growing faster than its needs are being cared for.

These are some of the reasons why religious poverty, as the Council tells us, may have to take on new forms in our times. Religious poverty must express itself in a way which carefully avoids giving the impression that Christians so despise the world that they are unconcerned about material progress for the benefit of mankind. The use of everything that religious possess needs to be geared in a very positive way towards developing all the true human values. All the resources of religious must be totally orientated towards the service of fellowman, in the likeness of Christ, the Servant of Yahweh.

For in the contemporary world situation, rendering material service to the destitute is clearly a rendering of spiritual service, since man cannot live a spiritual life of virtue when he is deprived of the basic necessities of life and is forced to live at a subhuman level. There are times when giving the material necessities to our fellowman is the only spiritual service we can render him. St. Thomas Aquinas wrote. "A man in hunger is to be fed rather than instructed."[2] And as General Booth, the founder of the Salvation Army, pointed out, when a man is drowning one doesn't stand on the shore preaching repentance to him. One jumps in and saves him.

Religious poverty, therefore, must take such a form that in no way will it impoverish this world while bearing witness to the

[2] *Summa Theologica*, 2a–2ae, Q. 32, a. 3.

next world. Pope Paul VI shows that it is precisely by bearing witness to the next life that Christian poverty enriches this life. For the living of gospel poverty is first of all an exercise of the virtue of hope, an expression of hope for the life to come. But this hope, far from destroying the values of this world, gives them their true dignity and function.

On this point, Vatican II declares,

> The Church teaches that a hope related to the end of time does not diminish the importance of intervening duties, but rather undergirds the acquittal of them with fresh incentives. By contrast, when a divine substructure and the hope of eternal life are wanting, man's dignity is most grievously lacerated, as current events often attest (GS 21).

Evangelical poverty, says Pope Paul,

> reminds us that the kingdom of God, the gift that Christ brings the world through his salvation, is not a gift of this world. . . . It does not enter into the sphere of the desirable things of this world, it does not consist in temporal riches. This brings about a relocation of the focal point of human desires and hopes, opens up the prospect of a human destiny different from and higher than the temporal one, instills in man an eschatological hope. . . .[3]

Christian poverty, then, is first of all an expression of eschatological hope. It is an act of hope even before it expresses itself in love, helping fellowman. It expresses self in service of neighbor only because it has the hope of bringing him, too, to the heavenly hope.

The secular city is not the only city. The religious, though in

[3] "Private Charity and the Poor," November 8, 1964, *The Pope Speaks,* X (1965), p. 162.

the world, is not of the world, and must never be totally absorbed into the secular city, but must ever remain a living sign of eschatological hope. But how else can eschatological hope shine forth in religious poverty unless, as in all past ages, the religious of today manifestly practise self-denial in the use of material things? And yet, in our times, this has to be in such a way that poverty is not interpreted as a denial of true temporal values. But, as the Pope's remarks bring out, the very hope of eternity expressed in Christian poverty guarantees the true value of temporal things. The eschatological hope instilled in man by the practice of evangelical poverty, he says, has important consequences:

"First, the true scale of values in life is spelled out." In the light of eschatological hope, economic values are no longer seen as supreme; but by that very fact their true dignity and function is guaranteed to them; for when one's heart is wholly set on the eternal hope, one can use material values well without being harmed by them. "The spirit of poverty removes the venom from economic values; it deprives them of their fatal power to deceive and tempers their tragic capacity for turning men into mortal enemies of each other."[4]

Seeing the true value of temporal things, we use them in moderation ourselves, and use them generously in providing for the necessities of others, thus enriching our fellowmen even in this life with true human values. Christian poverty and eschatological hope do not at all impoverish life in this world. "Gospel poverty is humility," says the Pope, "it is peace, it is even renunciation, but in reality, not such as to make the temporal and economic order any poorer, nor to weaken labor and its prodigious organization. . . . It humanizes labor . . . making it more functional and beneficial."[5] For the gospel attitude towards material values, instead of making material things an end in them-

4 *Ibid.*, p. 162.
5 *Loc. Cit.*

selves, directs man's labors toward the truly human values upon which a life of virtue and grace is engrafted. Christian labor aims at providing, in love, the conditions necessary for life in keeping with the true human dignity of the sons of God. Thus, the temporal and economic order is not at all impoverished by poverty of spirit and heavenly hope, but is endowed with its truest value.

The poverty of religious life in our times must be lived in such a way as to direct the attention of our fellowmen to these truly human values served by the economic order. It would seem that this purpose will be best accomplished when religious poverty expresses itself in a total dedication of all we are and have to the material and spiritual welfare of our needy fellowmen, helping them achieve the true human values which are necessary for their human dignity. Certainly religious help towards this goal in their educational and social work. And they need possessions and equipment in providing these services.

And religious communities, in which all the members work hard for the common good with sincere dedication to one another in providing both the material and spiritual necessities for a fully Christian life, should be living examples of the true value of work, and of the true fruits to be looked for from human labors. Perhaps the Council reasserted the obligation of work for all religious so that they might bear witness to the dignity of work in a mechanized era when technological progress has given many the vain hope of someday avoiding all labor, an era when the sense of service of fellowmen by our daily labors is being lost, when fewer and fewer see, as the Council tells us we should see, that the normal expression of Christian charity is the service we render one another in our daily labors (*GS* 67). We should bear witness to this truth at a time when ever so many workers do the very minimum they can get away with, looking only for a large pay check to take home, foolishly unaware that by their labors they should be perfecting themselves and finding fulfillment in loving service of neighbor, who benefits from the products of our labors.

Such are the things the Council has in mind when it states: "It is ordinarily by his labor that a man supports himself and his family, is joined to his fellowmen and serves them and is enabled to exercise genuine charity, and be a partner in the work of bringing God's creation to perfection. Indeed, we hold that by offering his labor to God a man becomes associated with the redemptive work of Jesus Christ, who conferred an eminent dignity on labor when at Nazareth he worked with his own hands" (*GS* 67).

The Christian concept of work as a service of fellowman in love, then, is a true expression of Christian poverty—for labor to serve fellowman counteracts the greed for possessions for their own sake, and the greed which wants everything for nothing and wants it in abundance, and clamors for it as something owed to us whether we work or not.

Religious, by their true poverty of spirit, expressed in hard work, in self-sacrificing dedication of all they are and all they have to the service of one another in the common life, and to the service of all their fellowmen, will be a sign both to the rich and to the poor. They will be a sign to the rich showing them how to be poor, in the sense that they do not hoard their possessions sheerly for themselves, but use all their economic resources in the service of the highest human values, helping their fellowmen to a life in keeping with their full human dignity as children of God. And by their hard-working dedication to their fellowmen in poverty, religious will be a sign to the poor showing them that the Church *is* concerned about human values, is interested in their welfare, material as well as spiritual. Her very hope for their eternal life causes her concern that they have all those good things of earth which they need for their Christian dignity here and now.

We see, then, some of the elements of the theology of Christian poverty. Gospel poverty is an expression of faith, and of hope in the things to come. In the light of this hope one sees the true value and function of the things of this world, and labors unselfishly in charity to provide the truly human values which are dependent upon these things. Religious poverty is indeed detachment, but it is never mere privation for its own sake; it is freedom from the slavery of greed; it is a very positive expression of the theological virtues of faith, hope and charity, which unite us to God and to one another in God. Christian poverty, by reason of the eschatological hope which it expresses, "tempers the tragic capacity of material things for turning men into mortal enemies of one another," and unites us in the charity which "needs the poor in order to develop its characteristic energy for good."[6]

[6] *Ibid.*, p. 163.

28. "The Gospel without Charge"

Vatican II seems concerned that religious should in no way give the impression that they are parasites, living an easy life on the alms of the faithful. In asserting that all religious are bound by the law of work, their dependence upon the alms of the faithful is de-emphasized (*PC* 13). Indeed, the Council puts far more emphasis on religious giving alms than on their receiving them.

But did not Jesus himself express his poverty by being dependent on the alms of those women who followed him, ministering to him from their means? (Lk. 8:3). St. Paul, on the contrary, refused to be dependent upon the alms of his converts, preferring to work with his hands and earn his own living. Was the poverty of St. Paul therefore more heroic than that of Jesus? No servant is greater than his master. Why could not St. Paul be like Jesus in this?

St. Paul was in a different situation from Jesus'. The manner in which one practises Christian poverty is determined in large measure by the situation in which one finds oneself.

Paul had a right to receive alms, for Jesus said that "the

laborer is worthy of his hire" (Lk. 10:7), and Paul "labored more than any of them" (1 Cor. 15:10). But Paul was in a situation where the spread of the Gospel required that he forego his right to support from the faithful. It seems that especially in Achaia, the area around Corinth (2 Cor. 11:10), it was most important that no impression of self-seeking be given in the preaching of the Gospel, perhaps because of the great poverty of most of the people who were drawn to the Gospel in that area (1 Cor. 1:26 f).

Moreover, certain false apostles who came to Corinth after St. Paul were taking pay for their labors, and they would have been only too happy to be able to point to St. Paul to say that he, too, received money for the Gospel (2 Cor. 11:12). But Paul refused to do so. "Did I do wrong when I humbled myself that you might be exalted, preaching to you the Gospel of God free of charge? . . . In all things I have kept myself from being a burden to you, and so I intend to keep myself. . . . This boast shall not be taken from me in the districts of Achaia" (2 Cor. 11:7–10).

We know that in another situation, when he was in jail and could not work, Paul did gratefully accept the alms of the Philippians.

The situation in the world today—widespread poverty, and workingmen in most of the world struggling for social justice—requires that religious take extraordinary care to give in no way the impression that they are parasites in the Church. Vatican II states: "In their assignments, religious should consider themselves to be bound by the common law of labor" (*PC* 13). As in Paul's situation, it has to be clear that they, too, deliver the Gospel without charge, and that they work for their keep.

This does not necessarily mean that all of them have to labor with their hands, as Paul did. But it does have to be clear that they are not parasites, as they are often accused of being—and as some of them in fact are. They must be fully earning their keep, as teachers, as nurses, as social workers, as hard-working students, as scholars laboring over books, employed in the service of the Church. When Jesus says of his apostles, "the laborer is worthy of his hire," in these very words he makes it clear that all his apostles are laborers. And indeed they must labor more abundantly than others, without benefit of labor unions or demands for rights, in total consecration to the spread of the Gospel, saying with the Apostle Paul, "Have we not a right to eat and to drink? . . . But we have not used this right, but we bear all things, lest we offer hindrance to the Gospel of Christ" (1 Cor. 9:4, 12).

St. Paul could not stand a parasite. "If any man will not work, neither let him eat" (2 Thess. 3:10). ". . . Let him labor, working with his hands at what is good, that he may have something to share with him who suffers need" (Eph. 4:28). And in his touching farewell to the clergy of Ephesus, whom he knows he will never see again, he says, "I have coveted no one's silver or gold or apparel. You yourselves know that these hands of mine have provided for my needs and those of my companions. In all things I have shown you that by so toiling you ought to help the weak and remember the word of the Lord Jesus that he himself said, 'It is more blessed to give than to receive'" (Acts 20:33–35).

So too Vatican II directs that religious, "bound by the common law of labor," should "gladly use their own goods for other needs of the Church and for the support of the poor, whom all religious should love after the example of Christ" (*PC* 13). In these days of widespread destitution, far from seeming to be parasites, religious must manifest their deep concern for God's poor and put their labors and their goods at their complete disposal. Christian poverty means keeping nothing superfluous for self; religious poverty, moreover, consecrates not only one's possessions but one's whole being—and all one's gifts and talents, and all one's time and energies—to serving the spiritually and physically needy. Religious violate this poverty when they luxuriate in leisure, thinking that long hours in comfort with a novel or before a television set are something owed to them.

Like Jesus himself, they must have the necessities of life, and recreation is one of these necessities. However, a religious never looks upon physical or mental work merely as a necessary evil taking him away from his leisure, but looks rather upon recreation as a necessary, and gratefully accepted and enjoyed, respite from his ardent service of God's cause. God's work is never done, God's needy ones are never adequately cared for. The zealous religious is always a bit uncomfortable spiritually when he is too comfortable physically, knowing how great is the harvest, how ready it is for harvesting, and how few are the laborers. He cannot in conscience plan long hours of leisure and comfort just for their own sake, as though this were something due to him. There is always someone to be served, by our prayers, or by our work, or by the hardships we suffer.

St. Paul gave a new twist to our Lord's words, "The laborer is worthy of his hire." Jesus meant that he who labors for the Gospel may accept alms with a clear conscience. But Paul says it this way: "The laborer is worthy of his reward" (1 Tim. 5:18). The reward will come in the future from God; here and now I wish to give the Gospel without charge, and unhampered by any care for possessions.

In the ages of faith, when most Europeans were still accustomed to seeing Christ in the poor, believers spontaneously and generously came to the aid of mendicant religious, religious who were frankly beggars, fulfilling a vocation to bear witness to heavenly realities. To the eyes of faith, those religious were not parasites. Their poverty was a penitential offering to God. But the situation has changed. The Church today prefers that religious poverty take a new form, and that religious follow the tactics of the Apostle Paul, earning their support, putting the emphasis on poverty as a giving, a self-sacrificing service, a keeping of nothing for self.

Some of our contemporaries think that the times require that religious go around in tatters, wearing the very poorest clothing they can find, even picking it from a trash can, and thus bear witness to the Church's solidarity with the destitute. Certain religious communities have had trouble with some of their members who refused to wear the neat and attractive habit of their order, insisting on going about in rags.

Certainly we must show our solidarity with the destitute, and perhaps the Holy Spirit intends that each order have chosen representatives living among the poorest of the poor and in the manner of the poor. "But," writes Father John M. King, O.M.I., "when one has manifested his solidarity with the poor, has he really done anything for the poor? He may have merely indulged himself in a spiritual egotism. The poor are not interested in having us assume their position in society. What they want is for us to aid them in overcoming their poverty. When Christ saw that the multitude was hungry, he did not merely take his place among them and say that he was hungry too. He fed them."[1]

If religious are to cope adequately with the destitution of our times, they are going to need physical resources and have techniques at their disposal. They will have to show their solidarity with the poor, not so much by reducing themselves to their level, as by laboring in unmistakable love to lift them to a level in keeping with their dignity. The poor will not resent the possessions of religious when these clearly possess them in the poverty of using them well for the material and spiritual salvation of others.

Perhaps some religious institutes, or maybe a few members of every institute, will be given the vocation to live with the destitute and in the manner of the destitute, to show the Church's love of the poor. But the majority of religious will be called to make good use of material resources in bettering the lot of man-

---

[1] "Report on Vatican II, The Decree on Religious Life," *Homiletic and Pastoral Review*, LXVI, No. 6 (March 1966), p. 474.

kind, fulfilling, as in times past, a variety of functions in the Church. And so Vatican II declares: "Religious communities have the right to possess whatever is required for their temporal life and work" *(PC* 13).

If it does become clear that the Holy Spirit requires that every religious institute have representatives working among the poorest of the poor, somewhat after the manner of the priest-at-work movement, these representatives will have to be carefully chosen and given a special intensive formation for this type of work—a specialized novitiate, one might say. One cannot rush forth into this work unprepared. Both Extension Lay Volunteers, and Papal Volunteers for Latin America have learned from experience to be more careful in accepting their candidates, and now seek only the more mature and experienced. So too the priest-worker movement has been restored in the Church, but only specially formed men will be allowed to function in it. Careful preparation, then, will be required for any work of religious among the destitute. Novitiates are ever necessary. The twelve apostles had three years' novitiate with Christ, and St. Paul spent his three years' novitiate in the desert of Arabia just after his conversion.

Perhaps the numerous defections from religious institutes by religious who claim to be eager to labor among the poor is a sign from God that all religious institutes should take the work among the poor most seriously, and assign a representative number of their members to the slums or other depressed areas. It has long been clear that the Church wills that all institutes come to the aid of South America and its increasing spiritual and material destitution.

But at the same time, the urgency of the poverty problem does not permit the abandonment of an institute's other works. Even in these times when the Church is so keenly aware that she is the Church of the Poor, her other children still need to be cared for. They too are poor in their way, in need of love's service. It is significant that the same Pope Paul VI who donated his papal tiara to the poor has also made a donation of $20,000 to the scholarly work of St. Thomas Aquinas Foundation, including the preparation of a critical edition of the works of St. Thomas. And all this while millions are starving. But the world is spiritually starving, too, and Pope Paul is convinced that it needs the help of Thomas Aquinas in finding the answers to modern problems.

Let us not think, then, that we should all be in the peace corps or in the slums or in other depressed areas. Let us not rob Peter to pay Paul. There are many, many tasks to be done in and for the Mystical Body of Christ, and being a good student is one of them.

29. Be Helpless
with the Helpless

If our charity for the poor, for the sick, for the sinner—for anyone in need—is to be genuine, we must become truly helpless with the helpless. This is a lesson learned from the compassionate Christ, who truly suffered all things with us, experienced all human infirmities, was "tried as we are in all things except sin ... For in that he himself has suffered and has been tempted, he is able to help those who are tempted" (Heb. 4:15; 2:18). St. Paul, perfect disciple of Christ, could say in full truth, "To the weak I became weak that I might gain the weak. I became all things to all men that I might save all." (1 Cor. 9:22).

Here we have expressed a basic principle of Christian service of neighbor: the necessity of becoming like the ones we serve. Genuine charity never serves neighbor from a position of superiority, but always comes down to the level of the one served, and indeed humbles self before him; humbles self not only before the poor and the suffering, but even before the sinner.

This apostolic principle of being like the ones we serve has often been misunderstood and misapplied. In his encyclical *Ec-*

246

clesiam Suam Pope Paul warns of the danger of becoming like the world in the wrong way, and reminds us of the need of being different from the world in the way Christ meant us to be different.[1]

It is a delicate problem indeed to know in what ways we must be like and in what ways we must be different from the people we are trying to serve. Some religious, misapplying this principle of likeness, are practically destroying religious life by their efforts to be just like laymen.

The misapplication amounts to this: they act as though the likeness were purely a material, external one; they fail to see that the likeness consists basically in an interior, spiritual attitude, flowing from charity's ability to identify self with the suffering one in genuine understanding and compassion.

If the likeness to those we are trying to help were only a material likeness, then it would follow that in serving the sick we would have to infect ourselves with their diseases and in serving sinners we would have to commit their sins. Some of our contemporaries have thought it necessary to go even to these extremes. Pius XII, in his encyclical on Holy Virginity, condemns those who teach that religious and seminarians ought to be exposed to all the occasions of sin so that they will really understand life.

Christ was like us in all things *except* sin. He did not have to be a sinner to understand sinners. On the contrary, sin is far better understood by a saint than by a sinner; for sin's true nature can be seen only in contrast to the holiness of God. One has to contemplate the holiness of God in purity of heart before he can have full understanding and compassion for sinners.

In what sense, then, *do* we come down to the level of the poor, the sick, the sinner, in order to serve them? There are counterfeits of charity in which the so-called charitable one acts from a position of superiority. With an air of superiority he "goes

[1] *The Pope Speaks,* X (1965), pp. 270–271.

slumming," patronizingly he condescends to the lowly in what he thinks is wonderful magnanimity. Then there is the so-called efficient apostle, who may indeed be expert in rendering physical services to the poor and suffering, but totally fails to understand and experience what the suffering one is enduring in the depths of his person. When we serve with the attitude of superiority, or from a position of power and riches, or if we blame the needy even while we help them, we can wound the very ones we think we are serving; we can crush them more deeply into their sense of inferiority and discouragement, and thus fail to render charity's true service of restoring them to a sense of their dignity and giving them the confidence to help themselves.

Therefore we must not come as rich and powerful to the poor and needy and sinners—remember how Jesus came in humility to the sinful woman at the well, as himself one in need, asking her for a drink. We must serve others from a position of humility and neediness, and with profound reverence for the ones we serve.

But how can we do this in all truth? Only by poverty of spirit. The poor in spirit are they who have an honest and sincere conviction of their own neediness before God. Before God, we are all beggars. As we help the sick, the hungry, the weak, the sinner, their helplessness should be a reminder to us that "All mankind is grass, and all their glory like the flower of the field. The grass withers, the flower wilts, when the breath of the Lord blows upon it. Though the grass withers and the flower wilts, the word of our God stands forever" (Isa. 40:6–8). Before God, each one of us is as helpless as the most helpless. Man's only hope is in Christ, the Word of God.

Only in this conviction of our own nothingness, accompanied by total trust in God, are we able to serve our fellowman with genuine humility, and avoid wounding and discouraging him by an attitude of superiority. Thus, when we help a sinner, we humble ourselves by acknowledging sincerely in our heart, with

St. Philip Neri, that "but for the grace of God, there went I." Each fall of a sinner that we witness should humble us, causing us to reflect that we too, without the grace and mercy of God, would also have fallen. Only if we are convinced of that truth will we be able to treat the sinner with compassionate love and humility and mercy, and so win his heart to God. Only the merciful obtain mercy. He who knows he needs mercy, he who has acknowledged his own helplessness before God, is the one who is most inclined to be merciful.

Likewise, in the presence of the sick and the suffering we humble ourselves, for we see the helplessness of the sick one as a striking reminder of our own mortality. But for the upholding providence of God, there too would I be, sick and weak. I am but dust and ashes and someday will be in that same helpless and hopeless condition. "All flesh is grass!"

How often we are inclined to resent the sick or anyone who needs our help, their presence is a burden or an inconvenience to us. Only a profound sense of our own neediness before God will enable us to experience, not resentment, but only compassion. They who have become like the needy, by acknowledging sincerely that they too live in perpetual need of God's merciful aid, are the quickest to show mercy.

In poverty of spirit, then, we become truly helpless with the helpless, we come down to the level of the needy one in genuine understanding and compassion; and with him and for him we hope only in God, asking God on his behalf for the help we desire so ardently to give. In poverty of spirit, we realize that we are receiving from God—even while we are giving it—the help which we bestow on the needy one. It is only in this way that our presence to the needy one is truly a presence of Christ, the Christ from whom we are receiving the very help we are giving. This sort of service of neighbor is sure to be genuine charity; this humble poverty of spirit guarantees that we will be loving with the Heart of Jesus, and not with some mere human counterfeit of charity.

For in our consciousness of our helplessness before the helpless, like St. Paul, in burning charity we "long for" the needy one "in the heart of Christ Jesus" (Phil. 1:8). When we are helpless with the helpless, we rush to the heart of Christ in which we find the divine creative love which does not love because a creature is lovable, but because God is love, and his love creates the creature's lovableness. When we love with this divine love, this love which we imbibe from the heart of Christ, then, like God, we are able to love others whether they are saints or sinners, whether they are worthy of love or whether they are not. Such love is creative also in the sense that it inspires a response in the loved one; it gives him a sense of his dignity, it encourages him to strive to become worthy of this love, by loving and serving in return.

Our likeness to the poor and needy, then, is basically a spiritual likeness—that is, it is poverty of spirit, a consciousness that all of us are beggars before God. Nevertheless, this spiritual poverty does desire expression in a tangible way. In some external way we have to express our likeness to the poor and needy ones whom we are trying to help. The most effective expression of this likeness is the vowed poverty of religious, when that vow is lived in all truth, when we really do live a life of physical poverty according to our vow. This visible poverty of the religious should be the eloquent expression of true poverty of spirit, of awareness of our own beggarliness before God, and our humility and trust in him alone. Religious poverty, then, when it is a tangible and sincere expression of inner poverty of spirit, is one of the best ways of becoming truly like the needy ones whom we wish to serve for love of God. Such poverty is truly apostolic.

If the helplessness of the needy ones we meet should ever remind us that we too are needy before God, this helplessness reminds us also of the divine love of Christ in which he became helpless with the helpless. But his helplessness is our strength. "The weakness of God is stronger than men," says St. Paul (1 Cor. 1:25). By his creative love, in which he has humbled himself before us, Christ has lifted us from nothingness all the way to the dignity of divine sonship. For God so reverenced his own image and likeness in men that he humbled himself to restore it.

Think of the reverence of Jesus for the woman at the well, for the woman taken in adultery, for Mary Magdalene; for he saw in them their God-given potentialities, he saw in them a nature created in God's own image, and therefore capable of loving with a divine love. He reverenced this in them and humbled himself before them, putting himself at their service, dying for them on the cross, exalting them to the very presence of God.

Therefore, whatever our works of service of one another— whether it be caring for the sick or bearing wrongs patiently, aiding someone in their studies or giving spiritual guidance, helping the aged in their infirmities or correcting and encouraging the young—whatever it be, let us do it with humility and patience and love, in the deep consciousness of our own infirmity, and with profound reverence for the likeness of God in our fellowman. This humble reverence, this creative love, encourages the needy one, lifts him up, restores his sense of his dignity as a child of God, as one created and redeemed by divine love.

30. Spiritually Uncomfortable in Material Comfort

The physical and spiritual destitution of so many of our fellow-men is a perpetual reminder of our own spiritual helplessness and neediness before our Creator and Redeemer, without whom we are nothing and have nothing, but from whom we hope for heavenly realities far surpassing the good things of this world.

In this consciousness, in this Christian poverty of spirit, we can never really find comfort in material things. Our sufficiency is not in possessions but in God; we never rest in possessions, but only in the Lord. We may have houses which are warm in winter and cooled in the summer, pantries well stocked with all the necessities of life, different weights of clothing for the different seasons, comfortable beds and easy chairs. But in the midst of all these comforts, if we are fully Christian, we are always a bit spiritually uncomfortable. We can never completely relax in material things.

Why? Not because these things are not good gifts of God, but because God himself, the Giver, forbids us to find our security and rest and sufficiency in them. Our Lord once told the story of a man whose fields bore such abundant crops that he tore down his barns and built bigger ones; and when everything seemed secure for the future, he said, "Soul, thou hast many good things laid up for many years; take thy ease, eat, drink and be merry." But God said to him, "Thou fool, this night do they demand thy soul of thee; and the things that thou hast provided, whose will they be?" (Lk. 12:19–21).

No matter how rich we are in the things of this world, then, we are poor and empty, for our true riches are not of this world. Christian poverty expresses eschatological hope; Christian poverty is an emptying of self that we might be filled with God, the true treasure. Material necessities must be cared for, of course, to make it possible to live in keeping with our dignity as human beings and children of the eternal Father.

There is a second reason why the true Christian is always a bit spiritually uncomfortable in the midst of his material comforts. Since in the solidarity of charity he is ever poor with the poor, his consciousness of the multitudes of the poor and the ignorant and the sinful in the world about him bothers him. He can never completely rest in his possessions, nor even in the security of his personal holiness, as long as he knows there are many others lacking the necessities of life and deprived of the message of the Gospel and without the grace of God. His Christian missionary spirit gives him no rest.

A religious especially, and precisely because he is a Christian taking his Christianity in fullest seriousness, is always a bit uncomfortable when he is too comfortable. If his community provides him with the material necessities a little more richly than is necessary, his conscience thinks twice before he relaxes in the use and enjoyment of these good gifts of God. Perhaps he can relieve his spiritual discomfort over these things by sanctifying them in thanksgiving. "God has created [these things]," says St. Paul, "to be partaken of with thanksgiving by the faithful and by those who know the truth. For every creature of God is good, and nothing is to be rejected that is accepted with thanksgiving. For it is sanctified by the word of God and prayer" (1 Tim. 4:3–5).

In this act of thanksgiving, we profess ourselves as poor before God, recognizing the divine love which has given us all things, thus resting in the Giver rather than in his gifts. We give thanks for the call to a community whose charity for us gives us all things in love: the physical necessities basic to our life as children of God, along with a superabundance of spiritual helps. And if we are provided with material aids more richly than is absolutely necessary, perhaps again it is an expression of community love which does not want our Christian life to seem in any way inhuman. If these good things are given to us in charity, it is because it is taken for granted that we are spiritually strong enough to use them well with thanksgiving and humility, and not as something which we demand as a right. We should be able to say with St. Paul, "I know how to live humbly and I know how to live in abundance (I have been schooled to every place and condition), to be filled and to be hungry, to have abundance and to suffer want. I can do all things in him who strengthens me" (Phil 4:12–13).

Our abundance is sanctified only when used in humble thanksgiving, and by sharing it with the needy; for the true Christian always considers his superfluity as somehow consecrated to and belonging to the poor. The real test as to whether we have really sanctified our abundance comes when we are brought low. Complaints over the lack of what we would like to have seem to show that we have not been schooled to live either in abundance or in want. In the midst of abundance we must school ourselves in the spirit of poverty by daily self-sacrifice in the use of material things, never demanding anything, never complaining over anything. Sincerity in doing this will prepare us to make the far-reaching adaptations in religous poverty which our times require.

A religious community's charity in providing its members with material things more richly than is necessary may sometimes be an unenlightened charity, which is doing more harm than good. The ideal way to find relief from spiritual discomfort in the midst of excessive material comfort would be to share these things with the needy. But if we are not able to do this because of our situation, then at least we must ever remain spiritually one with all the poor, suffering in our hearts over their material and spiritual neediness, keeping alive our spiritual solidarity with them by making whatever hidden sacrifices we can for them, offering our labors, for example, as a prayer to God that he will provide in some other way for those whom we cannot personally help.

One who is in daily touch with needy souls and is honestly laboring for their salvation with all his heart finds it easier to keep poverty of spirit alive in his heart. He has no time to get attached to material comforts, no interest in doing so. His heart is too much with others who are in need of Christ. Thus poverty is an expression of charity—because his heart is so attached to the souls to be saved, it is consequently detached from material things. One who is fully involved with all his heart in a laborious and exacting apostolate is free even if he has to live in the midst of plenty. But one who is merely doing a job under necessity, just waiting for the moment when he can return to his comfort, is the slave of his possessions.

We must labor, then, with all our heart at whatever task has been assigned to us in the Mystical Body of Christ, knowing that thus we are filling up what is wanting to the labors of Christ for his body the Church. If we are aged or sick and therefore retired from active service in the Church, our very retirement is a vocation in the Mystical Body. The sick and the aged remain spiritually poor in the midst of the comforts provided for them in community charity, if in their hearts they ever remain conscious of the multitudes of their fellowmen who are spiritually and materially in need, and therefore endure the hardships of sickness and age with patience, united with the sufferings of Christ, as a sacrifice for the salvation of all.

The true Christian, who sees physical poverty and sickness and weakness as a sign and reminder of the poverty of all of us before God, lives in the hope of the fullness of God, which the Lord wills to give to all those who have emptied themselves of all else to receive his fullness.

31. Charisms and Religious Obedience

It is often said that St. Albert and St. Thomas baptized Aristotle, just as St. Augustine had baptized Plato. That is, scrutinizing the works of these philosophers in the light of faith, these saints took everything that was good and true in them and put it to the service of Christian living. Vatican II has continued this procedure and, in the Holy Spirit, has baptized a good deal of contemporary philosophy.

This is part of the Church's function of "scrutinizing the signs of the times and interpreting them in the light of the Gospel" (GS 4), for the contemporary philosophies are themselves signs of the times. In their attempts to solve the problems of the day, these philosophies are products of the times, and in turn will help fashion the times to come. And lest they give a wrong direction to the course of human events because of any erroneous elements they may contain, it is imperative that the Church, under the Holy Spirit, hasten to develop in the fuller light of the Gospel the good insights of these philosophies. If this development of the true insights is vigorous enough, any errors which may be connected with them will wither away, and the good insights will help answer the needs of the times.

It is obvious that the Council has done some of this baptizing of contemporary philosophy in *Perfectae Caritatis* in speaking of religious obedience and authority. The references to liberty, maturity, dialogue, responsibility, dignity of the person are echoes of the special emphases of current personalistic philosophy.

The contemporary emphasis on the person, its uniqueness and liberty, is truly a blessing in the face of our assembly-line culture in which many a worker is hardly better than an automatic tool, and in the face of the utter disregard for the value of the individual person in the modern totalitarian state, where the state is god and the individual is expendable.

Christian spirituality has been responding to these needs of the times, and with the aid of new terminology borrowed from the philosophies of the day has gladly re-emphasized age-old ideas, now newly expressed in terms such as personal commitment, involvement, engagement, initiative. In this new spirituality tailored to our times, the alert Christian has a wonderful awareness of his personal, distinctive role in God's salvific plan.

In baptizing the good insights of personalistic philosophy, however, the Holy Spirit has granted to the Church certain complementary insights which correct the limitations and aberrations of this philosophy. Chief among these corrective insights is the Church's rediscovered awareness of the importance of the charisms in the lives of all the faithful. The doctrine on the charisms, we shall see, gives full recognition to the dignity and the function of each individual person in the People of God.

Charismatic Graces

Charisms are graces granted by the Holy Spirit primarily for the good of others—and especially for the building up of the Mystical Body—rather than for the personal good of the ones who receive them, although the person himself grows in holiness by using these graces well in genuine charity for neighbor.

The teaching on the charisms solves the so-called obedience crisis, which springs in part from certain exaggerations of personalistic philosophy; for both obedience and authority are charisms, special graces coming from one same Holy Spirit. When obedience and authority are truly lived as charisms, there can be no real conflict between them. It is necessary therefore that we consider the Council's doctrine on obedience within the fuller context of its teaching on the charisms.

In the paragraphs of *Perfectae Caritatis* dealing with obedience and authority, the chief emphasis is put upon obedience and authority as services rendered to the Church. The key word in the whole paragraph is *service*. But that is precisely what a charism is: it is a grace appointing and empowering one to serve the People of God. A charism is a grace which is given for the common good, for the building up of the body of Christ. St. Paul is speaking of charisms when he says, for example, "Our gifts differ according to the grace given us. If your gift is prophecy, then use it as your faith suggests; if administration, then use it for administration; if teaching, then use it for teaching. Let the preachers deliver sermons, the almsgivers give freely, the officials be diligent, and those who do works of mercy do them cheerfully" (Rom. 12:6–8 j). All these are charismatic graces, when carried out in the Holy Spirit.

The charisms are not restricted to only a few members of the Church but are distributed among the faithful of every rank. The charisms of the laity and of religious are as indispensable in the building up of the Mystical Body as are the powers of the clergy. Such is the teaching on charisms contained in *Lumen Gentium:*

It is not only through the sacraments and the ministries of the Church that the Holy Spirit sanctifies and leads the People of God and enriches it with virtues, but "allotting his gifts to everyone according as he wills" (1 Cor. 12:11), he distributes special graces among the faithful of every rank. By these graces he makes them fit and ready to undertake various works or offices profitable for the renewal and full building up of the Church, according to the words of Scripture, "To each is given the manifestation of the Spirit for the common good" (1 Cor. 12:7). Since these charisms, whether the more outstanding ones or the simpler and more widely diffused ones, first of all are adapted and useful for the needs of the Church, they are to be received with thanksgiving and consolation. Extraordinary gifts, however, must not be sought rashly, nor are the fruits of apostolic work presumptuously to be expected from them. Judgment concerning their genuineness and their orderly use pertains to those who are in authority in the Church, and to whose special competence it belongs not to extinguish the Spirit, but to test all things and hold fast to that which is good (1 Thess. 5:12, 19–21) (*LG* 12).

There is no faithful Christian who is without his proper charisms. "Every layman, in virtue of the gifts bestowed upon him, is both a witness and a living instrument of the Church itself 'according to the measure of Christ's bestowal' (Eph. 4:7)" (*LG* 33). That last phrase is a text from St. Paul in which he is speaking specifically of charismatic graces. After the statement, "To each one of us grace was given according to the measure of Christ's bestowal," the Apostle indicates that there is an order among the charisms, and the first five he enumerates have as their purpose the preparing of all the faithful for the exercise of their own special charisms: "He himself gave some men as apostles, and some as prophets, others again as evangelists, and others as pastors and teachers: for the perfecting of the holy ones for the work of ministering, for building up the body of Christ" (Eph. 4:11-12). St. Paul is saying that apostles, evangelists, prophets, pastors, teachers perfect the rest of the faithful so that the faithful can carry on their work of ministering—that is, their charismatic works in which they help the Church in her work of salvation and thus contribute to the building up of the Mystical Body.

Charisms, then, are given universally, to all the People of God; unless, of course, one puts obstacles in the way by negligences and infidelities to Christ. The Council insists that ruling authorities should acknowledge and reverence the charisms of the people subject to them. The following words apply as much to religious superiors as to pastors:

> Pastors . . . know that they were not ordained by Christ to take upon themselves alone the entire salvific mission of the Church toward the world. On the contrary they understand that it is their noble duty to shepherd the faithful and to recognize their ministries and charisms, so that all according to their proper roles may cooperate in this common undertaking with one mind. For we must all "practice truth in love, and so grow up in all things in him who is head, Christ. For from him the whole body, being closely joined and knit together through every joint of the system, according to the functioning in due measure of each single part, derives its increase to the building up of itself in love" (Eph. 4:15–16) (*LG* 30).

The Council points out the wonderful unity in this diversity of graces, and its words echo St. Paul, who speaks of three groups of charisms: graces, such as the gift of tongues and prophecy; ministries, such as ruling authority and teaching; and works, such as nursing and other works of mercy (1 Cor. 12:28).

In their diversity all these bear witness to the wonderful unity in the Body of Christ. This very diversity of graces, ministries and works gathers the children of God into one,

because "all things are the work of one and the same spirit"
(1 Cor. 12:11). (*LG* 32).

The words we have just read are from the chapter on the laity
in *Lumen Gentium*. But what about the charisms of religious?

The Charisms of Religious

The doctrine on the charisms is beautifully woven throughout
the whole structure of the decree on the religious life. To be
convinced of this, one need only notice in the document the frequent texts from St. Paul in which he speaks explicitly of charismatic graces. The decree's concern about the value of religious
life in the Church and world today is a concern for the charismatic value of religious life, its value as a grace of service of the
Mystical Body.

In the opening section of the decree the Church is described
as being adorned with a "wonderful variety of religious communities" each one of which is itself a charismatic gift to the
Church, making it "easier for the Church to be equipped for
every good work (2 Tim. 3:17) and 'perfected for the work of
ministering, for building up the body of Christ' (Eph. 4:12)"
(*PC* 1).

Each religious institute, then, is a charism, and all who give
themselves in obedience to that institute are consecrated to that
institute's specific service ordered to the building up of the People of God. Each community has its own special work assigned
by the Holy Spirit. This, of course, explains the decree's insistence that each institute, in making its adaptations to modern
conditions, remain faithful to the spirit, the aims, the ideals of
its founder (*PC* 2,b). The great founders were charismatic leaders
raised up by the Spirit of God. The hierarchy, guided by that
same Holy Spirit, adapted and approved the ways of life these
founders proposed (*LG* 45).

In the paragraphs of the decree dealing with the various types of religious institutes, much emphasis is again laid on their differing charismatic gifts. Thus, in section seven, the Council vindicates the strictly cloistered life of communities dedicated entirely to contemplation by indicating that this way is a special charism benefiting the whole Church, quoting a text of St. Paul in which he is speaking explicitly of charisms: "all the members do not have the same function" (Rom. 12:4). The Church needs an endless variety of charisms for her perfection.

Section eight, dealing with communities devoted to apostolic works, is practically a paraphrase of Romans 12: 5–8, a great text of St. Paul on the charisms:

> The gifts which these communities possess differ according to the grace which is allotted to them. Administrators have the grace of administration, teachers that of teaching, the gift of stirring speech is given to preachers, liberality to those who exercise charity, and cheerfulness to those who help others in distress (Rom. 12:5–8). "The gifts are varied, but the Spirit is the same" (1 Cor. 12:4).
>
> In these communities, apostolic and charitable activity belongs to the very nature of the religious life, seeing that it is a holy service and a work characteristic of love, entrusted to them by the Church to be carried out in its name *(PC 8)*.

"Holy service," "works characteristic of love"—these again echo St. Paul's terminology on charisms. Charisms, he says, are "manifestations of the Holy Spirit" (1 Cor. 12:7). He is the Spirit of divine love. As expressions of the spirit, the charisms are "works characteristic of love."

The Council takes special care to praise teaching and nursing religious. It expresses its high esteem for their charisms of educating youth and nursing the sick and other such ministries "so useful to the pastoral mission of the Church" *(PC 10)*. That word "ministries," we saw, is one of St. Paul's three synonyms for "charisms" (1 Cor. 12:4–6). Teaching and nursing are charisms, services to the People of God. The commission which drew up this decree explained that this section was included because the Conciliar Fathers wished to counteract a widespread recent tendency to depreciate the value of the apostolates of teaching, nursing and the like.[1]

Obedience and Authority as Charisms

From the terminology used by the Council in speaking of religious obedience, especially the recurrence of the words "service" and "building up the body of Christ," we learn that the grace of religious obedience is itself an outstanding charism, of immense value to the salvific mission of the Church:

> In professing obedience, religious offer the full consecration of their will as a sacrifice of themselves to God, and thus are united more permanently and more securely to God's salvific will. . . . Under the motion of the Holy Spirit, they subject themselves in faith to their superiors, who hold the place of God, and under their guidance are led to serve all their brothers in Christ. . . . Thus they are more closely bound to the service of the Church and strive to attain to the measure of the full manhood of Christ (Eph. 4:13) (*PC* 14).

They should realize that by their obedience "they are contributing to the building up of the body of Christ according to the plan of God" (*ibid.*).

The more perfectly one has given self into God's hands, the more likely it is that charismatic gifts will be given him abundantly for the benefit of the Church. It is to be expected, then,

[1] *Relatio super Schema Decreti de Accommodata Renovatione Vitae Religiosae*, p. 5.

that by reason of religious obedience Christ will measure out his charisms more abundantly to religious, since obedience so effectively puts them into his hands, uniting them "more permanently and more securely to God's salvific will," making them fit instruments of the Holy Spirit for every good work.

If obedience is a great charism, so too is religious authority, given by the same Holy Spirit. Charisms, we said, are graces given for the common good, appointing and empowering a person to serve the People of God. Superiors, says the Council, "should exercise their authority in a spirit of service of the brethren, expressing in this way the love with which God loves their subjects." Here again we have the idea that charisms, as "manifestations of the Spirit," are expressions of divine love. This is true both of the service rendered by the charism of ruling and of the service rendered in obedience.

The doctrine on charisms, we said, gives full recognition to the dignity and function of each member of the People of God. That is why this doctrine should be so appealing to those lovers of freedom who are wise enough to see that freedom is responsibility, and that responsibility can be carried out only in freedom. Only a free person can respond to a call and make a commitment, lovingly assuming and loyally fulfilling love's obligations. This the religious does in making and keeping the vow of obedience. In love's freedom he promises to obey, and in love's freedom he keeps that promise. The doctrine on charisms teaches that each son of God has his freedom under the Holy Spirit, his personal responsibility in carrying out God's salvific will, his unique role in building up the Mystical Body. It reaffirms St. Paul's view of Christian liberty as an opportunity to serve, in love. "For you were called to freedom, brethren; only do not use that freedom as an excuse for sensuality, but pledge your service to one another through love" (Gal. 5:13).

In treating authority and obedience as charisms, then, the Council baptizes contemporary philosophy's emphasis on the dignity of the human person. Any tendency of this philosophy to exaggerate human liberty at the expense of obedience and authority is duly corrected by seeing both obedience and authority as charisms from the one Holy Spirit who works in both. Counteracting the claims of exaggerated personalism, the Council declares that "religious obedience, far from lessening the dignity of the human person, brings it to a maturity in the broader liberty of the children of God" (*PC* 14).

Obedience gives this broader freedom, however, only when it fulfills the requirements laid down by the Council, i.e., only when one obeys intelligently and willingly, in keeping with his dignity as a human person. "Religious are to obey their superiors humbly, according to the norms of the rule and constitutions, in a spirit of faith and love for the will of God, using both the powers of their intellect and of their wills, as well as their gifts of nature and of grace, in executing the commands and fulfilling the duties entrusted to them, realizing that they are contributing to the building up of the body of Christ according to the plan of God" (*PC* 14).

In other words, the Council does not ask for simple passive submission, but desires that religious find the true fulfillment of their persons in an active, intelligent, willing response to authority, offering all their natural and supernatural endowments to the service of the Church under the guidance of their superiors. They must be able to see in faith that this is an outstanding way of lovingly putting one's complete personality at the full disposal of God's salvific will which is working in the Church.

The Council then goes on to instruct superiors to encourage fully this intelligent and willing response of their subjects. "Let them rule their subjects as children of God with respect for the human person, eliciting their voluntary submission. . . . Subjects should be led to cooperate with an active and responsible obedience in undertaking new tasks and in carrying out those already undertaken. For that reason superiors should willingly listen to their subjects and promote their cooperation for the good of the institute and of the Church, preserving intact, however, their authority to decide and command what is to be done" (*PC* 14).

In these last words, the Council definitely rejects the concept of "dialogue obedience." In the so-called dialogue obedience, "simple submission to the superior is set aside and the subject is at liberty to discuss with the superior until they come to an agreement which is acceptable to both."[2] The proponents of this false view of obedience contend that a subject has no obligation to obey until he is personally convinced by the superior of the wisdom of the superior's command. The Council rejects this view. After the debate on the schema on religious life in the Council aula, "four hundred and five of the Conciliar Fathers requested that 'the authentic concept of religious obedience be preserved intact' so that obedience should not be conceived as 'a dialogue wherein the superior tries to convince the subject.' "[3] In answer to this request, the decree states that even though superiors should willingly listen to their subjects and encourage their cooperation for the good of the institute, they should nevertheless maintain their authority to make decisions and to command what is to be done. The Council, then, is clearly against the concept of dialogue obedience.

But it strongly favors superiors consulting their subjects and seeking their help in arriving at their decisions.

What is the reason for this consultation? The dignity of the individual? This is not an adequate reason. The reason is that both the superior and the subject labor under the obligation of doing God's will. His will is not always clearly

[2] Schema II on the Religious Life, quoted by Archbishop Beck, "The Schema on Religious," *Doctrine and Life*, 15 (August 1965), p. 422.

[3] *Schema Decreti de Accommodata Renovatione Vitae Religiosae* (Rome: Typis Polyglottis Vaticanis, 1965), #167, p. 54.

evident; but it is, objectively, that which the real situation actually requires. So a search to discover his will must include a study of existing conditions.

Today it is impossible for the superior to possess the many separate competencies which will enable him to evaluate a situation. He is often surpassed in competence by many of his subjects. This will become more and more true as knowledge increases and society and religious life become more specialized. In order to discover what the will of God is in a given situation, the superior often has need of the competence possessed by his subjects. This is the reason why he must consult them. Furthermore every religious is open to the inspiration of the Holy Spirit and it is the community as such which must act, not simply the superior. There is no doubt that in the final moment, the decision rests with the superior. . . . However, it has often been overlooked that this right of the superior is operative in the final moment. Responsible examination and consultation must precede such a moment if there is to be a well-founded hope that the community will actually be doing what the will of God dictates in a given situation.[4]

The so-called "obedience crisis," we said, is resolved when both superiors and subjects have profound reverence for the special charisms of one another. Superiors should be firmly convinced that their subjects have charisms, too, and therefore all the initiative need not come from the superiors. "The Spirit blows where he wills." He gives special graces in every rank of the faithful. Ruling authority is one charism among many and is at the service of the other charisms, encouraging and coordinating them. "Judgment concerning the genuineness of the charisms and their orderly use," says the Council, "pertains to those

4 John M. King, O.M.I., "Report on Vatican II, The Decree on Religious Life," *Homiletic and Pastoral Review*, LXVI, No. 6 (March 1966), p. 465.

who are in authority in the Church, to whose special competence it belongs not to extinguish the Spirit, but to test all things and hold fast to that which is good" (*LG* 12).

That is why the decree on religious says that superiors should listen to their subjects. They should carefully evaluate their ideas and their complaints. With deep understanding and sympathy they should listen to the needs of their subjects and the needs of their apostolates.

When the Holy Spirit first began to move the boy Joseph, giving him dreams in which he saw his brothers and his parents bowing before him, his father Jacob's first reaction was to reprove him. But Jacob took second thought about the matter, and quietly pondered it in his heart (Gen. 37:10–11). The Holy Spirit does give charisms even to the very young sometimes, and through some of these youngsters he may very well be starting new trends in a religious community, more in keeping with the changing times. Superiors have an obligation to be on the lookout for the graces of their subjects, lest they extinguish the Holy Spirit, hampering his workings.

But at the same time the subjects, no matter how richly endowed they may be in charisms, must deeply reverence the charisms of authority, and are under obligation to subject their own charisms to the testing and directing of authority. The Council leaves no doubt on this point: "Judgment concerning the genuineness of the charisms and their orderly use pertains to those who are in authority in the Church" (*LG* 12).

Since in no way does religious obedience destroy, but rather enhances, the dignity and the freedom of the sons of God, what the Council says about the laity in their relationships with their pastors applies also to religious in their relationships with their superiors:

They should openly reveal to them their needs and desires with that freedom and confidence which is fitting for children of God and brothers in Christ. They are, by reason of the knowledge, competence or outstanding ability which they may enjoy, permitted and sometimes even obliged to express their opinion on those things which concern the good of the Church . . . Let this always be done in truth, in courage and in prudence, with reverence and charity toward those who by reason of their sacred office represent the person of Christ (*LG* 37).

Only when superiors truly listen to their subjects with a genuine interest and honest attempt to get to the truth in their hearts will they fulfill the requirement laid down by the Council for the exercise of authority; namely, "Superiors, as those who are to give an account of the souls entrusted to them (Heb. 13:17), should fulfill their office in a way responsive to God's will." They cannot mediate and manifest God's true will to their subjects unless they seek that will sincerely; and they will not find it unless by listening to their subjects they rightly appraise their situation, know what is in their hearts, know their genuine needs and their true charisms.

The Council warns superiors not to extinguish the charisms of their subjects (*LG* 12). But subjects can extinguish their own charisms, and one of the surest ways of doing this is by the attempt to use these gifts independently of ruling authority, which has the obligation to test the genuineness of the charisms and direct their use. One of the surest signs that a subject is not really being moved by the grace of the Holy Spirit, but a spirit of pride or some other perverse spirit, is his refusal to accept the decisions of superiors in the use of his gifts, unless the superior is manifestly commanding something sinful.

It may well be that the Holy Spirit had been moving the subject, initiating some good idea or work in him, but his rejection of the guidance of God's human representatives is enough to stifle what the Holy Spirit had begun. Precisely because we can be moved by various spirits—the Holy Spirit, evil spirits, or our own perverse spirit—God requires that we must submit our spirit to authority to be tested, even when it is the Holy Spirit himself who is moving us. "The spiritual gifts of God's inspired spokesmen," says St. Paul, "must be subject to the control of other inspired spokesmen of God" (cf. 1 Cor. 14:32). The works of our apostolates are no longer charisms when we carry them out independently of the Holy Spirit, and the surest way of breaking with the Holy Spirit is to break with those whom he "has placed to rule the Church of God" (Acts 20:28).

Even when a superior's decision may seem to hamper what the Holy Spirit has begun in us, if it is really the Holy Spirit who has been at work, he will prevail in his own good time, if we ourselves remain in harmony with him. The seeming frustration of his purpose is itself a stage in making his movement all the more efficacious in the long run. For the humility of the subject in accepting the decision of the superior in obedience more effectively delivers him into the hands of the Holy Spirit, and purifies him of any perverse spirit which could have hampered the Holy Spirit's work. For in carrying out even the best of desires inspired in us by the Holy Spirit, we have a way of mixing in motives which are still all too human, and of making foolish mistakes in our planning. So, in a sense, our very charisms need to be purified and corrected, and submission to the direction of authority is one of the most effective ways of doing this. Neither our personal sanctification nor our charisms in the service of others are ever purely a matter between ourselves and the Holy Spirit alone. They are the concern of the whole Mystical Body, and so need to be regulated by the ruling charisms of that Body.

Let us beware, then, lest what the Holy Spirit has begun in us be extinguished in us by a rebellious spirit in trying to do God's work in our own way. And let us pray that God will ever give us outstanding superiors who will not extinguish the Spirit by authoritarianism, a failure to reverence and encourage the charisms of their subjects.

If we are thoroughly convinced that all our charisms are services which we are to render to others in humble love, we will not extinguish the Spirit.

"For you were called to freedom, brethren," says St. Paul. "Only do not use that freedom as an excuse for sensuality, but pledge your service to one another through love" (Gal. 5:14).

32. Religious Obedience and Authority: Love's Service

The key word in Vatican II's treatment of religious obedience and authority, we have seen, is *service;* and it is a service of love, a following of Christ, who became the servant of all in loving obedience to his Father. In a religious community, both superiors and subjects are servants of their brethren, servants of the Church, servants of God's will to save mankind.

Perfectae Caritatis states first of all that obedience is the gift of self to God's saving will. "In professing obedience, religious offer the full consecration of their own will as a sacrifice of themselves to God, and thus are united more permanently and more securely to God's salvific will" (*PC* 14).

Obedience, then, is a union of man's will to God's will, to God's will to save us. Vowed obedience makes this union of wills firmer and more secure. Obedience is thus an openness to salvation. It is a concrete expression of the faith by which every intelligence is brought "into captivity to the obedience of Christ" to receive from him the salvation he wills to bestow (2 Cor. 10:5). For it is only in the obedience of Christ that man is saved; the vowed obedience of the religious is an especially intimate participation in this obedience. "After the example of Jesus Christ who came to do the will of the Father, and 'assuming the nature of a slave' learned obedience in the school of suffering, religious under the motion of the Holy Spirit subject themselves in faith to their superiors, who hold the place of God" (*PC* 14).

But if obedience, an expression of faith, is first of all a union of man's will with God's salvific will to receive the benefits of salvation, it also makes man the instrument of God's will in saving others. "Under the guidance of superiors," says the Council, "religious are led to serve all their brothers in Christ, just as Christ himself in obedience to the Father served his brethren and laid down his life as a ransom for many" (*PC* 14). The Council thus expresses the basic evangelical and theological principles of religious obedience.

However, religious obedience opens man to the benefits of salvation and makes him the servant of God's saving will only because religious authority is in the same loving service. "Superiors," says the decree, "as those who are to give an account of the souls entrusted to them, should fulfill their office in docility to God's will. They should exercise their authority in a spirit of service of the brethren, expressing in this way the love with which God loves their subjects" (*PC* 14).

It is clear from this that government by superiors is the true expression of God's love and saving will to the extent that superiors seek sincerely, through the exercise of their authority, to bring to their subjects the full benefits of God's saving will, and to employ their subjects to the best possible advantage in serving the work of salvation of others.

We see then the great importance of the Council's phrase, "superiors should fulfill their office in docility or responsiveness to God's will." As servants of this saving will, never may they use their authority arbitrarily. They must ever take care to seek in each situation precisely what is God's true will for their subjects, asking themselves, for example, "Does this assignment, or does my governing policy, dispose my subjects to receive the benefits of salvation, and help them to communicate these benefits to others? Does my exercise of authority in this instance contribute directly or at least indirectly to the work of salvation and growth in holiness?"

Only when superiors are truly servants of their brethren and servants of God's saving will does their exercise of authority express the love with which God loves their subjects. Obviously, such exercise of authority must be inspired ever and only by charity. According to the Scriptures, authority is essentially a service of love, and the person who possesses it is a servant in the likeness of Christ, who came not to be served but to serve and give his life a ransom for many (Matt. 20:28). "The kings of the Gentiles," he said to his disciples, "lord it over them, and those who have authority over them are styled 'Benefactors,' but with you it shall not be so. On the contrary, let the greatest among you become as the youngest, and the leader as the servant . . . I am in the midst of you as he that serves" (Lk. 22:25f, s).

Ruling authority in the Church, we have seen before, is a charism—a grace granted not for the benefit of the ruler, but for the benefit of the ruled. The efficacy of charismatic graces, however, can be impeded either by those who exercise them, or by those for whose benefit they are granted. Abuse of authority —failure to use it in the openness to God, the obedience to his will of which we have just spoken, can certainly be an obstacle to God's graces which would freely flow were authority used well. But bad attitudes on the part of the governed can likewise impede this flow of grace.

There is a time-honored saying that we usually have the kind of superiors we deserve. If our superiors seem to be failing us, perhaps it is because our resistance to them impedes the benefits God would otherwise be granting us through them. Consequently, our superiors seem to lose their charismatic qualities, perhaps more as a punishment of their subjects than because of their own failings; since, after all, charisms by their nature are for the sanctification of others, not that of those who possess them. God could grant these graces to these others even through a mediocre instrument, and would do so in proportion to the receptivity of these others—their faith and hope, their humility, sincerity and charity.

If then there is a woeful lack of charismatic qualities in superiors, all the blame is not necessarily due to the superiors—though, as we said, they, too, can impede the graces God would like to grant through them. An insubordinate spirit on the part of the governed, and especially a bitter, merciless spirit of criticism, a lack of charity and compassion for superiors and their human shortcomings, can utterly close the governed to the benefits which God's saving will would grant them were they submissive to his representatives in love and humility.

Carping, bitter criticism is in practice a denial of the faith, faith in the truth that God uses weak human instruments in his work of salvation, that he uses the weak to confound the proud. The fact that he uses vessels of clay is a test of our faith and humility and charity.

Attitudes of merciless criticism can actually paralyze a whole community, because the closed hearts of the critics—hearts closed to charity—are such an obstacle to the divine mercy and blessings which could flow to the humble of heart and the merciful despite the human imperfections of their governors.

The charismatic structure of the People of God is rooted in charity, and operates effectively only to the extent that there is unity in charity. St. Paul's great hymn to charity is the very heart of his treatment concerning charismatic graces: "If I have all the eloquence of men or of angels, but speak without love, I am simply a gong booming or a cymbal clashing" (1 Cor. 13:1).

Both authority and obedience, then, should be exercised in love, as a service of love. Vatican II clearly places religious obedience in the context of chairty, saying that it reproduces and bears witness to the charity and humility of Christ. We read in the Constitution on the Church:

> The Apostle . . . in urging the faithful to charity, exhorts them to have in them the mind which was in Christ Jesus, who "emptied himself, taking the form of a slave, becoming obedient unto death," and who "when he was rich, became poor" for our sakes. Since it is necessary that the disciples imitate this charity and humility of Christ and bear witness to it, Mother Church rejoices to find in her bosom many men and women who more closely follow the Savior's emptying of himself and more clearly manifest it, by embracing poverty in the freedom of the sons of God and by renouncing their own wills . . . subjecting themselves to man for God's sake, so that they may more fully conform themselves to the obedient Christ (*LG* 42).

A prime motive for religious obedience, then, is charity like Christ's own which expresses itself in service of neighbor. "Under the guidance of superiors, religious are led to serve all their brothers in Christ, just as Christ himself in obedience to the Father, served his brethren and laid down his life as a ransom for many, and thus they are closely bound to the service of the Church and strive to attain the measure of the full manhood of Christ" (*PC* 14).

In its treatment of obedience, then, the Council highlights in obedience as the gift of self to God's will to save the world, to be at the service of the Church and of mankind; whereas in treating of chastity, the Council has highlighted the theologal value of chastity, that is, its power to unite us firmly to God.

Some Interrelationships of the Three Vows

For in chastity, we have seen, the chief emphasis is on the gift of self to God alone, with an undivided heart. By chastity, in ardent charity, the religious roots self firmly in the transcendent Christ. That is why the Council gives chastity the fundamental place among the three vows of religion; for it is a grace of deeper participation in the Church's bridal union with the eternal Word of God, the total gift of self to belong exclusively and perpetually to him.

Poverty and obedience are inevitable consequences of this gift of self in chastity. For one who exists for Christ alone in virginal chastity can no longer exist for the purely temporal, and, by poverty in spirit and in fact, strives for increasing freedom from temporal bonds. And existing for Christ alone, one puts self at the disposal of his Church in obedience, to be used in the apostolate wherever the Church sees fit to use him, thus bringing to the world the fruits of one's virginal love of Christ. Consecrated chastity, says the Council, "is certainly a particular source of spiritual fecundity in the world" (*LG* 42). This fruitfulness, however, is communicated to the world chiefly in the service to the Church rendered in religious obedience. We see, then, the eminent apostolic value of religious obedience, which so effectively unites one to God's saving will in the service of the Church.

Religious chastity, then, is more directly theologal in value, uniting us immediately to the eternal Christ in faith, hope and charity, whereas obedience is more directly ecclesial and apostolic in value, intimately consecrating us to the service of the Church in the saving of souls, thereby bringing to the world the fruitfulness of chaste union with Christ. These two aspects are expressed in the words of the Council:

Impelled by the love which the Holy Spirit has poured into their hearts, religious live more and more for Christ, and for his body the Church. The more fervently they are united to Christ by this total life-long giving of themselves, the richer the life of the Church becomes and the more vigorous and fruitful its apostolate (*PC* 1).

The virginity of heart cultivated in fidelity to the vow of chastity makes it possible to love Christ with ever greater freedom and fervor, and to be united to him in ever increasing intimacy. That is why the Council can assert that religious life is a great help towards maturity of personality and the freedom of the sons of God:

> Let it be clearly known to everyone that the profession of the evangelical counsels, though entailing the renunciation of certain values which are undoubtedly to be esteemed, does not detract from a true development of the human person, but rather by its very nature is most beneficial to that development. For the counsels, voluntarily undertaken according to each one's personal vocation, contribute a great deal to purification of heart and spiritual liberty, continually stir up the fervor of charity, and are of special value in forming the Christian man in the virginal and detached life which Christ chose and which his virgin Mother embraced (*LG* 46).

The three counsels, then, "contribute to purification of heart and spiritual liberty." Purity of heart and spiritual liberty are practically synonymous. Purity of heart gives an inner freedom to love wholeheartedly. Virginity of heart in chastity, humility expressed in obedience, poverty in fact and in spirit, wonderfully free the heart from the various forms of selfishness which could hamper the power to love and to attain true fulfillment of personality in the loving gift of self to others. The virginal heart— that is, the detached heart, poor and pure—loves Christ and neighbor ardently; and the obedient heart is given in obedience to the full service of the Church and of mankind.

The Four Values of Obedience

In this chapter, then, we have seen the four values of religious obedience—the theologal, ecclesial, ascetic and christological values.

First, its theologal value, or its power to unite us to God; for obedience is a concrete profession of the faith which brings us into captivity to the obedience of Christ. "Religious, under the motion of the Holy Spirit, subject themselves in faith to their superiors, who hold the place of God" (*PC* 14).

Secondly, the ecclesial value of obedience, for these superiors guide them in the service of the Church in carrying out God's saving will.

Thirdly, its ascetical value in giving freedom from enslaving self-will, forming religious in what the Council calls "liberty strengthened by obedience" (*LG* 43). In obedience, they are guided by superiors in the religious discipline which exercises them in purity of heart and inner freedom, and opens them fully to the benefits of God's saving will.

And finally, its christological value, which unites and contains all the other values—and here we are back to our key word, "service." For religious "subject themselves to men for God's sake," says the Council, "so that they may more fully conform themselves to the obedient Christ" (*LG* 43), who in obedient love of the Father emptied himself, and came not to be served, but to serve, and give his life a ransom for many.

33. Secularized "Charity"

"When the appointed time came, God sent his Son, born of a woman, born a subject of the Law, to redeem the subjects of the Law, and to enable us to be adopted as sons. The proof that you are sons is that God has sent the Spirit of his Son into our hearts: the Spirit that cries 'Abba, Father!'" (Gal. 4:4–6, j).

Just about the first thing a newborn infant does is cry. The first breath that enters his tiny lungs comes out at once in a healthy yell. When the Christian is born of God, his very first cry is "Father!" The Holy Spirit's first breathing into our hearts comes out immediately in that cry.

"Father!" is the first cry of Christian love, for it is the first cry of Jesus himself, whose Spirit of love in our hearts likens us to him. "Father!" is the first cry, "brother!" is the second cry of Christian love, the infallible consequence of the first. For only when we know God as Father can we know our fellowmen as brothers in Christ—not mere brothers in humanity, but brothers in divine life.

These are truths which need profound meditation in these

days of Christian Atheism and its cry, "God is dead!" The Christian Atheists love to quote Bonhoeffer's catchword that Christ is essentially a "man-for-others." From this, however, they are only too likely to conclude that we no longer need the Father, we no longer need religion. Love of neighbor is all-sufficing. They speak of religionless Christianity.

This movement began, of course, as a healthy reaction against the sham, pharisaic religion of many Christians. But it should not be carried to the extreme of rejecting the true religion of other Christians. Many sham practitioners of religion do honor the Father with their lips while dishonoring him by their shameful lack of love for his children. But this does not mean that in reasserting love for the children we must now dishonor the Father directly in his own Person, and put up a tombstone for him marked "God is dead."

Though much of the God-is-dead theology is an attempt to kill only the false concepts of God, there are many brands of atheism which are dead serious about putting God to death. We need him no more. Man has come of age. Through his mature accepting of personal responsibility, he will henceforth do for himself what he used to expect God to do for him. Christ the man—the man for others—is all the God we need. Christ is a man who took heroic initiative in solving mankind's problems.

In what we are saying, we do not pretend to be presenting the full doctrine of Bonhoeffer or his predecessors, nor the full teaching of any stage of the evolution that this thinking has undergone among their successors. We shall merely sample various manifestations of the trend in order to bring out in contrast the whole truth which we are striving to recover. A reaction against one position almost always leads to the opposite extreme. Reaction against sham religion has led to such extremes as situation ethics and religionless Christianity. Consequently, there has to be a new synthesis of the truths contained in all positions.

In saying that Christ is essentially a man for others, Bonhoeffer

is stating a magnificent Christian truth. Jesus came "for us men
and for our salvation." But this becomes falsified when it is taken
out of the total context of the Gospel, when one loses sight of
the fact that this man for others is also God, Son of the Father,
and essentially a "man-for-the-Father." A true insight not integrated into the whole truth becomes a falsehood.

Therefore, even while the Christian rejoices in the truth that
Christ is a man for us, he also reasserts that first of all Jesus is
for the Father. And we, too, even while we endeavor to be men
for others, must above all be men for God. Providentially, Vatican II, so deeply concerned about men in the world today, first
of all, in its first document, the Constitution on the Sacred
Liturgy, reasserted the need of giving glory to God in fitting
worship. To be men for others, it is not necessary to espouse the
so-called religionless Christianity, and every form of institution.
We must not abandon the direct experience of God in prayer, we
must not condemn adoration of God as a waste of time, claiming
that God is to be found only in love of our brothers.

Love of neighbor which separates itself from reverential love
of the Father is secularized love. When we secularize love, it is
no longer divine love, it is merely humanistic. It is no longer
the divine *agape* which cries "Brother!" only because it first cries
"Father!"

Christ, says Bonhoeffer, is essentially a man for others. St. John
shows that Christ is also and first of all a man for the Father.
Zeal for the Father's house eats him up (Jn. 2:17). He does everything for the glory of the Father: "I have glorified thee on
earth, I have accomplished the work thou hast given me to do"
(Jn. 17:4).

If he is a man for others, it is because this is the Father's will,
this is why he has been sent. He loves and reverences the Father's
will because he loves the Father above all. It is because he loves
the Father that he lays down his life for his fellowmen. "The
Father loves me, because I lay down my life in order to take it

up again. No one takes it from me; I lay it down of my own free will. . . . This is the command I have been given by my Father" (Jn. 10:17–18, j). Jesus goes forth to battle Satan on our behalf "that the world may know that I love the Father, and that I do as the Father has commanded me" (Jn. 14:31).

Christ's entire life, then, is centered on the Father, and on his Father's will that he be a man for others. His whole life is a going to the Father, but he brings his brothers with him. "Jesus knew that the hour had come for him to pass from this world to the Father. He had always loved those who were his in the world, but now he showed how perfect his love was . . . Jesus knew that the Father had put everything into his hands, and that he had come from God and was returning to God" (Jn. 13:1–3, j).

He came from the Father, he goes to the Father. His kingdom is not of this world. If he goes out to his brothers, it is only to bring them back to the Father: "that he might gather into one the children of God who were scattered abroad" (Jn. 11:52).

Since Christ's entire life is a going to the Father, bringing his brothers with him, is it any wonder that when we are begotten of God by the Holy Spirit in the likeness of the Son, our first cry, and our every cry of love, is "Father!" We cry "Father" even when we cry "Brother," for in brother we see the likeness of the Father we love—unless, of course, our cry "Brother" is merely human, merely naturalistic, and not divinely inspired.

When we take the Father out of our brotherhood, when we deny the need of profound worship of the Father in intimate prayer, both public and private, our love becomes secularized, it becomes merely naturalistic humanitarianism.

"Be human in your love," they say. "Love in a human way." But love which is not regulated by a profound reverence for the will of the Father becomes sheerly secularistic and naturalistic. It is no longer divine love in the way of the children of God. "Love is the only law," say the proponents of situation ethics. But theirs is a secularistic love, cut off from love of the Father, for in the name of that love they violate the will of the Father, they break his commandments, saying that these are irrelevant to this situation or that.

Exaggerated personalistic emphasis on human fulfillment in human love is no doubt behind much of the abandonment of the priesthood and the religious life by those who were called to bear striking witness by celibacy to a heavenly fatherhood and a divine rebirth.

The sheer secularists—for whom God is dead because they no longer need a God—claim that they already have whatever is good in religion; and by good, they mean whatever is of use to mankind in this world—as if our God existed only for the good of man! They have nothing to learn from religion. They claim, for example, that personalistic psychology has taught us more about love's personal relationships and personal commitment than religion ever could; modern social science teaches us all we need to know about humanitarian problems; modern scientific progress, with its amazing advances in speedy communication with the entire world by jet flights and television and radio, will bring about the desired unity of mankind.

Religion may talk about love and unity and humanitarianism, but modern man has found how to make all these effective, and has learned them in a better way. Anything worthwhile that religion has to say, modern man already knows; anything which religion speaks about in addition to these things is irrelevant— irrelevant, because not useful in this world. The Holy Trinity, the indwelling of God in the soul by grace—all that is irrelevant to modern man; and so, they say, it is no longer true for modern man.

Truth is purely relative, says the existentialist and situationist. When a situation changes, and a truth is no longer relevant to it, it is no longer a truth, though perhaps once it was true. If you do not need a truth, it is not true for you. If someone needs the Holy Trinity, or the Blessed Virgin Mary, then these are still true for him. But a really modern man does not need them.

However, say the Christian Atheists, modern man does need Christ, the man for others. It does not need the remote God. That God is dead.

As we said, all these varying doctrines contain some wonderful insights, which are very attractive indeed; for every glimpse of God's truth is appealing. But, we said, partial truth not integrated into the whole truth becomes partial falsehood.

Partial truths have a way of masquerading as though they were the whole truth; and so these contemporary systems of thought often mimic Christianity so well that they even claim to be the true Christianity; and deceive, if possible, even the elect. That is how Jesus and St. John warned us it would be. The Antichrist would masquerade as the Christ. Though the proponents of these theories may be in good faith, Satan can take advantage of half-truths to build up the appealing masquerade.

Thus, in the Apocalypse, St. John tells us that the beast mimics everything that Christ does; his reign is a caricature of the reign of Christ.[1] Christ impresses the mark of the cross on his followers. The beast, too, has a mark for his followers—it is concern for the world, but not in the Christian sense of respecting and developing the true human values of this life in their relationship to the life to come. So to exaggerate the human side of Christ that one forgets he is also a man for the Father is a dangerous caricature of the truth. It is to care for the human needs of man in a secularistic context and to forget his heavenly calling. If man has only earthly needs, of course a doctrine concerning a Holy Trinity would be irrelevant. But man is called to fellowship with the Father in his Son (1 Jn. 1:3).

Therefore, if we are to be integral Christians, we must take care of all the needs of men these other systems are concerned

[1] See *The Jerusalem Bible*, notes on Revelations (Apocalypse), 13:3, 4, 15; 14.

about—and much more! In the Incarnate Word, we have to know how to be both human and divine in our approach, both for the Father and for our brothers.

Much modern atheism came into being because it really does look as if there were no God in the modern world—the lack of love of neighbor, the greed and hatred which has flamed into the world wars of our century, the mass murders in concentration camps, the total destruction brought by atomic bombs, the lying and cheating and infidelity and persecution and social injustice and race hatred so widespread among us, breeding further wars; with the world in such a state, can we blame the ones who say: "How can I believe in a God of mercy and justice and loving providence if he lets this sort of thing go on? There is no God in *this* world. It is therefore up to us men to assume the responsibility and make something of this world. We must be men for others, we must commit ourselves to our neighbor. We must put love where there is hatred."

How true all of this is! But it is only partly true, and dangerously partial. For to put secularized love into the world, a love cut off from the Father in heaven, is not enough.

If there is no God in the modern world, let us not blame God. St. Paul blames the evils of the pagan world on man's failure to acknowledge the God he knew: "Although they knew God, they did not glorify him as God or give thanks" (Rom. 1:21). That is why Paul could tell the Ephesians that before their conversion to Christ, they were "without God in the world" (Eph. 2:12). The modern world is in the same mess. But modern man explains the absence of God by saying that there is no God; at least, no God who cares about man, no personal God interested in man. So man on his own initiative has to remake the world.

It was man who expelled God from his world. Through the prophet Osee, God complains about lack of love among men, and brands it as lack of love for him (Osee 4:1-3); and he says: "I will go back to my place, until they pay for their guilt and seek my presence" (Osee 5:15).

We are not going to solve the godlessness of the world today, then, merely by being men for men, merely by a secularistic, naturalistic love. First of all we have to be men for God, seeking his presence in reparation and adoration through the sacrifice of Jesus, crying, "Abba, Father," winning his grace and the Holy Spirit of divine love, and bringing divine love into the world.

Even some Catholics have been tainted by the half-truths concerning brotherly love. There are some who refuse to look upon the Mass as a sacrifice of reparation and adoration, and see it only as a love feast, a banquet of brotherly love.

But at Mass, before we participate in the banquet in communion with our brothers, we say "Our Father who art in heaven"; and we say that only after we have offered the Eucharist as a true sacrifice, to glorify the Father and give him thanks; "Through him and in him and with him is to You, God the Father Almighty, in union with the Holy Spirit, all honor and glory, Amen!" Thus, with Jesus and in him we first cry "Father," and only after that does our cry "Brothers in Christ" ring true. Christianity, Christ's way, still *is* religion, worship of the Father —adoration, reparation, thanksgiving, petition—before it is a service of the brethren in love. Or, better still, the two are inseparable: it is one same movement of love which takes us to the Father in the sacrifice of Jesus and to neighbor in love's service.

God left the modern world when men stopped loving one another, when they failed to make him present through their love and justice towards each other. They must bring him back by loving one another again in the Holy Spirit of divine love— whom they receive from the Father when they go to him in the sacrifice of the Son. Like Jesus, they must glorify the Father by acting as sons in reverencing their brothers, in being men for others—in the way that Jesus was a man for others. He was a man for others because he was first of all a Son of the Father.

"The proof that you are sons is that God has sent the Spirit of his Son into our hearts: the Spirit that cries, 'Abba, Father!' "— the Spirit that impels us towards all as our brothers in Christ.

These considerations make it clear why Vatican II, even while it was concerned with the pastoral, incarnational aspect of Christianity, strongly reasserted also the eschatological aspect:

> In a striking analogy, the Church is compared to the mystery of the Incarnate Word. Just as the assumed nature inseparably united to the Divine Word serves him as a living instrument of salvation, so in a similar way the social structure of the Church serves Christ's Spirit, who vivifies it, for the building up of the body (*LG* 8).
>
> The promised restoration which we are awaiting has already begun in Christ, is carried forward in the mission of the Holy Spirit, and through him continues in the Church, in which we learn through faith the meaning of our terrestrial life, while we perform with hope in the future the work committed to us in this world by the Father, and thus work out our salvation (*LG* 48).

The "incarnational" approach, or "being men with men in the world," is worthless if we are not men sent from the Father, to whom we have already had access in Christ; our incarnational efforts are a failure if we do not succeed in taking back others with us to the Father. For such was the work committed to "the one whom the Father consecrated and sent into the world" (Jn. 10:36) and to his members. To be fully christological, we need to be eschatological as well as incarnational (and religious, Vatican II teaches, in a special way are eschatological witnesses—*LG* 44)—for he said, "My kingdom is not of this world" (Jn. 18:36).

We see again, therefore, why Pope Paul underlined both these aspects in stating the goal of aggiornamento in the religious life:

The aggiornamento of the religious life called for by the new demands of the times ought to make it easier in our day for each religious to conform to the divine model, Christ. It is certainly not a question of an aggiornamento that aims at catching up with the secular world. Rather, it is a sincere and loving pursuit of anything that will be of help and encouragement to a more faithful extension in the world of Christ's presence, his example, his sacrificial life that was expended for the glory of the Father and the salvation of the brethren.[2]

The updating is not to be a mere conformity with the secular world, nor does it aim at making the religious life easy. It aims at making it easier to live Christ's sacrificial life and make it present in the world today—for the glory of the Father, a glory achieved in the salvation of the brethren. For the Father will be fully glorified when all men have become truly his children, treating one another as such, in reverence for the Father of all, and all crying in unison with Christ, "Abba, Father."

Mary, too, in whom the mystery of the Church has been uniquely perfected, "who has entered intimately into the history of salvation" and has thus become the Mother of all, "invites believers to her Son and his sacrifice and to the love of the Father" (*LG* 65)—"that God may be all in all" (1 Cor. 15:28).

2 "The Religious Life and Aggiornamento," *The Pope Speaks*, X (1965), p. 331.

General Index

Index of Documents
of Vatican II

Key to the Symbols: